Good King Richard?

RICHARD III
Statue in Castle Gardens, Leicester, by James Butler RA 1980

Jeremy Potter

Good King Richard?

An Account of Richard III
and his Reputation

Constable
London

First published in Great Britain 1983
by Constable and Company Ltd
10 Orange Street London WC2H 7EG
Copyright © 1983 by Jeremy Potter
ISBN 0 09 464630 9 (casebound)
ISBN 0 09 468840 0 (paperback)
Reprinted 1983, 1985
Paperback edition 1989

Printed in the United States of America

'A minute study of the facts of Richard's life has tended more and more to convince me of the general fidelity of the portrait with which we have been made familiar by Shakespeare and Sir Thomas More.'

JAMES GAIRDNER

Preface to History of the Life and Reign of Richard the Third (1878)

'What is astounding about this statement is not so much that Gairdner supposes the sensational protagonist of the melodramatic *Richard III* to be a portrait of the real Richard but that he supposes it to be, in any way, the portrait of a human being.'

PAUL MURRAY KENDALL
Richard III (1955)

Contents

Illustrations

Chapter Headings
Boar Badge of Richard III Society

Tailpiece
Richard III's Signature (BL Vespasian MS)

Foreword

Richard III, the so-called 'last English king of England' and the wicked uncle of tradition, is the most controversial and enigmatic of monarchs. Could he really have been as black as he was painted by Tudor chroniclers and, if he wasn't, why do some historians go on saying that he was? Why is his enlightened legislation so little noticed? Is there any real evidence that he murdered his nephews, the princes in the Tower? Did he really have a hunchback or was it invented for him after his death as 'proof of villainy'? Is Shakespeare's Richard III a portrayal of the real Richard or no more than a character in a work of fiction? Was St Thomas More really a witness of truth?

Good King Richard? is an account of Richard III's life and times, character, appearance and reign, but above all of the Great Debate which has raged since his death between traditionalists and revisionists. Written to mark the 500th anniversary of his accession to the throne, this is a history of his reputation from 1483 to 1983.

The author, who is Chairman of the Richard III Society, makes no claim to impartiality. If it is permissible to borrow from politics and see traditionalists as ranged on the right and revisionists on the left, the perspective of this book represents a view from the inside left position. A balance is attempted nevertheless, and after chapters on the rival traditional and revisionist pictures of the king, the background of the fifteenth century and events of the reign, participants in the Great Debate are introduced and allowed to speak for themselves.

Contemporary writers whose works are examined include the author of a monastic chronicle, an Italian visitor to fifteenth-century London, a Flemish politician, a chantry priest in the Midlands and a London draper. Later protagonists whose involvement and views are recorded include a formidable array of quarrelsome historians and a colourful assortment of the famous. Among the latter are Jane Austen, Francis Bacon, Charles II, Sir Winston Churchill, Charles Dickens,

David Garrick, HRH the Duke of Gloucester, David Hume, Charles Lamb, Henry Cabot Lodge, Louis XVI, Sir John Millais, Laurence Olivier, Sir Walter Ralegh, Sir Walter Scott, Rex Stout, Horace Walpole, John Wesley and Sir Christopher Wren.

That Richard III has been seen by posterity almost exclusively through the eyes of his enemies and has as a consequence been grievously wronged in history, literature and legend is, in the author's view, scarcely to be denied. But was he, even so, a villain – and, if so, a villain by the standards of his own time and/or ours? This is an argument not only about the nature of truth and the credibility of tradition, but also about the exercise of power and whether public and private morality is indivisible. It should be noted that the title *Good King Richard?* contains the word 'king' as well as 'good' and a note of interrogation. Whether Richard was a good or a bad king may be understood as a question somewhat different from that of his alleged villainy. Witness Henry VI, the feeble-minded innocent whose rule brought disaster to England and an abrupt end to the Lancastrian line. Or, by way of contrast, the Yorkists' successful and wholly unscrupulous contemporary on the throne of France, Louis XI.

The author's debt to, and indeed dependence upon, those who have written about Richard III from the king's time to his own will be apparent. His acknowledgement and gratitude take the form of a bibliography, where their works are listed for reference and as a recommended guide to further reading. The absence of more detailed references in footnotes is to be regretted, but this is a work of historiography intended for the general reader.

Acknowledgement and gratitude for assistance and advice are due in particular to Margaret Potter, Caroline Bradford and Charles T. Wood, and to fellow members of the committee of the Richard III Society: Carolyn and Peter Hammond in their respective roles as librarian and research officer, and Geoffrey Wheeler for the illustrations.

York and Lancaster *simplified*

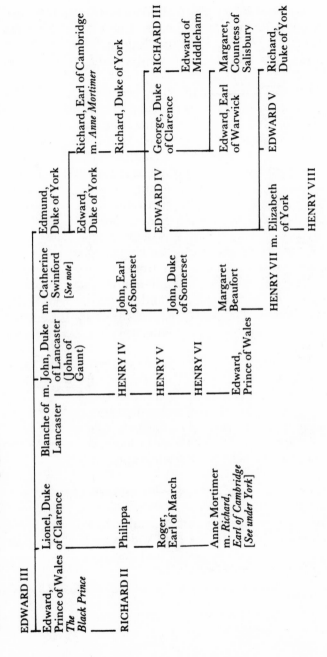

EDWARD III

Edward, Prince of Wales — *The Black Prince* — Lionel, Duke of Clarence — Blanche of Lancaster m. John, Duke of Lancaster (John of Gaunt) m. Catherine Swinford [*See note*] — Edmund, Duke of York

RICHARD II

Philippa

Roger, Earl of March

Anne Mortimer m. *Richard, Earl of Cambridge* [*See under York*]

Richard, Earl of Cambridge m. *Anne Mortimer*

Richard, Duke of York

John, Earl of Somerset — HENRY IV

John, Duke of Somerset — HENRY V

Margaret Beaufort — HENRY VI

Edward, Prince of Wales

Edward, Duke of York

EDWARD IV — George, Duke of Clarence — RICHARD III

Edward, Earl of Warwick — Edward of Middleham

Margaret, Countess of Salisbury

HENRY VII m. Elizabeth of York

EDWARD V — Richard, Duke of York

HENRY VIII

Note: John, Duke of Lancaster (John of Gaunt) married Catherine Swinford after the birth of their children, who were legitimised by Parliament, with the subsequent qualification by Henry IV: *excepta*

Descent of Richard III

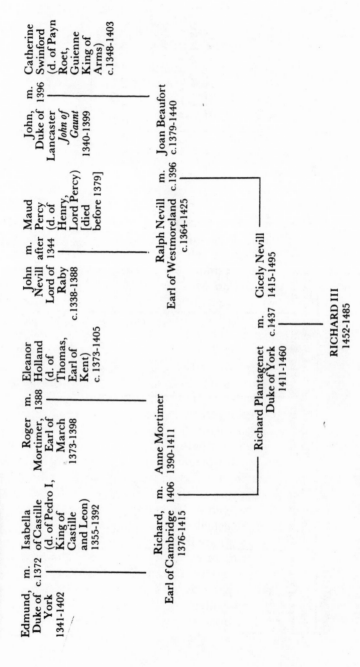

Deformed or Defamed?

History is not made by great men and women, nor by social and economic forces. It is made by historians. They it is who, scavenging among the relics of the past, select, interpret and speculate – and the more distant the period, the larger the element of speculation. Most who have subjected to this process what is known of events in England during the second half of the fifteenth century have not been kind to the last of the Plantagenet kings. They have been 'no smoke without fire' men, opting for the Tudor-inspired tradition and impatient with those who would question it. Yet, as others have recognised, there are different selections, interpretations and speculations which do not violate known facts.

Is history a bare record of known facts or the play of the imagination upon them? Neither definition is adequate. Any historian, however scrupulous, must find some facts significant and others not worthy of note, and in making such judgments is inescapably drawn into bias. History according to the Whigs is not history according to the Tories. History is the winners' version of what happened. If the great victories in the Hundred Years War at La Rochelle (1372), Baugé (1421), Patay (1429) and Chatillon (1453) are little known in England, it is because they were French victories. And, despite Bury's hopeful dictum that it is 'a science, no less and no more', much of what passes for history is transparently little more than guesswork, sometimes inspired, more often not. Jane Austen is one of those who have expressed surprise at what they were expected to believe about Richard III, and she conveys this view of history through the mouth of Catherine Morland, the heroine of *Northanger Abbey*, in one of her driest *mots*: 'I often think it odd that it should be so dull, for a great deal of it must be invention.' ('I am fond of history,' replies Miss Tilney, 'and very well contented to take the false with the true.')

From the confines of the Tower of London Sir Walter Ralegh saw history grandly as:

> Time's witness, herald of Antiquity,
> The light of Truth, and life of Memory.

More succinctly and prosaically, it has been described as lies about crimes, and to find support for this harsh verdict one has to look no further than the accusations – still widely believed on no evidence worth the name – that Richard III murdered successively the Lancastrian Prince of Wales, Henry VI, his own brother George of Clarence, and his own wife Queen Anne.

According to A. L. Rowse (in *The Use of History*), the historian must be two-minded, part scientific and part intuitive. This refinement of Bury enables him to know, not scientifically but intuitively, that Richard III murdered the princes in the Tower. He concedes that there are 'plenty of historians who allow their emotional prejudices to bedevil their judgment' and proves his own point by comparing Richard to Hitler.

This is in the great tradition of historians who see history in Lord Acton's terms ('history must be a judgment seat') and appear to derive much satisfaction from passing moral verdicts on the kings who have become their subjects. Vilification of the great became a popular pastime among eminent historians in Victorian times when Freeman indulged in character assassination at the expense of William Rufus, Stout roughed up King John, and Gairdner put the boot in on Richard III. Despite some attempts at first aid, these three battered monarchs are still the Bad Kings today, while others are held up for admiration whose reputations might seem no less vulnerable: Richard the Lionheart (the absentee extortioner), Henry V (the mass murderer of French peasants) and Henry VIII, who judicially murdered a couple of wives and was perhaps responsible for the destruction of more works of art than any other man in history. If English history has to have a monster king, Henry VIII one would have supposed to be the leading contender; instead he is known as Bluff King Hal and enshrined in the national consciousness as the most popular of all our monarchs.

Not only royal reputations, but turning points in history too, are the invention of historians. By this artificial device Richard III is seen as the fag end of medieval barbarism, while Henry Tudor is applauded for having ended the middle ages at Bosworth on 22 August 1485. Yet the last battle in the so-called Wars of the Roses took place in 1487, and it was between 1461 and 1471 that the House of York established a new system of government which was inherited and continued by the Tudors. No fewer than twenty-nine of Henry's councillors had been councillors to one or other of the Yorkist kings, nineteen of them to Richard III. There was continuity between the Yorkist kings and the early Tudors in government, the development of production and trade, the strengthening of law and order, and abandonment of the Lancastrians' war against France. Yet the argument of A. R. Myers (in *England in the Late Middle Ages*) that the natural break between medieval and modern England came, not with the death of Richard III, but with the dissolution of the religious houses in the social revolution of the 1530's has had little effect on entrenched attitudes and illusions, which are still to be found among many who teach history and in the narratives of general historians.

Such attitudes persist in reflecting traditional accounts of the deeds and reputation of Richard III, into which are woven strands of fiction and speculation. The king's character remains enigmatic and the events of much of his lifetime are poorly documented. Where so little is known, much must be guessed and, influenced by Tudor myth and the power of Shakespeare's imagination, posterity's guesswork has been almost wholly to Richard's disadvantage.

The reason for the myth is not hard to discern. The Tudor usurpation of the throne had to be justified. For more than a hundred years after his death it was a political necessity for a usurping dynasty to portray the last of the Plantagenets as a usurper, and an act of treason for anyone to suggest that he was a normal human being. With their own claim to the throne so shaky, the doctrine of absolute obedience to a crowned and anointed sovereign lord formed the constitutional bedrock of the Tudors' tyranny, and Henry Tudor's own act of rebellion and regicide could be explained and excused only by dubbing the man from whom he took the crown a monster. In the case of monsters, the natural order is suspended and one is entitled to waive the rules.

The legend of the wicked uncle, the evil hunchback, then created has endured for want of hard evidence to the contrary. At the bar of history Richard III has continued to be judged guilty because it is impossible to prove him innocent. The Tudors ride high in popular esteem. They are believed somehow to have rescued England from the middle ages, and their reputations still bask in the sunshine of the Renaissance which illuminated Europe during their rule. Recognition of Shakespeare's genius is undimmed, but it is seldom remarked that he was a writer of fiction and that his *Richard III* is an historical romance which would nowadays be described as 'faction'. Thomas More, whose scurrilous *History of King Richard III* exceeds all bounds of credibility, has been canonised, and the word of a saint is not to be doubted.

A fleeting occupant of the throne, Richard III is still today the most discussed and controversial of all English monarchs. He reigned for less than twenty-six months five hundred years ago, but the Great Debate about his qualities as a man and a ruler – his character, actions, motives and personal appearance – shows no signs of abating. Was he a cruel tyrant or (in Francis Bacon's words) a good ruler 'for the ease and solace of the common people'? Could he not have had a hand in the death of his brother Clarence? Did he really try to marry his niece Elizabeth? How did he come to lose the battle of Bosworth? The fate of his nephews and the truth about his hunchback are only the most famous of issues in contention.

The controversy raises wider questions too. Just how inaccurate and prejudiced were the early chroniclers and later historians? In historical studies how much value should be placed on tradition? How powerful is the influence of literary genius on history? Is a legend indestructible?

The Tudor writers include the historian Polydore Vergil and the chroniclers Hall and Holinshed, as well as Chancellor Thomas More and William Shakespeare. The Jacobeans include another Lord Chancellor (Francis Bacon), a Master of the Revels (Sir George Buck) and Sir Walter Ralegh. Horace Walpole and David Hume feature prominently in the eighteenth century, and there are Victorian bluestockings and a dramatic clash of eminent heavyweights in the nineteenth. The twentieth century sees the rise of an organised revisionist movement, the examination of what may or may not be the bones of the princes in the Tower, and widely differing views among modern historians.

As the genealogical tree of his descent indicates, 'the last English king of England' might more accurately be described as the most English of all the sovereign rulers of England for more than a thousand years. Before him there was a dominance of Danish and French blood in the royal family; after him some Welsh and much Scottish and German. The two royal brothers of the house of York alone had four English grandparents and, while Edward IV's birth-place was in Normandy, Richard was born in Northamptonshire in the heart of England. He was a brave soldier, a respected administrator, a benefactor to the church, and a good ruler. He died tragically and heroically at an early age, leading the last cavalry charge in the middle ages against an invading army of foreign mercenaries and traitors backed by England's hereditary enemy, the King of France. What a hero to set beside those other warrior kings: Richard I, the fearless crusader, and Henry V of Agincourt fame!

Yet this is the 'almost proscribed king' to whom history has awarded a hump which no one noticed during his life-time, and who is famous as the archetypal wicked uncle, although no one knows what happened to the nephews he is convicted by posterity of killing. The case against him is supported by many distinguished historians and a roll call of the illustrious. Against them stand arrayed what traditionalists see as a motley array of blindly perverse romantics, eccentrics and dilettanti intent on swimming against the tide.

The perspective of the revisionists is naturally different. They see their cause making gradual but perceptible headway, as the long-besieged traditionalists are forced to abandon successive bastions of error and defamation. They may not envisage a total capitulation or aspire to the triumph of a Galileo, but they are sustained by a consciousness that the

heresies of yesterday and today are not infrequently the orthodoxies of tomorrow. For them it is not Richard III who stands
in the dock, but history and historians. To them eccentricity in
the age of 'scientific' history is the hallmark of the few surviving
unregenerate traditionalists. Horace Walpole is the spokesman
in this pithy summary of their case: 'The reign of Richard III
has so degraded our annals by an intrusion of childish improb-
abilities that it places that reign on a level with the story of Jack
the Giant-killer'.

'The Great Debate,' writes Paul Murray Kendall in his
Richard the Third, 'has always been waged between amateurs
and professionals – scholars imperturbably holding ranks
against the irregular sallies of guerrillas. However, if, on the one
hand, the revisionists have been much too ready to build on
flimsy evidence or flat assertion, the traditionalists proved less
than willing to acknowledge undoubted errors and violent
distortions in More and Shakespeare. Furthermore, controversy over the "mystery" was concentrated on pushing back
and forth all-white and all-black counters labelled Richard,
instead of attempting to uncover the lineaments of the man and
to explore the accomplishments of the ruler.'

Defences of Richard III are greeted with cries of 'whitewash',
an accusation neatly encapsulating a pre-supposition that his
character was black. Revisionist frogmen submerged among
the mud hope to bring to the surface a Richard revealed in a
different, and more plausible, colour. Their aim is to transform
a monster into a man. They wish to replace devilification with
de-vilification, to convince the world that Richard was de-
famed, not deformed.

As Francis Bacon and Josephine Tey have reminded us,
truth is the daughter of time, and have five hundred years really
not been long enough? It seems not. 'It is terrifying' (Stendhal
once remarked) 'to think how much research is needed to
determine the truth of even the most unimportant fact.' The
mystery of the princes in the Tower, proclaimed as the greatest
crime in history, remains unsolved. History abhors a mystery
no less than nature a vacuum, and historians and laymen alike
feel the obligation to provide a solution. This is one topic where
history is very far from being a thing of the past. But if the truth
about their disappearance and Richard III's murderous or

virtuous character and dark or enlightened deeds may never be established by general agreement, at least the arguments for and against can be rehearsed and a balance of probabilities assessed.

2

The Monster of Tradition

In history classes at school generations of children have been taught that there are Good Kings and Bad Kings and, of them all, the most wicked who has ever sat on the throne of England was King Richard III. In English lessons the verdict of history has been seen to be confirmed in one of the most famous and powerful works of the most respected writer in the language. To those precocious enough to question the authenticity of a dramatist's version of history the reply has been that Shakespeare may not be, strictly speaking, an historian, but he followed contemporary historical accounts closely and knew human nature better than anyone before or since. 'However little the noble poetry of Shakespeare may agree in detail with the results of historical research,' wrote one eminent German critic in the nineteenth century, 'fundamentally both reach the same goal.'

What has been taught in schools about this king – and is often still taught, mostly by older teachers – is the view of the traditionalists or, as Sir George Buck first named them, the antiRichards. This is the account passed down to posterity by the king's enemies, so that (in the words of A. R. Myers) 'by the end of the sixteenth century the facts of his real appearance, character and deeds had been buried under a great mound of tradition. He had become the archetypal tyrant-king, incarnate evil enthroned.'

In this version of English history, immortalised by Shakespeare, Richard III is the fifteenth-century protagonist whose death dramatically brings down the curtain on the Wars of the Roses, the Plantagenet dynasty and the whole period designated as the Middle Ages.

The wars were the outcome of a family quarrel between the various Plantagenet heirs of Edward III, who fathered too many sons for the good of his country. Richard II, the recognised heir who had succeeded his grandfather, was deposed by his cousin, Henry Bolingbroke, the son of John of Gaunt, Duke of Lancaster. Bolingbroke became Henry IV and was succeeded without dispute by his son as Henry V and his grandson as Henry VI. But Henry VI was at first an infant king and then, as an adult, proved incapable of ruling. The Hundred Years War with France was lost, and with it nearly all the English possessions across the Channel. Weak authority and national humiliation provided the opportunity for a rival Plantagenet, Richard, Duke of York, to advance a claim to the throne allegedly superior to that of the usurping Lancastrian Henrys. A century of fighting against the French was to be succeeded by thirty years of civil war.

The youngest son of the Yorkist claimant, Richard III grew up during this period of violence. He did not become a big, handsome hero like other Plantagenets, but was (so tradition asserts) small and dark and physically misshapen, with a hunchback and withered arm. These were outward and visible signs of the evil which lay concealed within, for he was determined to become king and allowed no scruple – or human life – to stand in his path to the throne. When his father and elder brother (the Duke of York and Edmund, Earl of Rutland) were killed at Wakefield by Lancastrians he was still a child. A few months later, when his eldest brother (Edward, Earl of March) had avenged their deaths in fighting at Mortimer's Cross and Towton and seized the crown as Edward IV, he became Duke of Gloucester and suddenly stood next in line to the throne after his other surviving brother, George, Duke of Clarence.

When Clarence turned traitor with his cousin, Warwick the King-maker, and they re-instated the Lancastrian king, Henry VI, on the throne, Richard did not join them. He escaped abroad with Edward and, returning with him, fought with Edward's victorious army at the battles of Barnet and Tewkesbury which re-established his brother as king. After the fighting at Tewkesbury (so tradition asserts) he stabbed to death the

Lancastrian heir, who had been captured, and presided over the execution of the Duke of Somerset and other prisoners of war. In London, when it was decided that Henry VI must die, he willingly assumed the role of executioner (so tradition asserts) and personally completed the task of extinguishing the legitimate line of Lancaster.

In spite of this, Richard's chances of becoming king were receding. King Edward had married and had two sons. Clarence, whose wife was the King-maker's elder daughter, also had a son, and Clarence had returned to Yorkist allegiance. Richard's search for a rich heiress resulted in his marrying the King-maker's younger daughter, Anne. This aroused furious opposition from Clarence, and in their greed the two brothers quarrelled bitterly over the division of the Warwick estates. Richard's prize, Anne Nevill, was a young widow. Her previous marriage had been to Edward, the Lancastrian Prince of Wales, whom Richard was said to have murdered.

Fortunately for Richard, Clarence again fell out of favour with their brother Edward, and Richard, while pretending to be his friend, is said to have been responsible for plotting his death as a traitor. According to Shakespeare, Edward, overcome with remorse, countermanded the order for Clarence's execution, but Richard contrived to have him killed before the reprieve could reach the Tower. Clarence's attainder as a traitor meant that his son was unable to inherit his titles and estates and was therefore barred from the succession. Richard's secret objective was two steps nearer achievement.

Once secure upon the throne, Edward IV became degenerate, over-indulging a gargantuan appetite for food, drink and, most especially, women. This proved a crowning piece of good fortune for his ambitious brother, for it caused his early death while his two sons were still minors. Not suspecting that his brother's loyalty to him was wholly self-interested, Edward made a will in which he appointed Richard as Protector of the Realm and entrusted the young princes to his care.

At that time Richard was living in the north of England, where he had ruled on his brother's behalf as lord of the north for the past eleven years, building a power base and biding his time. Although himself the father of two illegitimate children, he had publicly exhibited a puritan distaste for the debaucheries at his brother's court. His disapproval was also seen as hostility to the influence of the queen and her Woodville relations, powerful and rapacious upstarts who were unpopular among the older nobility.

On the news of his brother's death Richard, according to tradition a cunning and practised hypocrite, at once sent a reassuring message to London, promising fealty and obedience to Edward's elder son as the new king. He travelled to York, where he attended a solemn mass for his brother's soul and ordered a ceremonial avowal of allegiance to his nephew, publicly acknowledging him as Edward V. He then moved south to meet the new king, a boy of twelve, who was being brought to London by a Woodville uncle, Earl Rivers, from his home at Ludlow castle on the marches of his principality of Wales.

The king's party failed to keep the appointed rendezvous at Northampton, but Rivers arrived to explain that they had moved on to Stony Stratford, fourteen miles nearer London, to ease the problem of accommodation. A large escort of two thousand men was accompanying the king while Richard had only three hundred retainers, but he had been joined at Northampton by the Duke of Buckingham (another Plantagenet and the senior nobleman in the realm after Richard himself), whose retinue was also three hundred strong.

After an amicable supper with the two dukes Rivers retired to bed, only to find himself under arrest in the morning. The dukes then rode to Stony Stratford, plucked the king from his entourage and ordered the armed escort to disband. His Woodville half-brother, Lord Richard Grey, and his chamberlain, Sir Thomas Vaughan, were also arrested. With Rivers, they were sent as prisoners to Yorkshire and later executed without proper trial. Edward IV's appointment of Richard as Protector was explained to the young king to reassure him, and he was shown all due respect and deference by his uncle. After a short delay they rode into London ceremonially together. In view of the delay and the need to make all due preparations, a new date was fixed for the coronation, which the Woodvilles had attempted to hurry through before Richard's arrival. Meanwhile all business was conducted in the new king's name.

Reports of Richard's coup and the arrest of her brother and

one of her sons had so terrified Edward IV's widow that before Richard could reach London she took herself and the rest of the late king's children into sanctuary at Westminster Abbey. One of her brothers, Sir Edward Woodville, fled the country, taking the fleet and part of the treasury with him. Another brother, Lionel, Bishop of Salisbury, and her eldest son by her first marriage, Thomas Grey, Marquess of Dorset, joined her in sanctuary with the rest of the treasure.

An ally on the king's council awaiting Richard was Lord Hastings, Edward IV's chamberlain and closest friend. He had been Richard's first informant of the news of Edward's death and had worked hard to prevent the Woodvilles from seizing power before Richard could arrive to exercise the protectorship which the late king had willed to him. But as soon as it became suspected that Richard intended to usurp the throne from Edward IV's rightful heir Hastings turned against him, was seized at a meeting of the council and summarily executed. An announcement was made that he had been plotting against the Protector's life, but no evidence was produced and there was no trial. Other respected members of the council were arrested at the same time (but later released): the Archbishop of York, the Bishop of Ely and Lord Stanley.

A few days afterwards the queen was persuaded to allow Edward IV's younger son, Richard, Duke of York, to join his brother in the royal apartments in the Tower of London. The way was now clear for Richard's final coup. He sent urgently to the north for an armed force to march on London and ordered a public proclamation that because Edward IV had been illegitimate and his marriage to Elizabeth Woodville was invalid (by reason of a pre-contract with another lady) the two supposed princes were bastards and Richard was therefore the rightful king of England. Under threat of the impending arrival of his army from the north, this story, although disbelieved, was reluctantly accepted, and it enabled Richard to have himself crowned instead of his nephew.

His life-long ambition was now achieved, but there could be no security while his nephews were still alive. Sir Robert Brackenbury, the Constable of the Tower, refused to be a party to their murder, but while Richard was away from London on progress after his coronation he is said to have sent a trusted retainer, Sir James Tyrell, to have them smothered to death and their bodies secretly buried. Nothing of this was known for certain at the time, but when the princes were no longer to be seen playing in the Tower gardens, fears for their safety were widely felt. One contemporary writer records that he had seen many men burst into tears and lamentations when mention was made of the boy who had, so briefly, been their king.

Within weeks rumours of the fate of the princes caused such revulsion against Richard that not only the Woodvilles but even loyal Yorkist supporters of Edward IV made common cause with their remaining Lancastrian enemies, led by Henry Tudor, who had taken refuge in Brittany. Insurgency broke out across the whole breadth of southern England, and at the head of the rebellion was none other than the Duke of Buckingham, who had done more than any man to put Richard on the throne. Yet even against this united opposition Richard's luck held. The rebels were disorganised, the expeditionary force from Brittany failed to land, and the muster of Buckingham's forces in the west were disrupted by bad weather which flooded the river Severn. Buckingham himself was betrayed, captured and executed – without being granted a hearing by Richard, despite his pleas.

The usurper had dated his reign from 26 June 1483, he was crowned on 6 July, the princes disappeared in August or thereabouts, and the Buckingham rebellion took place in October. In January 1484 a cowed parliament formally confirmed his title to the crown. In a series of bold and brazenly unprincipled strokes Richard had accomplished his purpose, ridden out the storm and secured his position. Yet only two months later his luck began to run out. The first victim of Nemesis was his only legitimate child, Edward of Middleham, who died leaving him with no direct heir and a barren wife.

Other misfortunes followed fast. Augmented by fleeing rebels the previous autumn, the opposition in exile with Henry Tudor continued to grow. An attempt to capture Henry narrowly failed and he fled to the territory of the French king, who was more willing and able than the Duke of Brittany to supply him with the necessary men, money and ships to launch an invasion of England. The Earl of Oxford, a determined and (to Richard) dangerous Lancastrian, escaped from imprisonment in one of the fortresses within the pale of Calais and crossed the French border with the lieutenant, Sir James Blount, who connived at his escape and deserted with him to join Henry in Paris.

The support which the Lancastrian claimant received from disaffected Yorkists was conditional on a promise to consummate the union between the two factions through a marriage with Edward IV's eldest daughter, Elizabeth of York. To frustrate Henry and strengthen his own position, Richard let it be known that he intended to marry Elizabeth himself, although she was his niece. Anne Nevill, his barren wife, was in ill health and expected to die soon; which she conveniently did (in March 1485) amid suspicion of being hastened to her grave with the aid of poison. But after her death the incestuous Richard was forced by his own supporters into the humiliation of a public announcement that he had never intended to marry Elizabeth.

Preparations to meet the threat of Henry Tudor's invasion impoverished the treasury, and Richard, always extravagant, was forced to raise money through the renewal of unpopular taxation which had been formally abolished by his own parliament. When the invasion at last took place, Henry was able to recruit further deserters from Richard, for whose cause few wished to fight.

The king assembled his forces at Nottingham and the armies met near Bosworth. Richard's forces were superior if he could count on the contingents led by the Earl of Northumberland and by Lord Stanley and his brother, Sir William. In the event Northumberland stood aloof, refusing Richard's order to engage the enemy, while the Stanleys changed sides at a crucial moment during the battle, bringing about Richard's defeat and death despite a furious last charge in which he attempted to kill Henry with his own hand. So hated was the dead tyrant that his body was stripped naked, publicly exposed like that of a common felon, and buried in obscurity.

After his victory Henry was hailed as the saviour of England, an angel sent to liberate and purify the country from tyranny. He was crowned as Henry VII and duly married Elizabeth of York to unite the white rose with the red in the cause of peace and harmony. He and his Tudor successors brought England out of an age of darkness and bloodshed – of civil strife and lawless brutality so aptly represented by that epitome of evil, the last Plantagenet king – into the glorious dawn of modern civilisation.

Such, in summary, is the traditional version of Richard III's life and times which, over a period of five hundred years, few have chosen to challenge. Even today, when history is studied more scientifically than ever before, many people, while perhaps conceding some elements of bias and exaggeration, still find it in substance a true account and a just verdict. It is, they will point out correctly, hallowed by time and tradition and blessed by an almost apostolic succession of historians, acting as the professional guardians and official spokesmen of received wisdom. We are Sir Oracles, some have sternly insisted in quelling dissenters, and when we ope our lips let no dog bark.

3

The Revised Version

In the latter half of the twentieth century, on the Sunday nearest to 22 August, an annual memorial service is held in the parish church of the Leicestershire village of Sutton Cheney. There Richard III is presumed to have heard his last mass on the eve of the battle which took place on Redmore plain, between Sutton Cheney and Market Bosworth, on 22 August 1485. Worshippers come from every part of England, and the church is sometimes so full that some have to stand and others listen outside the door. Usually there are representatives from countries undiscovered in Richard III's day – Canada, Australia, New Zealand. Often there is a coach party of Americans who are devoting their summer vacation to a Ricardian tour of Britain, visiting the places associated with him. Hymns are sung in praise of King Richard, and one year, by a not unforeseeable slip of the tongue during his sermon, the preacher referred to St Richard.

After the service an expedition is made to the battle ground, where in 1974, as a result of this public interest, way-leaves were obtained from farmers by the Leicestershire County Council and the site was formally inaugurated as a National Park. There at the opening ceremony, to a salute by trumpeters in period costume, Richard III's battle standard was run up on a flag-staff at the top of Ambion Hill where he had spent the last night of his life and drawn up his forces for battle. Twenty-one feet in length (the regulation footage for kings according to some medieval authorities), it depicted the cross of St George for England, the sun in splendour of the House of York, and the white boar which was the king's personal emblem.

The standard was raised for the first time since 1485 in the presence of two dukes of Plantagenet descent: the Duke of Gloucester, descended from Richard III's niece, Queen Elizabeth of York, and the Duke of Rutland, descended from Anne, Duchess of Exeter, one of his sisters. HRH the Duke of Gloucester, who is the present Queen Elizabeth's cousin, spoke in the king's favour. Among the gathering of local notables and members of the general public, press correspondents and radio interviewers found no shortage of further 'copy' in favour of Richard but searched in vain for someone who would say a good word for the man who had won the battle. Even men from the BBC's Welsh service were sporting white boar badges.

Such public manifestations of partisanship by revisionists – or, as they now call themselves, Ricardians – occasion a curling of lips and shaking of heads (more in anger than sorrow) among traditionalist historians. Yet some of the scepticism exhibited is shared by other historians, who have found the commonly accepted assessment of Richard III unconvincing. That 'he was very far from being the distorted villain of tradition' is the judgment of the late E. F. Jacob, sometime Chichele Professor of Modern History in the University of Oxford and author of the volume on the fifteenth century in the Oxford History of England (1961). Of the princes in the Tower he writes: 'It is unlikely that the circumstances of their death will be known', and certainly, whatever the truth about their fate, the traditional story seems to revisionists a transparent fabrication. They regard it as a myth like King Alfred and the cakes, King Canute and the waves, and Robin Hood's re-distribution of wealth at the expense of King John. All these are amusing fairy tales. But how can it be that the one about Richard, more appropriate to a pantomime like The Babes in the Wood, is actually taught as history? The facts as revisionists see them are different.

Throughout the fifteenth century no King of England enjoyed an undisputed claim to the throne, but on his brother Edward's death Richard was indisputably the male adult heir of the Plantagenets, who had ruled England for more than three centuries. The unsuitability of King Edward's sons to rule was generally accepted, either because the marriage of their parents was believed to be invalid under canon law or because

no one wanted the weak and uncertain rule of a boy king with
the likelihood of further civil war. Richard became king by the
assent of lords and commons, subsequently confirmed in a
formal parliament. The city of London supported his accession,
and his coronation at Westminster was one of the best attended
in English medieval history.

Henry Tudor, on the other hand, was plainly a usurper, a
rebel, a regicide. His claim to be the Lancastrian heir was
flawed. It derived from his mother, a Beaufort, who was
descended from a bastard son of John of Gaunt and his
mistress, Catherine Swinford. To oblige his uncle, Richard II
had declared the Beauforts legitimate by royal edict, but Henry
IV, John of Gaunt's only genuinely legitimate son, had
cautiously had this amended by parliament so that the
Beauforts and their descendants were specifically excluded
from succession to the crown. Thus when Richard III was
killed there were, it has been estimated, twenty-nine people
alive with a better claim to the throne than the man crowned as
Henry VII. The country had to be persuaded that it was
Richard who was the usurper and, for good measure, a monster, and the disappearance of the princes provided a ready-
made pretext for wholesale vilification.

Communication was haphazard in the fifteenth century, the
public ignorant, gullible and superstitious. Important truths
often lay beyond discovery, and improbable rumours were
readily believed – even supernatural stories of the sky raining
blood and women giving birth to animals. A weeping foetus was
seriously reported from Huntingdonshire, and the voice of a
headless man crying out in the air somewhere between Leicester and Banbury was solemnly recorded by no less a personage
than the master of a Cambridge college (John Warkworth). In
Richard's case documents may have been destroyed by Henry
VII, who made a determined attempt to expunge his predecessor's reign from the record and encouraged Polydore Vergil to
rewrite English history. Then with the good fortune which the
Tudors have continued to enjoy in what would nowadays be
called their press relations and the promotion of their public
image, the story was taken up successively by the three intellectual giants of the English renaissance – Thomas More, William
Shakespeare and Francis Bacon.

Revisionists are quick to point out that More was not a contemporary authority, as is often supposed. He was aged six at the time of Bosworth and brought up in the household of Cardinal Morton, who had committed treason against Richard III. The portrait of Richard drawn by him achieved permanence through the genius of Shakespeare, who, like Bacon, took for true a Tudor tale which was the political apologia of a usurping dynasty with a precarious hold on the crown.

The real Richard, claim the revisionists, was a very different person. He was royally descended from no fewer than three of the sons of Edward III – through the male line from Edmund of Langley, Duke of York (no. 5), through the female line from Lionel of Clarence (no. 3), from whom the superiority of the Yorkist claim was derived, and also (although seldom mentioned) from John of Gaunt (no. 4), father of the first Lancastrian king. His parents were Richard, Duke of York and Cecily Nevill, daughter of the Earl of Westmorland. His elder brothers had been born abroad during their father's periods of service as viceroy – Edward and Edmund in Rouen and George in Dublin. Of the boys who survived infancy, Richard alone was English by place of birth. He was born in the family castle at Fotheringhay on 2 October 1452.

In June 1461, back from a period abroad as a political refugee at the tender age of eight, he rode into London in triumph beside his victorious brother, who had become Edward IV and soon made his infant brother not only Duke of Gloucester but also a Knight of the Bath, a Knight of the Garter, and Admiral of England, Ireland and Aquitaine. He was probably dark-haired, pale-faced, slight and by no means robust. There is no contemporary evidence that he was deformed, only some suggestion that one shoulder was slightly higher than the other, possibly the result of sword drill at an early age.

Shortly after his seventeenth birthday he became Constable of England and exercised almost viceregal powers in Wales, where he put down a revolt. On his eighteenth birthday – such were the hazards of power in the fifteenth century – he once more became a refugee, setting sail from King's Lynn for the Low Countries with his brother Edward, who had been dethroned by Warwick and Clarence. Barely six months later he returned with Edward and a perilously small band of supporters. Gambling with their lives against desperate odds, they recaptured the crown in two hard-fought encounters: the great Yorkist victories at Barnet and Tewkesbury.

There is no argument over the facts of Richard's early career, only a failure to accord him just recognition as a young hero of great courage and unswerving devotion. And his loyalty was in marked contrast to the behaviour of his brother George, Duke of Clarence, who received more favours from Edward but proved an incorrigible 'quicksand of deceit'.

It is after the triumph at Tewkesbury, in which he played a leading part, that the first of the various crimes alleged against him in Tudor times is said to have been committed. He is accused of murdering Edward, the Lancastrian Prince of Wales, in cold blood after the battle. Yet there happen to be no fewer than two major and nine minor contemporary sources referring to the battle, all of which state or imply that the prince was 'slain on the field', none mentioning Richard as the slayer. The only chronicle which refers to any of the Yorkist leaders in this context says that the prince 'cried for succour to the Duke of Clarence'.

After the battle the Duke of Somerset and twelve other Lancastrians were executed as traitors. Their trial was conducted by Richard and the Duke of Norfolk in their respective offices of Constable and Marshal of England. That was the extent of Richard's involvement. Whether or not the executions were justified, the decision would have been King Edward's.

The next accusation concerns the mysterious death of Henry VI, which occurred in the Tower of London shortly after the battle. Much has been made of a passage in John Warkworth's chronicle which records that Richard was in the Tower on the night in question. Less is heard of the fact that the full record runs: Richard 'and many others'. If Henry was indeed killed, the decision would have been made by the king and council and their mandate may have been conveyed to the Tower by Richard as Constable. One contemporary chronicle states that King Edward caused the secret death of King Henry. None accuses Richard, and it is surely obvious that if Henry was anyone's victim he was Edward's, as Edward would have been Henry's if the battle at Tewkesbury had gone the other way. According to a modern historian not usually well disposed

towards Richard (Charles Ross), the Tudor saga's inclusion of
the murders of Prince Edward and King Henry in the catalogue
of Richard's alleged crimes is 'quite unrelated to the mundane
facts of historical evidence'.

There is no evidence, either, to connect Richard with the
death of his brother Clarence, who was later executed on King
Edward's orders after a public slanging match between king
and accused. If there was a dark influence at work it is likely to
have been that of the queen, who regarded both George and
Richard as enemies and obstacles to Woodville domination of
the king. In this instance the Tudor saga lacks support from its
own side. Not only is there no contemporary source which
implicates Richard, but even Henry Tudor's historian, Polydore Vergil, places the responsibility squarely on Edward.

Blame for these deaths is assigned to Richard without evidence by a process of back-derivation. Since he had to be a
monstrous usurper he must have murdered his vanished
nephews. Since he murdered his nephews he becomes readily
convertible into an all-round assassin, even before he became
king and had the necessary power and authority. Shakespeare
even has him slaying the Duke of Somerset in the first battle of
St Albans, which would have been an undeniably monstrous
act because Richard was two years old at the time.

After the fighting in 1471 Edward was firmly back on the
throne. 'In the space of twelve fierce months' (writes Paul
Murray Kendall) 'Richard had become the king's first general,
the chief prop of his throne, and his most trusted officer. He was
not yet nineteen.' From the following year he was lord of the
north. Such was Edward's confidence in him that he became
effectively ruler of the whole of the north of England, a quasi-
king beyond the Trent. There he spent eleven years – one third
of his life – bringing order and justice to an unruly region and
establishing an admirable record of public administration.

In 1482, after Louis XI of France had persuaded James III of
Scotland to break his truce with England, Richard captured
Berwick (which has remained English ever since) and went on
to capture Edinburgh too, with no casualties and no molesting
of the inhabitants. According to Mancini, a contemporary
writer generally unfavourable to Richard: 'The good reputation of his private life and public activities powerfully attracted

the esteem of strangers.' In Henry VIII's reign Lord Dacre, Warden of the West March, complained to Wolsey that he should not be expected to rival Richard's achievements. Wolsey replied that he must provide the same effective rule.

Richard was thirty when King Edward died. He had scarcely more than two years to live, and the record of his career was unblemished. What then of the reputedly dreadful tyranny of those two remaining years which effaced from memory all that had gone before and transformed him from paragon to demon?

If kings are to be judged by the impact of their rule on their subjects, Richard's reign was the very opposite to what the Tudor-inspired legend would have posterity suppose. It was motivated by concern for the poor and helpless. One contemporary wrote that 'he contents the people where he goes best that ever did prince'. There was a programme of law reform which included measures to correct injustice in the ownership and transfer of land, measures to safeguard the individual against abuses of the law in matters affecting juries and bail, measures to prevent the seizure of goods of those arrested but not yet found guilty, and the abolition of a much resented form of taxation known euphemistically as benevolences. Richard insisted on fair dealing in the law courts, which had been notoriously lacking during a period when the nobility flouted the law and took it forcibly into their own hands.

His policy of protection of the weak against the strong would have made him unpopular among some of the nobility, but to ordinary people he may well have been Good King Dickon. When he was killed the citizens of York, with considerable courage since they had to live under the rule of his successor, had their grief minuted in the official city records: 'This day was our good King Richard piteously slain and murdered, to the great heaviness of this city.'

If the legislation of Richard's reign had been oppressive, this would have been taken to confirm the worst judgments of posterity. That it was, on the contrary, exceptionally enlightened has proved a source of embarrassment to those who wish to see the blackness of his traditional villainy unrelieved. Yet even in Tudor times the true facts could not be entirely concealed, as an exchange between Wolsey and the mayor and aldermen of London in 1525 reveals. They were protesting against his demand for a benevolence in contravention of Richard III's statute. 'I marvel that you speak of Richard III, which was a usurper and murderer of his own nephews,' he reprimanded them. 'Although he did evil,' they replied, 'yet in his time were many good Acts made.'

AntiRichards attribute Richard's creditable record as a legislator not to any desire on his part to do good, but to a need to buy popularity. This is a guess about motivation which can be neither proved nor disproved. It is a speculative accusation which may be brought against almost any political leader in any age. From the point of view of the governed and their welfare it is scarcely relevant.

What kind of man do the revisionists read in this record? Richard was loyal, taking as his motto: *Loyaulte me lie* – loyalty binds me. His badge was the wild boar – a symbol of courage. He was generous and unwisely forgiving: his friends were treated munificently and his enemies allowed to live to fight another day. He declined free gifts from the cities he visited, saying that he wanted their hearts, not their money. He was not remote, suspicious and vindictive like the Tudor Henrys.

He was religious and puritan, conscientious, earnest and involved. The clergy in convocation praised his 'most noble and blessed disposition'. A bishop declared that God had 'sent him to us for the weal of us all'. A dedicated patron of the Church, he gave large sums of money for the building of King's College chapel in Cambridge and the completion of St George's at Windsor, both now so covered with Tudor and Beaufort emblems that it is hard to find any acknowledgment of his benefactions. He founded ten colleges or chantries, was a liberal benefactor to the university at Cambridge and encouraged education generally. He founded the Council of the North, the Court of Requests for poor litigants, and the College of Arms. Further evidence of his interest in heraldry and chivalry is to be found in the dedication to him of Caxton's *Order of Chivalry*. Those brought up to regard him as dating before the dawn of civilisation, ushered in by the Tudors, should be reminded not only of his piety and patronage of Caxton but of his company of scholars and the fact that the music at his court was famous throughout Europe.

All this is of no significance to a Tudor-trained traditionalist.

There is none so blind, remark the revisionists, as those who do not wish to see, and where the facts cannot be disputed they are disguised under Tudor gloss. In Sir Clements Markham's words: 'If Richard performs kindly acts, and many such are recorded, he is trying "to get unsteadfast friends". If he punishes treason he is a "venomous hunchback". If a rebellion is put down during his reign he is an inhuman tyrant. His ability is cunning, his justice is cruelty, his bravery is fury, his generosity is artfulness, his devotion is hypocrisy.'

George II led his troops at Dettingen, but Richard III was the last King of England actually to fight in battle while king. It is untrue that he was so unpopular that the nobility deserted him en masse at Bosworth. The pattern of self-interest was unchanged throughout the Wars of the Roses, and the absenteeism and cross-currents of allegiance discernible at Bosworth were par for the period. As Professor Ross has demonstrated, more than half the nobility of military age are known to have fought on Richard's side, and more may well have done so: not one joined Henry Tudor between his landing and the battle. Richard was brought down by the desertion on the battlefield of one earl, one baron and one knight.

The manner of his death was a heroic disaster. He showed supreme courage in leading a small band of his household to charge and challenge the Tudor pretender man to man. Even Polydore Vergil could not suppress admiration: 'King Richard, alone, was killed fighting manfully in the thickest press of his enemies.' He was the crowned king, the Lord's anointed, sanctified with the holy oil at his coronation at Westminster. Yet when he was dead, his body, riddled with the sword thrusts of traitors, was carried back to Leicester strapped across the back of a horse, stark naked, with a felon's halter round its neck, and publicly exposed in the town. Then it was buried in a friary church, where it lay only until the dissolution of the religious houses by Henry Tudor's son, when it is said to have been thrown into the River Soar. The treatment of his reputation has been not dissimilar to the indignities suffered by his corpse.

This is the Richard III remembered by those who gather at Sutton Cheney for their annual service of commemoration. This, they believe, is a good king, who was murdered in the flesh by traitors and in reputation by the lies of his enemies. As

Shakespeare wrote in another context: 'Who steals my purse steals trash. . . But he that filches from me my good name Robs me of that which not enriches him, And makes me poor indeed.' Some revisionists are motivated by a sense of injustice, some by sentiment and compassion; others are puzzle-solvers or simple seekers after truth. To all of them Richard was a man as other men are, but better than most: a man of honour and piety. For as long as the traditional tales are believed, they and others after them will persist in a self-imposed mission 'to strip the bandages of error from the eyes of men'.

Even now the bandages are slipping. Give or take a wart, this re-drawn portrait of Richard III has at last achieved some measure of academic respectability, accepted in part at least by historians of the period as well as the faithful at Sutton Cheney. Enlightenment, however, has yet to reach some general historians, many school-teachers and the public at large.

One summary of the attitude of the not unsympathetic historian is provided by Professor J. R. Lander (in the first edition of *Conflict and Stability in Fifteenth-Century England*, 1969): 'Richard was an able soldier and administrator, a cultivated man, fond of music and architecture, a patron of learning and deeply pious. He introduced into Parliament a useful programme of reforming legislation. Had he come to the throne through the normal workings of the succession he might well have enjoyed a long and successful reign. According to the Bishop of St Davids, writing probably in September 1483, everywhere he went he was popular amongst the people. The men of the north long remembered, to the embarrassment of Henry VII, his firm administration of justice in those parts in the last years of his brother's reign. Unfortunately for Richard's reputation neither Edward V nor his younger brother were ever seen again after the end of August 1483 and soon rumours widely spread that he had made away with them in the Tower of London.'

What continues to divide Ricardians from the specialist as well as the general historian are the two main charges against Richard: usurpation and infanticide. Yet if these commonly made accusations are well founded, the admirable record of a Richard Jekyll must be reconciled with the perpetration of two heinous crimes by a Richard Hyde.

4

Fifteenth-Century Attitudes

'Who shall be king, he who has the title or he who has the power?' asked Pepin the Short, father of Charlemagne. 'He who has the power,' replied the Pope obligingly, and Pepin proceeded to overthrow the Merovingian dynasty of Frankish kings. This was an early contribution to the creation of a lasting tradition in medieval Europe that kings could be lawfully deposed: specifically a bad king (one who broke laws) and *rex inutilis* (one who was incapable: a madman or a child). So if Richard III was indeed a usurper, was his usurpation unlawful, and was it undesirable?

Other and more recent precedents would have been in men's minds when Edward IV died unexpectedly on 9 April 1483, leaving a widow and a child heir. Neither the rule of boy kings nor the behaviour of queen mothers would have inspired much confidence in just administration and the maintenance of law and order, and the life expectancy of a Protector would not have been highly rated. During the preceding century and a half Edward III, Richard II and Henry VI had all been boy kings, and the purpose of this chapter is to illustrate that, so far from his behaving unnaturally in the context of his time, Richard's actions after the death of his brother were exactly what might have been expected from the example of those reigns, and that the actions of others, so far from being reactions to any unnaturalness on his part, were wholly in accord with the consistently self-interested behaviour of the nobility of that age. A man cannot be understood without an understanding of the times in which he lived, and the fourteenth and fifteenth centuries were periods of armed struggle and domestic violence among the members of the feudal families.

After they deposed and murdered Edward II, Queen Isabella and her bed-fellow, Roger Mortimer, had ruled scandalously in the name of her young son, Edward III, until he came of age three years later and rallied sufficient support to overthrow them. Edward III's successor, Richard II, had reigned unhappily, dominated by uncles and a council of quarrelling nobility, until he too was deposed and murdered. On Henry VI's accession to the throne as an infant, government had once more been exercised by a royal council. When as an adult Henry was still unfit to rule, civil war had broken out and the leadership of his cause was assumed by his termagant queen, Margaret of Anjou. As strong-willed as he was feeble-minded, it was she who led armies, executed opponents and, alone among Lancastrians and Yorkists, permitted her troops to indulge in pillage – at Ludlow and during her march on London after victory at Wakefield.

Edward III had become king in name at the age of fourteen; in fact at seventeen. Richard II, who was aged ten when he succeeded him, remained a puppet ruler for most of his reign. Henry VI, aged nine months, formally ascended the throne before he could walk, and became king in his own right at fifteen. In April 1483 Edward V was aged twelve and a half and might therefore be expected to be ruling as well as reigning after two and a half years. What then of the likely influence of his mother, Elizabeth Woodville, before and after his coming of age?

At Tewkesbury twelve years before, Margaret of Anjou had failed disastrously to establish her son, Edward of Lancaster, on his father's throne. Edward IV's widow was no less strong-willed and much better placed to ensure her son's succession and her own rule in his name until he came of age. Margaret had to lead an invasion force from France, but Elizabeth was already established in London at the centre of power. Her relatives and their allies represented a dominant faction on the council; over the years she had built a powerful affinity through a network of marriages between her family and the old nobility; and her son was safely in Woodville hands.

The queen was widely suspected of being behind her husband's decision to execute his brother George, Duke of Clarence (who, with Warwick, had been responsible for the execution of her father and her brother John). After Clarence's death there was only one remaining obstacle in her path to power, one sure rallying point for those opposed to the Wood-villes taking over the country as Isabella and the Mortimers had done: her husband's brother, Richard, Duke of Gloucester. And in that superstitious age those with knowledge of the past might well have caught their breath at a Duke of Gloucester being named Protector.

The first duke had been Thomas of Woodstock, the youngest son of Edward III. When his nephew succeeded to the throne as Richard II, he became Constable of England and the most powerful man in the realm. After the young king had broken free from his uncles and made himself unpopular through the arbitrariness of his personal rule, it was Gloucester who led the nobility against him, seized him, crushed his friends and supplanted him as *de facto* ruler. When Richard regained his rightful authority there was a period of reconciliation followed by the arrest of the duke, who was taken to Calais and there murdered.

The story of the second duke, good Duke Humphrey, youngest son of Henry IV, was also strangely apposite to the circumstances of 1483. When Henry V died of dysentery at the age of thirty-five while campaigning in France (a premature death like Edward IV's) the elder of his surviving brothers, John, Duke of Bedford, became Regent in France while Hum-phrey, Duke of Gloucester, appointed Protector in Henry's will (the precedent followed by Edward IV), attempted to secure the regency in England. Appointment as tutor to the infant king would, if all went well, have brought him power for at least thirteen years. But his ambitions were frustrated by the opposi-tion of Cardinal Beaufort, and the royal authority became vested, formally, in the lords spiritual and temporal as a body and, in practice, in the council, where Gloucester, although gaining the titles of Protector and Defender of the Realm as well as Chief Councillor, was no more than *primus inter pares*. When his power waned he was inevitably charged with treason, dying while under arrest in the custody of his enemies, probably murdered like the first duke.

Only seven years later (in 1454) parliament had to meet to decide yet again how a realm with an incapable monarch should be ruled. Since August of the previous year Henry VI had been suffering from what would nowadays probably be diagnosed as catatonic schizophrenia and Richard III's father, Richard, Duke of York, who had assumed the surname of Plantagenet but not yet advanced his claim to the throne, was demanding the royal authority as the king's closest adult relation, in competition with the queen, who unsuccessfully sought the appointment of Regent.

Like Humphrey of Gloucester, York was denied any title which would 'import authority of governance of the land', although named as Protector of the Realm. Governments in the fifteenth century ruled without police or regular military forces at their disposal, and he became, in effect, a commander-in-chief with no army except his own retainers. Even this appointment was short-lived because the king recovered his sanity early in the following year, and matters moved towards a more decisive and violent outcome with the 'scuffle in a back street' known as the first battle of St Albans.

That these events and the civil war which succeeded them are likely to have been in the minds of Richard and the more learned of his friends and advisers in Middleham castle in April 1483 does not warrant the assumption, now enshrined in legend, that he at once determined to seize the crown for himself. Uncertainty would seem a more plausible reaction. What authority would the protectorship carry in theory and in practice? Would it prove strong enough to overcome the queen's bid for power? How long would it last and what would happen to them all when it ended? In the remoteness of the north Yorkshire dales much would have been unknown, most crucially the views and likely actions of members of council not attached to the Woodville cause, the other powerful magnates of the realm, and the city of London. Richard had no choice but to assume the role his brother had bequeathed to him. If he allowed himself to be outwitted by the queen and she were to trump his protectorship with a regency of her own, no one could be in doubt what would follow. The urgent necessity for him to take physical possession of Edward V to prevent the boy being used as a Woodville pawn would have been generally understood and agreed. Other decisions would have waited upon events.

Above all others, the example of his father, after whom he was named and whom he is said to have resembled, must have been vividly in Richard's mind. The Duke of York had been confronted with a very similar set of circumstances in May 1455. He had fumbled for the crown and it had cost him his head. In 1459 a Lancastrian parliament at Coventry had passed an act of attainder condemning him and members of his family for treason. They were to be hanged, drawn and quartered (a punishment including castration and dis-embowelment while still alive) and their heirs disinherited for ever. Such would have been the penalty for failure.

All this may serve to explain why, after the attempted coup by Hastings and other councillors, Richard decided or allowed himself to be persuaded that the limited authority of a Protector would protect neither England from further civil war nor himself and his supporters from, sooner or later, the mortal vengeance of the Woodvilles. Seen against the background of his own and earlier times, Richard's eventual decision seems both natural and inevitable, and the general acceptance of him as king at the time confirms that that was the view of most of his contemporaries. What ruined his reputation was not usurpa-tion but the subsequent disappearance of the princes and the defeat at Bosworth which deprived him of the opportunity of proving his worth as a king and left his good name in the hands of his enemies.

What of the behaviour of the nobility? Traditionalists con-tinually assert that desertions at Bosworth were caused by revulsion against a tyrannical usurper, but the defection of the Stanleys and Northumberland should be viewed in the context of contemporary custom and practice in warfare. By the fifteenth century the age of true chivalry, like the age of true monasticism, was over. In the French wars, in the words of K. B. McFarlane, men 'made no pretence of fighting for love of king or lord, still less for England or for glory, but for gain'. It was Polydore Vergil and, after him, Shakespeare who bestowed an *ex post facto* halo of patriotism on Henry V and his army of marauders. Nationalism was a concept unknown at the time. Henry claimed France as a personal possession and was attempting to assert his rights as a property-owner, and his army was no less acquisitively self-interested.

During the Wars of the Roses there was not much warfare and precious little display of heraldic roses. Estimates of total time occupied in active campaigning during the entire period between 1455 and 1487 vary from three months to 428 days, and few of the armed encounters between members of the nobility and gentry and their retainers merit description as a battle. Towton, fought in a snowstorm on a Palm Sunday, was bloody; so was Barnet, fought on an Easter Sunday in a fog. But usually casualties were light, tactics amateur, and hearts not in the fighting. Those participating in the conflict were more concerned with their own private disputes over landed property and legal rights than with whether York or Lancaster should wear the crown.

The objective of most of the nobility, in council or in arms, was not to commit themselves irrevocably to either side. In 1454 when parliament was summoned to make a critical decision between the Duke of York, who was urging his claim to be Protector, and the queen, who was demanding to be appointed Regent, such a large number of lords failed to answer the summons that, for the only time in English history, fines were introduced for non-attendance. In some cases the political undesirability of commitment was so strong that prominent peers were seized with miraculous fits of piety and disappeared hurriedly on pilgrimages to the Holy Land. Among the few who became irreconcilably committed was John de Vere, Earl of Oxford, who as well as restitution of the confiscated de Vere estates sought revenge for the death of his father and brother (not killed in battle but executed by Edward IV for conspiracy).

The Percys and the Stanleys, who in the end betrayed Richard, characterised the age. Changing sides on the battlefield was a common ploy, by no means peculiar to Bosworth. At Ludlow in 1459 Andrew Trollope and his contingent from Calais had crept out of the Yorkist lines in darkness to join the Lancastrians on the eve of battle. A year later at Northampton Lord Grey of Ruthin had deserted the Lancastrians as soon as the fighting began, bringing victory to the Yorkists. At the second battle of St Albans, Loveless, captain of a contingent of

Kentishmen, tipped the balance by deserting York for Lancaster.

Treachery at Bosworth should not therefore have taken Richard by surprise, nor be interpreted by responsible historians as the revulsion of honourable men against a monster king. Henry Percy, the fourth Earl of Northumberland, was the head of a family of Lancastrian supporters whose loyalty to Edward IV had been spasmodic and suspect. The Percys behaved like kings themselves in the north, where their court (like those of other magnates) was modelled on the royal household. Their enemies were the other northern families, their rivals for supremacy: the Dacres, the Cliffords, but above all the Nevills – and Edward and Richard were Nevills on their mother's side.

The Percys, moreover, were a family with an unfortunate battle record. The fourth earl's father, the third Earl Henry, had been killed in action in 1461 at Towton, where he commanded the Lancastrian vanguard. His grandfather, the second Earl Henry, had been killed in action in 1455 at St Albans, fighting against Richard's father. His great-grandfather, Harry Hotspur, had been killed in action in 1403 at Shrewsbury fighting against Henry IV. The fourth earl's lack of enthusiasm for taking part in the fighting at Bosworth is therefore understandable, particularly as it would have meant fighting for a Nevill, a Yorkist king, and the man who for eleven years had been placed above him as the leading magnate in the north of England.

Lord Stanley had already played at Blore Heath the same waiting game as he played at Bosworth. Paul Murray Kendall has written of him: 'In a century of civil strife, fierce partisanship, betrayals, broken causes, in which many among the lords and gentry had been brought to ruin or extinction, Lord Stanley and his brother Sir William had thrived. They thrived by daring to make politics their trade, by sloughing off the encumbrances of loyalty and honour, by developing an ambiguity of attitude which enabled them to join the winning side, and by exploiting the relative facility with which treason in this age might be lived down, provided it were neither too passionate, overt nor damaging.' The family motto could not have been less apt. It was *Sans Changer*.

Although providing an outstanding example of a family on

the make during this period, the Stanleys were not atypical. For all their solemn oaths, loyalty was not a prime consideration among the nobility and gentry. Instead they were obsessed with what Professor Lander has described as the 'near-sanctity of inheritance'. What they worshipped was the possession of land, offices and titles, from which alone wealth and power derived. What they looked for from a ruler was the assurance that these 'rights' would remain in the family and pass down within it from generation to generation.

The issue between York and Lancaster was itself a question of inheritance. Richard's father had based his claim on the superiority of the right of an heir general over that of an heir male. The fact that the Lancastrians had sat on the throne for more than half a century he dismissed as irrelevant: however long a claim remained dormant, it was not for that reason extinguished. As a later historian put it: 'If a man steals a guinea it is no more his own after keeping it twenty years than it was the first day.' Or, in the words of the Duke of York himself (overdoing the negatives in his vehemence): 'Though right for a time rest and be put to silence, yet it rotteth not nor shall not perish.' That was a statement which the establishment of the fifteenth century would have found unexceptionable. What was less easy to agree upon was the tricky matter of the respective rights of Edward III's heirs general (passing through females) and heirs male (passing through males, but a junior branch).

When in 1399 Henry Bolingbroke had forced Richard II to abdicate and usurped the crown as Henry IV, he disregarded the claims of the Mortimers, Richard's heirs general. And it would not have gone unnoticed that Bolingbroke's son, Henry V, claimed the throne of France as heir general to the House of Capet (through Edward III's mother, Isabella of France) while a precisely similar argument in respect of the throne of England led to the inescapable conclusion that the rightful heirs were not his father and himself but the Mortimers and afterwards, by descent from them, the House of York. Property being the obsession of the medieval magnate, Bolingbroke had received strong support when Richard II deprived him of his rightful inheritance, the duchy of Lancaster, on the death of his father, John of Gaunt. But as a king he could never command total loyalty, not so much because of the brutal murder of Richard, but because he in turn had deprived the Mortimers of their rightful inheritance.

These attitudes explain why Richard III's accession to the throne may have been as popular as the large attendance at his coronation suggests. At a time of lawlessness and disorder, when powerful criminals were often too well connected to be brought to justice, those with a stake in the established order of society would be relieved at the prospect of firm government by one who held a similar stake. As a member of the long-ruling royal house of Plantagenet and a man of good reputation for sound and honest administration in the north, he was a much safer bet than a puppet of the upstart and predatory Woodvilles.

The cause for concern would have been, not the usurpation of the throne, but the usurpation of the rights of Edward IV's heirs. Disinheritance remained a crime against society, a threat to every member of the establishment; it could not be accepted without justification. This was forthcoming through a formal, legal and constitutional declaration that Edward IV's marriage was invalid. Since his children were no longer his rightful heirs, the fabric of society remained intact. To some this solution to the problem was doubtless no more than a convenient fiction, but for others, well aware of Edward's reckless wenching, it was probably a welcome truth.

If this interpretation is correct, Richard's 'usurpation' was not an act of tyranny but an expression of the general will. Some opposed it, others like the Archbishop of Canterbury and the Bishop of Lincoln are believed to have accepted it reluctantly,· but without the backing of most of the nobility and representatives of the commons, acting rationally in what they judged to be their own interests, it seems doubtful whether it would have been attempted. There is no evidence that the (ill-armed) force which Richard summoned from the north for his protection terrorised a London opposed to his coronation, and it was sent home immediately afterwards. Without encouragement, or at least acquiescence, in high quarters, he would have been forced to make what he could of the protectorship and resign himself to the fate which would have overtaken him when Edward V came of age. If the boy's deposition is seen as a crime, the guilt must be shared by many who did not have this excuse.

Constitutional or not, was Richard's accession in the best interests of the country? Contemporary events in France offer some support for the belief that the reign of Edward V, if continued, would inevitably have resulted in a renewed outbreak of civil war. Louis XI died on 30 August 1483, some five months after Edward IV, leaving a thirteen-year-old heir (Charles VIII). Power was formally divided between the boy's sister, Anne of Beaujeu, who became Regent and had charge of the king's person, and a council of twelve who were charged with responsibility for the affairs of state. The council proved ineffectual, Madame ruled supreme in her brother's name, and civil war ensued.

When passing moral judgments on Richard, Tudor chroniclers and later antiRichard historians might have found it salutary to take an imaginative step backwards into the ambience of the later middle ages and let their readers know what they themselves would have done if they had been in his shoes facing the unsought predicament in which he found himself between April and June of 1483.

5

Accession to the Throne

The true tragedy of Richard III – the event which led to the ruin of his life and reputation – was the early and unexpected death of his brother Edward IV. A struggle for power was the unavoidable outcome. Richard won the first round, taking the crown with widespread support and little bloodshed. But then, so far from becoming the ruthless tyrant of legend, he was soon 'piteously slain and murdered' largely as a result of clemency shown towards known enemies and traitors.

Its constitutional validity apart, his assumption of the crown may be judged as sensible, perhaps even inevitable. After the anarchy of the Wars of the Roses and the relative calm under Edward IV the country needed, not a precarious protectorship, but a strong ruler permanently enthroned to avert a relapse into barbarism, and Richard of Gloucester was already experienced in government and war. If his accession was a usurpation, then there was good cause and good precedent, but it should be more widely recognised that the man who has become history's most notorious usurper became king by title of inheritance, with the full support of the city of London and after a petition by the Lords and Commons of the realm subsequently confirmed by a formal parliament in an Act for the Settlement of the Crown upon the King and his Issue. 'Ironic though it may be,' writes Professor Charles Wood (in an article in *Traditio*, 1975), 'Richard III, legendary usurper and tyrant, has some claim to having been the one possessor of a genuinely parliamentary title during the entire middle ages.'

The chaos of events during April and June 1483 strongly

suggests that there was no prepared plot to seize the throne, merely indecision. Professor Myers judges Richard to have been 'probably an anxious and nervous man rather than a cruel and merciless one', and his accession seems, not an example of successful scheming, but a good illustration of Oliver Cromwell's dictum that 'no man often advances higher than he who knows not where he is going'. Sudden alterations of plan do not suggest premeditation, and it appears likely that Richard was perplexed by conflicting advice.

Of all the influences upon him the most potent seems to have been Henry Stafford, second Duke of Buckingham, a man of about the same age as Richard and himself a Plantagenet, descended from two of Edward III's sons. His mother was a Beaufort and his branch of the family had supported the Lancastrian cause, his father being mortally wounded fighting against Richard's (at St Albans in 1455) and his grandfather killed in battle against Edward IV (at Northampton in 1460). As a minor he was Elizabeth Woodville's ward and suffered a possibly much resented disparagement through marriage to the Woodville queen's sister Catherine. In the events of Edward IV's reign he is most notable as an absentee, presumably living in disgrace or sulking on his vast estates. Ambitious and unstable, he gallops out of oblivion on to the pages of history at Northampton on 29 April 1483 and fills them until his execution six months later. Amid the confusion and high drama of those months Buckingham is dominant and decisive, a new Warwick playing the role of kingmaker. While Richard appears in the centre of the stage, at times somewhat bewildered, there is always a suspicion that Buckingham is the author or impresario, the equivocal promoter of a protagonist whom he has no cause to love.

On the evening of the critical meeting in Northampton Earl Rivers must have gone to bed satisfied that he had hedged successfully. He was the queen's brother and there is little doubt that his objective was to bring the boy king to London under his own protection in order to have him crowned as quickly as possible and a new pro-Woodville council formally appointed before Richard could take up the reins of government. By that means the protectorship willed to Richard by the dead king could be effectively nullified. By leaving Edward V in

Stony Stratford, Rivers had brought him within striking distance of London without actually delivering him into the
Protector's hands. But he had kept the rendezvous himself and
been well received. It was after his retirement, when Richard is
said to have talked long into the night with Buckingham, his
fiery new ally, that the next day's seizure of the king's person is
likely to have been planned and the situation become transformed.

On arrival in London Richard behaved with exemplary
propriety, immediately mounting a public ceremony at which
the lords spiritual and temporal and the city dignitaries, himself at their head, swore fealty to Edward V. A meeting of the
council on 10 May formally appointed him Protector and a new
day was fixed for Edward's coronation, the original date for
which had passed. Writs and warrants were issued in the name
of King Edward V 'by the advice of our dearest uncle, the Duke
of Gloucester, Protector of our realm during our young age, and
of the Lords of our Council'. The late king's last wishes had
been fulfilled. The Woodville bid for power had failed. An
armed conflict had been averted thanks to the bold action of the
two dukes. A period of calm ensued.

On 5 June letters were written in the king's name to some fifty
esquires, who were commanded to 'prepare and furnish
yourselves to receive the noble order of knighthood at our
coronation on 22 June and be at the Tower four days before'.
On 8 June Richard wrote a routine letter to the city of York. On
9 June there was no news of importance, or hint of trouble, to be
reported in a letter from Simon Stallworth, one of the chancellor's staff, writing from London to a friend in the country. Then,
five weeks after the entry into London, the storm broke. On 10
June Richard sent urgently to the north for reinforcements:
there was a plot by the queen's 'blood, adherents and affinity' to
murder and destroy the two dukes and the old royal blood of the
realm. The tone of the despatch to the city of York, heightened
by the importance of its bearer (Sir Richard Ratcliffe), strikes a
note of panic.

Committed antiRichards among historians deny the existence of a plot: to them the brouhaha is, of course, a charade. Yet
there seems no good reason to doubt that Richard – and others
– believed his life to be in danger. Lord Hastings, in May

confirmed in his appointments as royal chamberlain and Captain of Calais, had now turned against the Protector. As the late king's closest friend and the head of his household, he was the natural leader of the loyalists supporting their old master's heir. The question which some see as crucial to Richard's reputation is whether his conspiracy sprang from knowledge that Richard had all the time been secretly intent on dispossessing his nephew. Was the Hastings plot the result of Richard's aiming for the crown, or was it the cause, bringing Richard to the realisation that he and his friends would never be safe unless he occupied the throne himself? There are no sure answers.

During May Buckingham had been well rewarded for his support of Richard. The grants he received gave him almost kingly powers in Wales. His meteoric rise is not likely to have pleased Hastings who, as Richard's earlier ally against the Woodvilles, must have hoped to retain the influential position which he had occupied under Edward IV but which he now saw usurped by the egregious Buckingham. The two were also rival magnates in the north Midlands, where the traditional dominance of Buckingham's family (the Staffords) had been overturned by Clarence, to whose ascendancy in the area Hastings had succeeded.

Whatever the gravity of the emergency, the summary execution of Hastings on 13 June has remained an ineradicable blot on Richard's record. For Richard it was an uncharacteristic act, and he afterwards treated Hastings' widow and family with generosity. Buckingham may therefore have been the instigator. William Catesby, who seems to have acted as a go-between, was a lawyer serving both Hastings and Buckingham, and it is possible that Buckingham used him to gain information about Hastings' treachery and transmit it to Richard, either accurately or in an exaggerated form. Convincing evidence that there was indeed a plot of some kind was apparently produced at a subsequent meeting of the council and made public. Whether or not he was the prime mover against Hastings, Buckingham was certainly involved in his arrest and execution and received all his offices after his death.

With Hastings dead and his fellow conspirators (Rotherham, Morton and Stanley) under arrest, the opposition was crushed. On 16 June the queen was persuaded to allow the king's

younger brother, Richard, Duke of York, to leave sanctuary at
Westminster and join the king in the Tower. Then on 21 June,
as we learn from another letter by Simon Stallworth, London is
in a ferment: 'with us is much trouble and every man doubts
other'. On 22 June, a Sunday, the uncertainty is ended.
Richard's claim to the throne is publicly asserted for the
first time – in a sermon preached to the citizens of London by
the mayor's brother (Dr Ralph Shaw) on a text taken from The
Wisdom of Solomon denouncing 'the multiplying brood of the
ungodly': 'Bastard slips shall not take deep root'. On 24 June
Buckingham makes an eloquent speech on Richard's behalf to
the city fathers assembled in Guildhall, and two days later lords
and commons unanimously approve a petition calling upon the
Protector to assume the crown. This he does on the same day:
Thursday 26 June.

Richard's accession was backed by only the most limited
military force (his own and Buckingham's retainers, augmented by some of Hastings'). The troops summoned from the
north did not arrive until after the coup. When they did come
they proved to be raw recruits, 'evil apparelled and worse
harnessed' according to one scornful contemporary Londoner,
and were soon sent home. So much for Richard's alleged show
of force and the cowing of a hostile populace. In the words of the
historian Malcolm Laing (in Robert Henry's *History of Great
Britain*): 'Instead of a violent usurpation we discover an accession, irregular according to modern usage, but established
without violence on a legal title.'

Meanwhile the only other deaths incurred in the course of the
accession had taken place at Pontefract on 25 June, when the
Earl of Northumberland presided over the execution of Rivers,
Grey and Vaughan. The decision would have been made by the
council in London. If More is to be believed, one of Hastings'
last acts was to give his assent to these executions. He and
Rivers had quarrelled over their amours and been bitter rivals
for the captaincy of Calais. Rivers was also a rival to Buckingham's supremacy in Wales. In the power politics of the time
there is no reason to see him and his two associates as the
victims of Richard alone.

It is possible that the parting of ways between Richard and
the faction headed by Hastings occurred at a council meeting

held on 9 June, when one matter which may have been discussed would have shattered the fragile harmony of conflicting interests by casting doubt on the legitimacy of the king. Robert Stillington, Bishop of Bath and Wells, came forward, at this time or later, with a story that Edward IV had been troth-plight to Lady Eleanor Butler, daughter of John Talbot, Earl of Shrewsbury, the hero of the French wars. Edward's marriage to Elizabeth Woodville was therefore null and void, for under canon law if a man was precontracted to one woman he was not free to marry another, and Lady Eleanor had not died until 1468, four years after the Woodville marriage.

Most historians dismiss this pre-contract as a hollow pretext for usurpation, but support for it has come, surprisingly, from James Gairdner, the antiRichard scholar of Victorian times. In his *Life and Reign of Richard the Third* Gairdner writes: 'The ecclesiastical theory of pre-contracts which prevailed before the Reformation was the source of great abuses. Marriages that had been publicly acknowledged, and treated for a long time as valid, were often declared null on the ground of some previous contract entered into by one or other of the parties. In this way King Henry VIII, before putting Anne Boleyn to death, caused his marriage with her to be pronounced invalid by reason of a previous contract on her part with Percy, Earl of Northumberland. Bulls of divorce were sometimes procured from Rome, even by the party that had done the wrong, dissolving a marriage that had endured for years, on the ground of a pre-contract with another person. Mere betrothal, in fact, was no less binding than matrimony, and could not be canonically set aside without a dispensation; for, as consent constituted the essence of a marriage, the marriage might be in itself a complete thing, even before it was celebrated *in facie ecclesiae*.'

'The evidence of Edward IV's pre-contract with Lady Eleanor Butler,' Gairdner continues, 'rested on the single testimony of Robert Stillington, Bishop of Bath and Wells. It is certain that Edward indulged in several lawless amours before his marriage, and, according to the bishop, Lady Eleanor yielded to his desire on a secret promise of marriage made before himself, which he was obliged to conceal so long as King Edward lived, for fear of his displeasure. Sir George Buck . . . informs us that the Lady Eleanor, after having a child from this unacknowledged connection, retired into a monastery, where she died not long afterwards; and though he gives no authority for this statement, the fact seems highly probable.'

'Another point, which is perhaps rather an evidence of the truth of the story,' Gairdner adds, 'is the care afterwards taken to suppress and to pervert it. When Henry VII became king, and married the daughter of Edward IV and Elizabeth Woodville, any allusion to the pre-contract was treated as disloyal. The petition to Richard to assume the crown was declared to be so scandalous that every copy of it was ordered by Parliament to be destroyed. The allegations contained in it were misinterpreted; the pre-contract was said to have been with Elizabeth Lucy, one of Edward's mistresses, instead of with Lady Eleanor Butler, and the name of the latter lady was omitted from the story. Thus, in Sir Thomas More's history, a courtesan of obscure birth is made to take the place of an earl's daughter as the person to whom Edward was first betrothed; and such is the version of the story that has been current nearly ever since. It was only after the lapse of a century and a quarter that Sir George Buck discovered the true tenor of the parliamentary petition in the manuscript history of Croyland; and again, after another like period had passed away, the truth received ample confirmation by the discovery of the very Roll of Parliament on which the petition was engrossed. Fortunately, notwithstanding the subsequent statute, all the copies had not been destroyed.'

Stillington's revelation was certainly a convenient tale to tell in the circumstances of the time, but it is not for that reason necessarily an invention. Stillington was far from being a provincial nonentity. He had been Edward IV's chancellor for seven years (1467–73) and was seemingly so pre-occupied with affairs of state throughout his political career that he paid no more than a single visit to his diocese during his twenty-six years as its spiritual father. At the time of Clarence's death he was removed from office and imprisoned. If Edward's marriage to Elizabeth Woodville was invalid and their children illegitimate, Clarence would then have been the true heir to the throne. Did Stillington tell his tale to Clarence – and Clarence confront Edward with it? Was that what lay behind Clarence's execution? Historians continue to argue the answers, but it may be relevant that one of the first arrests ordered by Henry Tudor after Bosworth was that of Stillington.

The matter of the pre-contract, justifying Richard's claim to the throne, is fully set out in the Act of Settlement (otherwise Titulus Regius) passed by his only parliament, which met at Westminster on Friday, 23 January 1484. As Gairdner says, when Henry Tudor became king it was ordained that all copies of this Act must be destroyed, and in the version of the story recounted by Tudor chroniclers the name of Elizabeth Lucy, a well-known lady of easy virtue whose name would effectively discredit the tale, was substituted for that of Eleanor Butler (regardless of the fact that Dame Elizabeth's son by Edward – Arthur Plantagenet, later Viscount Lisle – would then have been the rightful king).

But this was not the only argument advanced in the petition and Act for setting aside the claims of Edward IV's children. By implication Edward's own legitimacy was called into question. He had been born in Rouen, not in England under the eye of the court and council, and (although this is not mentioned in the Act) during his reign rumours had been circulating that he was really the son of a common soldier – an archer. According to More, this tale was even given some credence by his mother, Cecily, Duchess of York. In exasperation, when his secret marriage to a commoner became known, she herself is said to have denounced him as illegitimate.

There is in the Act, too, an accusation of sorcery and witchcraft. In an age when dabbling in the occult was fashionable this was a charge to which high-born ladies were vulnerable. A first step in the downfall of the previous Duke of Gloucester holding the office of Protector had been the trial of his wife, Eleanor Cobham, for practising the magical arts. This, in 1441, had ended with a sentence of life imprisonment. A similar charge against Elizabeth Woodville and her mother may therefore be seen as essentially political, although it will not have escaped notice in those superstitious times that, to consummate his surreptitious marriage, Edward IV stole away during the night of 30 April/1 May, which was Walpurgis night, a grand sabbath in the witches' year, an occasion for orgiastic revelling with the Devil.

'And here also we consider,' runs the relevant passage from

the Act so nearly consigned to oblivion by Richard's enemies (but published in 1783 in the original English text of the one surviving copy), 'how that the said pretensed marriage was made privily and secretly, without edition of banns, in a private chamber – a profane place and not openly in the face of the church after the law of God's church, but contrary thereunto and the laudable custom of the church of England.'

From all this it followed that because 'the said King Edward and the said Elizabeth lived together sinfully and damnably in adultery against the law of God and of his church . . . all the issue and children of the said King Edward [were] bastards and unable to inherit or to claim anything by inheritance by the law and custom of England'.

It may be thought that the Act doth protest too much, that the very enumeration of a variety of causes for invalidating the claim of Edward IV's children argues a lack of confidence in the persuasiveness of any one. On the other hand, it should be recognised that there was at that time no general acceptance of rules and laws governing the succession. Usurper is a term which has been applied to every King of England in the fifteenth century: Lancastrian, Yorkist and Tudor. In defence of Richard's claim it can be argued that, once King Edward V had become, by the will of lords and commons, no more than Edward the Lord Bastard, what Richard was petitioned to occupy was a vacant throne.

6

King from the North

'Every one that is acquainted with English history must know that there is hardly any part of it so dark as the short reign of this king: the Lancastrian party which destroyed and succeeded him took care to suppress his virtues, and to paint his vices in the most glaring colours.' These are the words of a northern antiquarian, Francis Drake, the eighteenth-century historian of York.

Southern historians have persisted in presenting the disappearance of the princes as the highlight of Richard's reign. Deposition was customarily a sentence of death. Edward II and Richard II had been murdered after the loss of their thrones, and probably Henry VI too. In the light of precedent and the absence of evidence to the contrary, the murder of Edward V and his brother by his successor became a natural presumption. Rumours to that effect would have been spread whatever the truth of the matter, and we know that some were inspired by interested parties hostile to the new king, contributing to the outbreak of Buckingham's rebellion and strengthening the hand of the Tudor pretender.

Certainly the so-called Buckingham rebellion in October 1483 was more than its name implies. Disaffection was widespread in the southern counties – in Kent, Essex and Hertfordshire, for example, far from Buckingham's estates and influence in South Wales and the west country. The quick collapse of his part in the enterprise is evidence of the slender support which Buckingham himself could command. The real inspiration of the rising is said to have been Edward V, although it is not clear whether in that case the objective was to rescue him, since he was thought to be alive, or to revenge him, since he was thought to be dead. Among those who were punished after the rebellion had been put down were former members of Edward IV's househould as well as the Woodville affinity and unregenerate Lancastrians such as Margaret Beaufort, Henry Tudor's mother.

The fifteenth century was a raw age, lived in the shadow of death from the moment of birth. Children were plentiful and infant mortality was high. (Richard's grandfather, the first Earl of Westmorland, fathered twenty-three children, and the fourth earl ran out at eighteen; in a succeeding generation not one of Dean Colet's nineteen brothers and sisters reached adulthood.) The cult of the Holy Innocents placed special emphasis on children as sacred trusts, treasures of God, but it is improbable that many men and women stood aghast at the possibility that the deposed boy king had been murdered. If there was anything to be gained from expressions of horror – as there was by supporters of the Tudor pretender – they would express it. But since the death of the princes was essential if their own candidate was to succeed, this is evidence of little more than hypocrisy.

Among the devout and those loyal to Edward IV's family there would have been genuine concern and a reaction against Richard if the fate of the princes was unknown and the worst suspected. But, generally, there seems a more potent cause for disaffection, which may be identified through the fact that there was none in the north. 'It is plain,' writes Drake, 'that Richard, represented as a monster of mankind by most, was not so esteemed in his lifetime in these northern parts.' What stirred the southern gentry in October 1483 was not an outburst of moral outrage but the justified belief that they were losing power and influence to intruding northerners.

Then, as now, England was two nations, and the events of Richard III's reign are best seen in focus through the perspective of north versus south. To the southerner England north of the Humber was, like Scotland, a barbarous region inhabited by savage brutes, the Ostrogoths of Britain, who represented an ever-present threat to the lives and livelihoods of the prosperous and civilised south. The terror inspired by the march of Margaret of Anjou's pillaging army from the north in 1461 is recorded in the *Rose of Rouen* and the Croyland Chronicle. It was Warwick's rough northerners who brought down Edward IV in 1470. The power of the Nevills lay in the north and when Richard married the Kingmaker's younger daughter and inherited his northern estates he succeeded to that power. Control of the northern barons by the king in London had been tenuous for centuries, and Edward IV must have been pleased to have contrived this assumption of northern leadership by his brother and well satisfied with its success. With his own council and almost regal authority, Richard ruled the unruly from the great Yorkshire strongholds of Middleham, Sheriff Hutton and Pontefract, leaving Edward secure in his self-indulgence in the soft south.

As A. J. Pollard has pointed out, the six northern counties at that time were under-populated, economically backward and growing even poorer. Foreign visitors remarked on the contrast between their desolate moors and forests and the rich gardens and orchards of Kent. Covering a quarter of the land mass of England, they contained no more than fifteen per cent of the population. Their support for their own viceroy as the ruler of all England must have been wholehearted. He had proved himself not only a good and just administrator but also a strong and victorious general who had brought them the priceless protection of Berwick, captured from the Scots. In 1483 the men of the north would have viewed southern England much as the Scots did more than a century later, when the crown of England at last fell into the lap of their king, James VI, and at the head of what was seen by some southerners as little less than a plague of locusts he led his impoverished nobles and their threadbare retainers out of a barren land into one flowing with milk and honey.

When after Richard's death Henry VII's tax-collectors visited the northern counties 'the people upon a sudden grew into a great mutiny' and said that they neither could nor would pay the tax, according to Francis Bacon in his *History of the Reign of King Henry the Seventh*. 'This (no doubt) proceeded not simply of any present necessity, but much by reason of the old humour of those countries, where the memory of King Richard was so strong that it lies like lees in the bottom of men's hearts, and if the vessel was but stirred it would come up.'

It came up with a vengeance when the Earl of Northumberland, who had betrayed Richard at Bosworth, assumed the role of Henry's chief tax-gatherer in the north. Then 'the meaner sort ranted together and, suddenly assailing the earl in his house, slew him and divers of his servants'. Doubtless the taxes were more in their minds than Richard III, but they are likely to have been all too conscious of the loss of his protection. Later, in the Pilgrimage of Grace, the men of the north were to mount what was indeed a great mutiny against Henry Tudor's son, and another against his grand-daughter, Elizabeth I.

In the south the great metropolitan city of London had little hesitation in accepting Richard as king and never turned against him during his lifetime. To commercial interests the preservation of law and order was all-important, and Richard's parliament legislated for the protection of English merchants against unfair competition from overseas. The rewards and favours bestowed on northerners by this king from the north were at the expense, not of southern merchants, but of the southern nobility and gentry, for it was natural that he should find places in the royal household for those who had served him in his administration as lord of the north and Steward of the Duchy of Lancaster in the north. Nor is it surprising that this and similar exercises in patronage should have caused resentment among those supplanted, so that some who had been close to Edward IV became participants in the October rebellion.

Afterwards, when the southern estates of the rebels were confiscated and given to northerners, the division between northern and southern interests grew even deeper. Inability to heal this breach was the dire political failure of Richard's reign and, more than any other, the reason for his downfall, but it is hardly a cause for moral stricture. Those who joined Henry Tudor were not reacting like a bench of Victorian bishops, rebelling in righteous indignation against an assassin of Holy Innocents: they wanted their estates back.

Unsupported by standing armies, medieval kings ruled largely through the exercise of patronage. This was their only weapon against overmighty subjects, who were sometimes richer in resources and armed retainers. To maintain his position after the defeat of the Woodville affinity, Richard needed to secure the adherence of only a handful of magnates who stood at the top of the pyramid of power. With Hastings he failed despite initial success. With Buckingham he failed despite loading the 'untrue creature' with honours and estates.

With John Howard he achieved success. Howard had been appointed Constable of the Tower for life by Edward IV, only to be superseded by the queen's son Thomas, Marquis of Dorset. He had been deprived of his share of the Norfolk inheritance after the death of the infant Anne Mowbray, when Edward IV (with dubious legality) kept it for his younger son, Anne's child husband. One of Richard's first acts as king was to create John Howard Duke of Norfolk and this favour was rewarded with loyalty until death.

Another success was with the De La Poles. The head of the family, the Duke of Suffolk, was a political nonentity married to Richard's sister, Elizabeth. Brothers-in-law could not be taken for granted (another, Sir Thomas St Leger, was executed for his part in the Buckingham rebellion) and Suffolk himself avoided all attachments and battles, but his eldest son, John, Earl of Lincoln, became Richard's heir, his viceroy in Ireland and the Yorkist leader after Richard's death.

It is ironical that the crucial failures in Richard's exercise of patronage were with the two major beneficiaries of the favours which he distributed among northerners: Stanley and Northumberland. Their bread was buttered thickly enough to preserve their loyalty during Buckingham's rebellion, but at Bosworth they took the decision that Henry Tudor's gratitude, inexperience and likely preoccupation in the south would serve their interests even better.

With these magnates, it may be argued, Richard did all that could have been expected of him, but the considerable amount of new patronage placed in his hands as a result of forfeitures after the Buckingham rebellion he used unwisely. Shaken by the failure of his policy of conciliation towards Edward IV's household men, 'rather than using the patronage at his disposal to build up a new affinity among the gentry of southern England,' writes Rosemary Horrox (in her Introduction to *British Library Harleian Manuscript 433*), 'he chose to "plant" trusted members of his northern affinity in the areas most badly affected by the rebellions. The resulting influx of northerners into the southern counties was enormously unpopular.' Under threat of further revolts throughout his brief reign, Richard continued unwilling or unable to broaden his power base. Surviving documents reveal a pattern of 'positive discrimination' in his patronage. Of seven vacancies in the Order of the Garter, for example, six were filled by northerners. The three bishoprics which became vacant were all filled by northerners.

Richard's exceptional clemency towards rebels only made matters worse for him. In November 1483 there were few executions and many pardons, leaving those disgruntled by forfeitures and the plantation of northerners alive and at liberty to join Henry Tudor. A foolish policy of leniency allowed John Morton, Bishop of Ely, the most dangerous of the Hastings conspirators, to accompany Buckingham to Brecon 'in protective custody' instead of remaining in the Tower of London where he could do no further mischief. After her involvement in the Buckingham rebellion Henry Tudor's mother (formally in the custody of her then husband, Lord Stanley) remained free in London to continue conspiring and organising an invaluable intelligence service for her son. It would have been elementary prudence, too, to have moved such an important Lancastrian prisoner as the Earl of Oxford from Hammes, a fortress on the edge of French territory, to the security of a castle, like Pontefract, in the heart of a loyal region. With the benefit of hindsight it can be seen how little more was needed in firmness of rule and a correct assessment of political expediency for Richard to have enjoyed a successful reign of normal duration. Without the injudicious plantation of northerners in the south, without the aid of Morton, Margaret Beaufort and Oxford, Henry Tudor's pretensions would surely have foundered and the illegitimate Lancastrian become a footnote in history like a Perkin Warbeck or the 'White Rose' Earl of Suffolk.

What of the life of the spirit and the mind during this 'dark' reign? Despite the uncivilised pursuit of self-interest among the propertied class, England was not an uncultured society during the period of Richard's rule. Piety was more practised then than now, not least by Richard himself. Among the arts music was cultivated and the beauty of the perpendicular architecture of the period has scarcely been excelled before or since. Humanism, spreading from Italy, took root, so that when Erasmus arrived in England early in the following century he found the ideals of the Renaissance already flourishing among English scholars. Some monasteries – Christ Church, Canterbury in particular – rivalled Oxford and Cambridge as centres of educational excellence famous throughout Christendom.

Apart from the occasional Duke Humphrey or John Tiptoft, Earl of Worcester, English learning at that time was exclusively in the hands of ecclesiastics, who controlled the universities as well as acting as ministers of state and running the civil and diplomatic services. As councillors they served the Yorkist kings well. Many had studied in Italy and enjoyed a European reputation for scholarship. For his Keeper of the Privy Seal Richard chose John Gunthorp, a renowned scholar and bibliophile; for his domestic chaplain Cardinal Bourchier's nephew, John Doget, educated at both Padua and Bologna, the author of a commentary on Plato's *Phaedo* and a member of a select European circle of neo-Platonists. In recommending John Shirwood, Bishop of Durham, for a cardinal's hat, Richard felt able to boast to the Pope of the bishop's exceptional learning in Greek as well as Latin. A decree of the University of Cambridge, dated 16 March 1484, bears witness to Richard's personal interest in 'conferring very many benefits' on the university, 'also with most devout intention founding and erecting the buildings of the King's College, the unparalleled ornament of all England'.

But a ruler should be judged, above all, by the impact of his rule upon the lives of his subjects – most particularly the humble, who have more need of his protection than the great – and since assertions that Richard III may actually have been a good king are apt to be greeted with scepticism or worse, it should be recalled that on the very first day of his reign he summoned all the judges to Westminster Hall to convey to them in person his royal command 'in right strait manner' that 'they justly and duly minister his law without delay and favour'. Those are the words of *The Great Chronicle of London* and they are repeated by another chronicler (whom historians refer to, by his Cottonian Library shelf number, as Vitellius A XVI): 'giving them straitly in commandment to execute his laws justly and indifferently to every person as well as to poor as to rich'. Two weeks later, when the nobility were about to return to their estates after attending his coronation, he commanded them to ensure that 'the countries where they dwelled' were 'well guarded' and that 'no extortions were done to his subjects'.

A few months afterwards the point is reiterated in a royal proclamation to the people of Kent after Buckingham's rebellion (as recorded in the Harleian manuscript 433 in the British Library): 'The king's highness is fully determined to see due administration of justice throughout this his realm to be had and to reform, punish and subdue all extortions and oppressions in the same'. All the 'grieved, oppressed or unlawfully wronged' should therefore make a bill of complaint to be heard by the king himself 'at his coming now into his county Kent'. 'For his grace is utterly determined all his true subjects shall live in rest and quiet and peaceably enjoy their lands, livelihoods and goods according to the laws of this his land which they be naturally born to inherit. And therefore the king chargeth and commandeth that no manner of man, of whatever condition or degree he be, rob, hurt or spoil any of his said subjects in their bodies or goods upon pain of death.'

This insistence on law and order, on equality before the law and on justice without delay was a constant theme throughout the reign. 'Fully determined' and 'utterly determined' is not the language of empty formality. Such phrases vividly express personal concern, and this is demonstrated also in Richard's institution of the machinery of legal aid for the poor which developed into the establishment of a Court of Requests in Tudor times. An entry in the Calendar of Patent Rolls dated 27 December 1483 records a grant for life of twenty pounds and the office of clerk of requests and supplications to the king's servitor, John Haryngton, for his service to the council, 'especially in the custody, registration and expedition of bills, requests and supplications of poor persons'.

This concern for the poor was recorded also by John Rous, the Warwickshire antiquary. Richard was not only 'a mighty prince' but an 'especial good lord': he 'ruled his subjects in his realm full commendably'. Rous is an unreliable witness and his real opinion of Richard, whom he later scurrilously abused, is unknown, but the grounds on which he chose to base his flattery are significant in corroborating similar evidence from other sources.

The legislation of Richard's reign has won the praise of lawyers. In 1962 H. G. Hanbury, Vinerian Professor of English Law at Oxford, judged that it gave much protection to the liberty of the subject and the sanctity of his property and concluded that Richard was 'a singularly thoughtful and enlightened legislator'. In his *Lives of the Lord Chancellors of England* (1845) a nineteenth-century Lord Chancellor and Lord Chief Justice, Lord Campbell, declared: 'We have no difficulty in pronouncing Richard's parliament the most meritorious national assembly for protecting the liberty of the subject and putting down abuses in the administration of justice that had sat in England since the reign of Henry III.'

AntiRichard historians find such encomia hard to bear. In *Richard III and His Early Historians 1483–1535* Alison Hanham does her best to deprive Richard of any personal credit: 'As Gairdner said, "The public Acts of this Parliament have always been noted as wise and beneficial", but how far the ordinary legislation of this (or any) parliament was initiated by the king in person is a debatable point. So much has been made of Richard's good government that it ought to be said that he was in no position to enact oppressive measures, even had he wished to do so; that the abolition of benevolences was probably a concession to popular feeling; and that specific acts dealing with commerce are likely to have been inspired (as usual) by discussions between the council and interested parties among the merchant community. More generally, no study has yet been published which would test the claim that the day-to-day administration of justice and government during the reign was unusually fair and efficient.' Richard's role in history is to be responsible for the bad, not the good.

Bosworth was not, as is popularly believed, the last encounter between York and Lancaster. Two years later there was a battle at East Stoke, near Newark. The Yorkist commanders were John, Earl of Lincoln (Richard's nephew and heir), Francis Lord Lovell (his friend and chamberlain) and the pretender Lambert Simnel. They were defeated by the Earl of Oxford, with Henry in attendance as a non-combatant, as at Bosworth; but what if they had won? Richard as king is mostly a might-have-been. He was allowed no time to achieve the greatness some believe was in him. If Henry VII, defeated at

Stoke, had also been a two-year king, how would history have judged their respective records?

This is Paul Murray Kendall's verdict: 'In stability of rule, establishment of order, vigour of diplomacy, development and execution of policy, and concern for the welfare of the people, the government of Henry Tudor hardly challenges comparison with the government of King Richard. . . Precisely from *what* [Henry] rescued England remains mysterious. From disorder, *The Earlier Tudors* remarks, rather as if the answer were self-evident. But the disorder of Henry's reign exceeded that of Richard's and the last half of Edward's. England as a whole neither needed nor wanted to be rescued. It doubtless learned of Richard's defeat with surprise, it accepted Henry's victory with apathy, and it afterwards resented Henry's harsh rule.'

All the principal contemporary sources for Richard's time, whether narrative or documentary, emanate from southern England. If the northern view had prevailed, the verdict of history might have been very different. It was a Westmorland man (Thomas Langton, Bishop of St David's) who told an assembly that God had sent Richard for the weal of them all. It was the city of York which hailed him as 'the most famous prince of blessed memory' and recorded grief at his death. The most English of our kings was not a Londoner and evidently not fond of metropolitan life and southern ways. He was bred in the Midlands, lived most of his adult life in the north, and died as he had been born in the rural heartland of the country. To the establishment of his day he was an outsider, and has remained so to the southern establishments of succeeding generations.

7

Death on Bosworth Field

The two most crucial battles fought on English soil both ended in surprise. On each occasion the victors were invasion forces with slender prospects; on each occasion there were misjudgments by the invaded which proved fatal. Harold should never have lost at Hastings, nor Richard at Bosworth.

To meet the threat of Henry Tudor's invasion, Richard made his headquarters at Nottingham, a stronghold strategically placed in the centre of his realm. There he assembled his army and then advanced through Leicester to bring the issue to a quick conclusion before the enemy could gather further support. Henry's landing had been unopposed and after a recruiting drive through the land of his father by way of Cardigan, Aberystwyth and Welshpool he had entered Shrewsbury 'without any annoyance received' and was marching along Watling Street via Lichfield and Tamworth. London was his objective, but he could not afford to leave the royal army in full strength behind him. Like it or not, Henry had to stand and fight: it was his long awaited moment of truth. The occasion was also long – and more eagerly – awaited by Richard. Two years of defiance and disaffection were over; the rebel pretender and his fellow traitors had at last ventured within his reach. Richard was an experienced general; Henry had no military pretensions.

Yet Bosworth proved to be Richard III's Waterloo or, more aptly, his Hastings. Like Napoleon and Harold, he was vanquished in an encounter from which, with only a narrow margin of better luck and judgment, he would have emerged victorious. As it turned out, defeat sounded the death knell for him, his dynasty and his reputation. In the eyes of his enemies God, who had spoken once when Richard's only legitimate son died, spoke again, decisively, at Bosworth. Sentiments from the Holy Bible such as 'Vengeance is mine, I will repay, saith the Lord' and 'to Me belongeth vengeance and recompense', however questionable as Christian concepts, enjoyed a wide acceptance at that time. God's displeasure with Richard, made manifest at Bosworth, was seen as retribution for the usurpation of his nephews' rightful inheritance. The outcome of the battle was proof of guilt.

Henry's small band of English exiles had crossed the Channel with men, money and ships supplied by England's enemy, the King of France, without whose help a successful invasion would have been impossible. According to traditional accounts, the men were sweepings from French gaols; yet as soon as Henry had landed (at Dale in Pembrokeshire) and sung Psalm 46 ('God is our refuge and strength, a very present help in trouble. . . The Lord of hosts is with us; the God of Jacob is our refuge') the Welsh flocked to join him and as he marched towards England his army was strengthened by ever growing numbers of English deserters, keen to abandon the cause of an unpopular and discredited king. By the antiRichards Bosworth has always been presented as a battle between good and evil. Henry, although outnumbered, achieved victory because of the rightfulness of his cause, and in the end the monster king was killed fighting like a demon, almost alone. Of Richard's four generals, the Duke of Norfolk was killed, Lord Stanley and his brother, Sir William, switched sides in the middle of the battle, and the Earl of Northumberland refused to fight. Thus Richard's tyranny received its due deserters and deserts. In fact, however, although there were some important deserters to Henry's cause before the battle, they were few.

Richard's loss of the battle is sometimes ascribed to a death wish, occasioned by guilt. By this argument, he was deeply depressed by the deaths of his wife and son and obsessed by remorse at his treatment of his nephews. His coffers were emptying and the realm becoming ungovernable through discontent and the desertions of the disaffected. In a reckless mood, gambling against the odds, he joined battle before all his troops were assembled (the contingent from York arrived too

late) and despite awareness of the treasonable activities of the
Stanley brothers (Lord Stanley was married to Henry Tudor's
mother and Sir William Stanley was arraigned as a traitor
before the battle) and of the ambivalence of Northumberland
(who under a different king would have much higher hopes of
regaining the traditional Percy domination of the north). Thus
Richard's final charge against vastly superior forces, while
exposing his flank to the Stanleys, is interpreted as something
more than an act of desperation. Crying 'Treason, Treason,
Treason', the shunned king even refused the offer of a new horse
when 'White Surrey' was killed beneath him. He allowed
himself to be hacked to death in what was no less than a
premeditated suicide. Life had turned sour for the last Plantagenet and he wanted no more of it.

The Ballad of Bosworth Field, which dates from the following
decade, describes how a knight brought the king a horse and
urged him to flee when it became clear that the Stanleys were
going to join Henry:

> 'Here is thy horse at thy hand ready
> Another day thou may thy worship win
> And for to reign with royalty
> To wear the crown and be our king.'

But Richard would not be persuaded, and, faced with death,
the legendary villain becomes a legendary hero:

> He said: 'Give me my battle-axe in my hand,
> Set the crown of England on my head so high!
> For by Him that shaped both sea and land
> King of England this day I will die.'

This ballad, written by a northerner, lists the names of ninety
noblemen, gentry and other leaders who fought on Richard's
side, predominantly from the north and Midlands. It effectively
gives the lie to those who would present him as a deserted
pariah. 'Except for the few already outlawed or committed in
advance to Henry's cause, no peer of England joined the
invaders,' remarks Kendall. Indeed most of the able-bodied

nobility obeyed Richard's summons to arms, and they were a
significantly larger number than those who turned out for
Henry at Stoke in similar circumstances two years later.
Richard's death wish, too, is surely imaginary. He was eager to
win, not to die. Over-eager perhaps, for impatience and impetuosity were his downfall – that and the failure of his personal
and political relationships with three men: the two Stanleys
and Northumberland.

One of the most important battles fought on English soil (a
'seminal milestone' according to one historian), Bosworth is
also one of the worst documented. There are no surviving
eye-witness accounts of the brief encounter which extinguished
a dynasty and, if the arbitrary demarcation lines of historians
are accepted, brought the middle ages to a tidy conclusion. The
resulting uncertainty has intensified the spell cast by battles
long ago, and Bosworth has been persistently re-fought.

Over the years since 1485 the bare heath of Redmore plain
has become enclosed and cultivated. Two hundred years ago, it
is recorded, 'not one human being resides upon this desolate
field, or near it; as if that place was studiously avoided which
had been the scene of blood'. But today a marsh has gone and a
canal and two or three farmhouses arrived. A railway line and
station have appeared and disappeared, and more recently car
parks have been constructed for country walkers and battlefield
enthusiasts. Even so, those who fought over it for little more than
a couple of hours one Monday morning in August 1485 would
probably still recognise the terrain.

From the gentle prominence flattered by the name of Ambion
Hill, where Richard encamped on the night before the battle
and drew up his forces the next morning, the view is still
uninterrupted. The most visible works of man, now as then, are
the churches: Market Bosworth (beyond the fields where one or
both of the Stanleys waited to be sure of coming in on the
winning side), Sutton Cheney (in the direction where Northumberland and his men did nothing so decisively) and Stoke
Golding (where after the fighting Richard's fleeing supporters
were butchered). To one side is an eighteenth-century cairn
marking King Richard's Well 'where Richard quenched his
thirst'. Ahead the ground slopes down to a road and a brook.
This is the scene of the famous last charge, the swansong of

medieval chivalry. The meeting of this path and stream has been identified as 'Sandeford within the shire of Leicester' where, according to a proclamation of Henry VII, Richard was killed. Today the site is marked by The Death Stone, a twentieth-century menhir often adorned with tributes of white roses and sprigs of rosemary for remembrance from the faithful.

The leading historian of the battle is William Hutton (1723–1815), a topographer of the Midlands and author of histories of Birmingham and Derby. In Birmingham he was a prominent dissenter and his house was looted by the mob rioting against his nonconformist friend, Joseph Priestley. His work on Bosworth, which occupied him for eighteen years and was published in 1788, is fully entitled: *The Battle of Bosworth Field between Richard the Third and Henry Earl of Richmond, August 22, 1485, Wherein is Described the Approach of Both Armies, with Plans of the Battle, its Consequences, the Fall, Treatment, and Character of Richard, to which is Prefixed, by Way of Introduction, a History of his Life till he Assumed the Regal Power.*

Hutton's narrative is racy and unreliable (for example, he identifies Shrewsbury instead of Salisbury as the place of Buckingham's execution). As befits a good radical, he is a plague-on-both-their-royal-houses man, dismissing the libels of the Tudor chroniclers with contempt ('idle tales beneath the notice of history . . . the Tudors degraded Richard below every degree of truth'), but not letting Richard off lightly either.

Was Richard guiltless when Edward IV had Clarence executed? 'Richard stood high with his sovereign. He might have been gratified with any favour for asking. One word would have saved Clarence. He did not utter that word.' And then: 'the death of Edward the Fourth opened a new and extraordinary scene, in which Richard showed himself a most accomplished and wicked actor. There is not in the whole history of the English kings a similar instance of a prince forming a design upon the crown, laying so able and deep a scheme, in which were so many obstacles; surmounting them all, and gaining the beloved object in eight weeks!'

As a refreshingly neutral participant in the Great Debate, Hutton surveyed the battle through the eyes of a committed non-combatant: 'Richard was an accomplished rascal, and Henry not one jot better. Which had the greatest right to the throne is no part of the argument; neither of them had any.' By Hutton's calculation the united strength of all parties in the battle 'did not exceed 28,000 men'. Because only the front lines were engaged, the slain did not exceed nine hundred, nearly all on Richard's side and mostly during pursuit after the battle proper. By way of contrast he enumerates with improbable precision the slain at the other battles in the Wars of the Roses. The tally for Towton is 36,776.

After an hour's fighting there was not much advantage to either side except that Richard had lost Norfolk, the commander of his vanguard. Then a scout reported that Henry was lurking behind a hill 'with a slender attendance' and Richard 'fired at the news'. Hutton does not subscribe to the death-wish theory: 'Richard is presented as having lost the battle and, disdaining to survive the disgrace, rushed into the heat of the action to sell his life at the dearest rate. Here seems another mistake; for this desperate plan, formed in a moment, was not an ill-concerted one; he was still uncertain whether Stanley would declare for Henry, and as Henry was thinly guarded, he stood a fair chance, by a bold stroke, of being instantly dispatched, and then the field was won. Besides, Richard's courage was invincible, ten such men might have withstood a hundred. This was one of those daring enterprises which is condemned or applauded according to its good or ill success.'

After killing Henry's standard-bearer, Sir William Brandon, with one stroke of the sword and unhorsing the powerful Sir John Cheney he cut his way towards the false Richmond, 'the spirit of the hero growing into that of the mad-man'. 'These were not the acts of a little, puny, decrepit fellow, with a withered arm!' But then Richard was overwhelmed by Sir William Stanley's 3,000 men. 'The ferocity of Richard would have terrified a better man than Henry', so that if Sir William had delayed 'but one minute', 'Henry must either have fallen or fled'.

'But as the sturdiest oak must give way to a multitude of axes, Richard at length fell, fighting an army! His body was covered with wounds. His helmet, which, like a cullendar, was full of holes, had lost the crown. . . Thus fell Richard the Third, one of the greatest heroes and one of the most dishonest men recorded in history.' Hutton's obituary of Richard is similarly balanced.

It judges Richard to have been a bad man with the potential of a good king. But losing the battle was his greatest crime.

'Former writers drew Richard's character from prejudice, but as time has diminished that prejudice their successors will, with more justice, draw it from facts. Perhaps he had a greater number of enemies than any person in the whole system of English history. It was said of Sir Robert Walpole, when he guided the helm under George the Second, that *he* had more than any man living. But *his* were only the enemies of a day; Richard's continued for ages! They were diligent in wounding his fame, while his friends, if he had friends, were condemned to silence. Although many crimes were laid to his charge, yet the greatest of all was *that of losing the battle of Bosworth!* This added emphasis to his guilt, gave his antagonist the ascendant and enabled Henry to raise against him the clamour of ages. Had Richard been prosperous, he would, with all his faults, have passed through life with *éclat*. His errors, like those of other monarchs, would have been lost in oblivion, and himself have been handed down to posterity as an excellent king. History would then have taken an opposite turn, and the odium have fallen upon Henry.'

Hutton's description of the fighting at Bosworth (and his estimate of the casualties) is taken from the prime source – an account by Polydore Vergil, Henry Tudor's historian. This was written more than twenty years after the battle, presumably based on the oral evidence of survivors from the winning side. There is no reason to doubt its general accuracy, but topographically Vergil has created confusion among later commentators by having Henry Tudor draw up his forces so that his right flank was protected by a marsh and the sun shone from behind him. In conformity with the lie of the land he could have done either but not both, and much ink has been expended by Hutton and subsequent historians in moving the now vanished marsh from point to point around the site of the battle or the battle from morning to afternoon.

In 1895 James Gairdner addressed the Society of Antiquaries on the subject at some length, desperately wheeling the rival armies round and round so that the sun could shine from Polydore Vergil's direction. More profitably, he speculated on the cannon balls which had been dug up on the site: hard evidence that the arrows and battle-axes of medieval warfare had been supplemented by artillery. Richard's serpentines could fire four-pound balls to a range of a thousand yards and, unexpectedly, Henry too was armed with guns, taken (Gairdner supposed) from Tamworth castle, which was in the possession of Sir Thomas Ferrers, a brother-in-law of the arbitrarily executed Lord Hastings.

Gairdner emphasised a point which may have been crucial to the outcome of the battle: that, since Sir William had been proclaimed a traitor and Lord Stanley was still formally loyal when the battle began, the contingents of the brothers would have been separately positioned and under separate commands. Prone to bouts of diplomatic sweating sickness when summoned to arms, Lord Stanley was such a notorious ditherer that Richard may have felt confident of his not making a move until the battle was irretrievably won or lost. He had been a prominent absentee from the battles at Towton, Barnet and Tewkesbury, and probably took no part in the fighting at Bosworth. But his younger brother's temperament and interest were different. Sir William might have been restrained if the Stanley forces had been together under a unified command, but the advantage to the family of divided armies was clear. The elder brother could hold himself ready to come in on Richard's side should the issue be seen to be running in the king's favour.

The inaction of the other commander in the field may or may not have been treachery. Commanding the rearguard of the royal forces, Northumberland stood idly by while his king was killed and the battle therefore, according to the custom of the period, deemed to be concluded. Did he ignore an order to engage the enemy, as is traditionally believed, or was he still properly holding his forces in reserve when Richard's impetuosity determined the issue of the day prematurely?

In Northumberland's favour is the fact that Henry's gratitude to him after the battle took the form of a prison sentence, albeit brief, and it is possible that, stationed on lower ground behind the height of Ambion Hill and unable to see the course of the battle for himself, he may simply have been waiting for orders which never came. Afterwards it would have been strongly to his advantage to claim that he had refused to fight against the victor. But Kendall's judgment remains the general one: that this perfidious Percy was 'the shame of the North, and four years later the North would avenge its shame by killing him'.

One contemporary source from whom a full record might have been expected is disappointingly skimpy. The Croyland chronicler's interests were more ecclesiastical than military. Richard, he tells us, left Leicester 'on the Lord's day before the feast of Bartholomew the Apostle'. 'At daybreak on the Monday following there were no chaplains present to perform divine service' on his behalf; nor was there any breakfast for him, so that, unrefreshed after a night of dreadful visions, his countenance was even 'more livid and ghastly than usual'. Henry, by contrast, had the advice and spiritual support of three bishops or bishops-to-be (Courtenay, Morton and Fox) as well as Christopher Urswick (who refused a bishopric) and, by implication, ate a hearty breakfast too.

Of the actual fighting the chronicler reports only: 'A battle of the greatest severity now ensuing between the two sides, the Earl of Richmond, together with his knights, made straight for King Richard; while the Earl of Oxford, who was next in rank to him in the whole army and a most valiant soldier, drew up his forces, consisting of a large body of French and English troops, opposite the wing in which the Duke of Norfolk had taken up his position. In the part where the Earl of Northumberland was posted, with a large and well-provided body of troops, there was no opposition made, as not a blow was given or received during the battle.'

The false report that Henry charged Richard instead of vice versa (as recorded even by Vergil) and the libel that Norfolk, Brackenbury and Richard's chief supporters from the north fled without engaging the enemy, although in fact they were killed, 'brings to its nadir', in Kendall's words, 'the increasing unreliability' of the chronicle.

Today's official guide to the battlefield, with its description of the disposition of the armies and the course of the battle, is the work of D. T. Williams, an historian at Leicester University. Dr Williams refutes the death-wish theory by pointing to surviving letters of array sent by Richard before the battle. These are mentioned by the Croyland chronicler: 'In the meantime, in manifold letters he despatched orders of the greatest severity, commanding that no men, of the number of those at least who had been born to the inheritance of any property in the kingdom, should shun taking part in the approaching warfare; threatening that whoever should be found, in any part of the kingdom after the victory should have been gained, to have omitted appearing in his presence on the field, was to expect no other fate than the loss of all his goods and possessions, as well as his life.'

By Dr Williams' account Richard's strategy was to assemble his forces from the north at Nottingham and then march south to Leicester, where he would be joined by the southern contingents: his knights of the body from London and the Duke of Norfolk's army raised in East Anglia. Dr Williams calculates that when he marched out of Leicester he was at the head of 12,000 men, but other estimates put Richard's army at 9,000, 3,000 of whom were Northumberland's men, leaving the king a fighting force of only 6,000 under his direct command. On the other side Henry's army had swollen to some 5,000, and after a secret meeting with Sir William Stanley he was counting on a further 3,000 from each of the Stanley brothers, making 11,000 in all.

After study of the topography Dr Williams greatly enlarged the marsh which protected Henry's right wing at the foot of Ambion Hill. According to Polydore Vergil this wing was commanded by Sir Gilbert Talbot, uncle of the young Earl of Shrewsbury, while the Earl of Oxford had command of the main force, and the left wing, in the initial absence of the expected Stanleys, was led by Sir John Savage, with Henry himself. Henry was therefore strongly protected on the right and dangerously weak on the left. As Charles Ross has pointed out, this disposition is curious. Henry should have commanded in the centre, and where was his uncle, that experienced commander Jasper Tudor, sometime Earl of Pembroke?

At the top of Ambion Hill Richard had a 400-feet advantage in height but was forced to draw up his forces in column rather than line, with Norfolk commanding the van, Richard himself the centre, and Northumberland the rear. The marsh prevented an attack on Henry's right flank, but the left was temptingly exposed if the Stanleys could be trusted to remain loyal or even neutral. Richard could have – as matters turned out, should have – waited and forced the enemy to attack uphill, as Harold did with initial success at Hastings. Instead, after an exchange of artillery and long-bow fire, he ordered his van to advance downhill in a bold bid to overwhelm the enemy's main contingent. For this his numbers proved insufficient, for they encountered Oxford's force, which was mainly composed of the hard core of Henry's army – professional French soldiers under the experienced command of Philibert de Chandée.

The size and importance of the foreign element in Henry's army has been deliberately understated and underplayed. As Charles Ross has remarked, his invasion force was 'very much an army of foreign troops'. It included Bretons and Scotsmen from France as well as the French contingent which played the decisive role. (It is suggestive that the Croyland Chronicle refers to Oxford's 'French and English' troops, not 'English and French'.) So far from being rabble or gaol sweepings, these Frenchmen were veteran soldiers from the military base at Pont l'Arche, on the payroll of the King of France, and despatched to Henry's aid by the order of Philippe de Crèvecoeur, the Marshal of France. Henry was notoriously niggardly with honours, as in all else, and the elevation of the French commander to the earldom of Bath after the battle reinforces the probability that the man who actually won the battle of Bosworth was de Chandée, a name almost unknown in English history.

Although the result of the opening engagement was a draw, the attack was a miscalculation which cost Richard the battle, for the enemy had not been overwhelmed. Richard was forced to break the ensuing deadlock and check the spread of demoralisation following Norfolk's death by a desperate move against Henry's left flank with an even more inadequate force. At this point in the battle Dr Williams has raised some eyebrows by enlarging Richard's traditionally small bodyguard into '1,000 or more knights', so that it was Henry who was outnumbered in Richard's furious charge and 'the unblooded Richmond fought with cool courage and skill' – even though Dr Williams has him intercepted by Richard while in the act of leaving the battlefield (not to run away, as his supporters might have feared, but supposedly to parley with Sir William Stanley).

There is, however, no evidence either for the '1,000 or more knights' or for Henry losing his unbloodedness. According to one critic (P. W. Hammond in his Introduction to *The Battle of Bosworth* by James Gairdner, 1975): 'In all probability there were not even 1,000 knights actually capable of fighting in the whole country. It can be shown that Edward IV in 1475 had approximately 200 knights in what was probably the best equipped medieval army (of nearly 12,000 men) ever to leave British shores. . . The king would not have had a mounted reserve in any case, since retaining a large body of men ready mounted was not the English practice in fifteenth-century warfare. . . We thus return to the usual picture of the final charge composed of Richard and his household knights.'

The Duke of Wellington's comment on Waterloo may be applied to Bosworth too. It was a 'damned nice thing – the nearest run thing you ever saw in your life'. England's only king from the north was narrowly defeated through the treachery of three rival potentates from the north. He had survived disaffection in the south and heaped favours on his northern supporters, among whom Northumberland and Lord Stanley were the most powerful and the leading beneficiaries of his largesse. Yet (unless Northumberland is to enjoy the benefit of a slim doubt), jealous and self-seeking, they brought him down, ending the north's brief dominance in English history and leaving his reputation in the untender hands of southern chroniclers.

His reign abruptly curtailed, his good intentions as a king can be judged only as promise largely unfulfilled. Yet there seems no good reason to doubt that the English renaissance would have dawned at least as gloriously under Yorkist as under Tudor rule. It is not implausible to suppose that the great centres of English faith and learning, the richness of beauty and culture destroyed by Henry Tudor's son, would have survived in some form. Edward IV and Richard III maintained close and good relations with the church of England, but permitted little interference from Rome. Richard and his successors could have loosened the spiritual and temporal bonds of Rome, as earlier Plantagenets had done, without the senseless destruction precipitated by Henry VIII's financial ineptitude, frantic urge for a male heir, and unbridleable wilfulness.

It is hard to avoid the conclusion that the chief architect of his defeat was Richard himself. Bosworth was a short engagement with little fighting and few casualties, scarcely a battle on the scale of Towton or Barnet, which Edward had won against worse odds. Richard failed politically in not securing essential loyalties and militarily against de Chandée's Frenchmen. Dynastically, he committed the mortal sin of dying without a direct heir. The penalty has been half a millennium of ill repute.

8

The Croyland Chronicler

How can posterity know what really happened in Richard's reign? The writings of some contemporaries survive. The problem is to evaluate them correctly.

At Crowland in fenland Lincolnshire stand the ruins of one of the least known of the great abbeys of England. A Benedictine house founded by King Ethelbald of Mercia in 716, Croyland, as it was formerly known, had become rich and powerful even before the Norman conquest. Although never achieving the grandeur of an abbot of St Albans or Glastonbury, its head qualified *ex officio* for what would today be called membership of the House of Lords. Whenever a medieval King of England felt obliged to convene a parliament, among those summoned on the roll of the lords spiritual of the realm would be the Abbot of Croyland: he was thus a mitred abbot, ranking as a bishop. During the turmoil of the second half of the fifteenth century Croyland's importance was recognised by successive royal visits from the Lancastrian Henry VI and the Yorkist Edward IV (accompanied by his brother, Richard of Gloucester).

Ingulph's History of the Abbey of Croyland, known as the Croyland Chronicle, was written within the walls of the monastery. It contains both national and local history, touching on great events but concentrating for the most part on the abbey's own story, with much emphasis on territorial claims and disputes, mainly against the neighbouring (and much hated) fraternal Benedictine house at Peterborough. The manuscript survived the dissolution, the first part being printed in 1596 by the Elizabethan scholar, Sir Henry Saville; but the full (Latin) text

was not published until 1684 (in Fulman's Oxford edition).
The chronicle is in five parts: Abbot Ingulph's history (up to
1091), Peter of Blois' continuation (until 1117) and three
further, anonymous continuations, covering the periods 1144–
1469, 1459–1486 and 1485–86. It is now accepted that the
earlier parts are spurious, Ingulph's contribution dating from
long after his death, but there is no reason to doubt the
authenticity of the anonymous continuations. It is the second of
these, the so-called 'second continuation' ('third' in the Bohn
English edition of 1854) which is of importance to Ricardian
studies. The author is remarkably well informed and must have
been an eye-witness of some of the events of the reign. From
internal evidence he seems to have been a doctor of canon law
and a member of the royal council. Here is an exceptionally
knowledgeable source unvarnished by Tudor gloss.

This section of the chronicle was discovered by Sir George
Buck in manuscript form and first used as an historical source
in his History, written during James I's reign. The most
startling revelation which it contained was the substance of the
Act of Settlement of 1484, the Titulus Regius, which had been
repealed by Henry VII's first parliament with the order that all
copies be destroyed. Thus only when the Tudor dynasty had
ended did it become public knowledge that Edward IV's
marriage had been declared invalid because of his pre-contract,
not with a courtesan, but with a daughter of the Earl of
Shrewsbury.

However, the general tenor of the text does little for Richard
III's reputation. It plainly reveals the dislike of the author of
the second continuation for Richard, and this has led some
revisionists to detect in it the malign hand of John Morton, at
the relevant time Bishop of Ely. If there was in truth any malign
influence at work it would have been more likely to be that of
Henry Tudor's mother, Margaret Beaufort, whose family
owned the neighbouring manor of Deeping and who was herself
at one time a 'sister' of the abbey. But it was the proximity of
Croyland to Ely which aroused Sir Clements Markham's
suspicions, and he (misleading the novelist Josephine Tey) mis-
takenly supposed it to be within the diocese of Ely and therefore
subject to Morton's influence.

In fact, except on the rare occasion of an official visitation,

Croyland was not subject to episcopal authority, and it lay within the diocese of Lincoln, whose bishop, John Russell, was a long-serving member of Edward IV's council and held the office of Chancellor of England under Richard III, possibly with some reluctance, until relieved of it a few weeks before Bosworth. The second continuation was written in April 1486, and in the third continuation we are told that the bishop stayed a month at Croyland at that time 'with a retinue of twenty persons'. Today John Russell is the most favoured candidate for second continuator, but it seems as likely to have been a member of his retinue: one identification is the proto-notary Henry Sharp. There may be a parallel here with Morton, who did not himself set down his version of events but disseminated it to others, More and Polydore Vergil obliging with the written record.

Whoever he was, the Croyland chronicler believed that, whatever the circumstances, Richard should not have taken the crown from his nephew, whom all the senior administrators (clerics and lawyers) who had served his father must have wished to see safely enthroned in accordance with proper precedents and procedures. The disorderly and dangerous events of June 1483 would have been a traumatic experience for bureaucrats in or near the eye of the storm.

As a cleric, the author disapproved of Richard executing Buckingham on a Sunday, and he seems to have held some post carrying responsibility for government funds, for at times he writes like a financial controller, denouncing Richard as a profligate spender. Of the suppression of Buckingham's rebellion he records that Richard 'triumphed over his enemies without fighting a battle, but at an expense not less than if the two armies had fought hand to hand. Thus was commenced the waste, in a short time, of those most ample treasures which King Edward supposed he would leave behind him for a quite different purpose'. The loss to Richard of a large part of the treasure in the Tower, stolen by the Woodvilles, is not mentioned.

In similar vein is the chronicler's sour account of Richard's successful campaign against the Scots in 1482: 'A tremendous and destructive war was proclaimed by Edward against the Scots, and the entire command of the expedition was given to

Richard, Duke of Gloucester, the king's brother. What he effected in this expedition, what sums of money, again extorted under the name of benevolences, he uselessly squandered away, the affair in its results sufficiently proved. For no resistance being offered, he marched as far as Edinburgh with the whole of his army, and then leaving that most opulent city untouched, returned by way of Berwick, which town had been taken upon his first entrance into that country; upon which the castle, which had held out much longer, not without vast slaughter and bloodshed fell into the hands of the English. This trifling, I really know not whether to call it "gain" or "loss" (for the safe keeping of Berwick each year swallows up ten thousand marks), at this period diminished the resources of the king and kingdom by more than a hundred thousand pounds.'

The author is self-evidently a southerner concerned at the threat posed by northerners, not with their protection from the Scots. His exaggeration of their presence in London in 1483 is a measure of the depth of his antagonism towards them and towards Richard as their leader: 'From this day these dukes [Gloucester and Buckingham] acted no longer in secret, but openly manifested their intentions. For, having summoned armed men, in fearful and unheard-of numbers, from the north, Wales and all other parts then subject to them, the said Protector Richard assumed the government of the kingdom, with the title of king. . . However, it was at the time rumoured that this address had been got up in the north, whence such vast numbers were flocking to London. . . These multitudes of people accordingly making a descent from the north to the south under the especial conduct and guidance of Sir Richard Ratcliffe, on their arrival at the town of Pomfret, by command of the said Richard Ratcliffe, and without any form of trial being observed, Anthony, Earl of Rivers, Richard Grey, his nephew, and Thomas Vaughan, an aged knight, were, in presence of these people, beheaded. This was the second innocent blood which was shed on the occasion of this sudden change.'

The first 'innocent blood' had been that of Hastings: 'The lord Hastings, on the thirteenth day of the month of June, being the sixth day of the week, on coming to the Tower to join the council was, by order of the Protector, beheaded. Two distinguished prelates also, Thomas Archbishop of York and John Bishop of Ely, being, out of respect for their order, held exempt from capital punishment, were carried prisoners to different castles in Wales. The three strongest supporters of the new king being thus removed without judgment or justice, and all the rest of his faithful subjects fearing the like treatment, the two dukes did thenceforth just as they pleased.'

In neither case does the chronicler offer any explanation for the executions. He omits to mention that Edward V's relations on his mother's side may have been guilty of conspiracy in a coup to seize power or that Hastings, disappointed at Buckingham's influence overshadowing his own, may have been plotting with them against the Protector's life. The 'two dukes' are seen as outsiders, backed by savages from the wilds of Yorkshire and Wales, and when confronted with an emergency they do not observe the established forms and proprieties of an ordered administration. Nevertheless, while he was almost certainly denied a fair trial, Hastings is unlikely to have been wholly innocent. In the case of the other executions there is some evidence that the Earl of Northumberland presided over, at least, a drum-head court-martial.

After Buckingham's unsuccessful rising the author's worst apprehensions about predatory northerners were realised: 'Attainders were made of so many lords and men of high rank, besides peers and commoners, as well as three bishops, that we do not read of the like being issued by the Triumvirate even of Octavianus, Antony and Lepidus. What immense estates and patrimonies were collected into this king's treasury in consequence of this measure! All of which he distributed among his northern adherents, whom he planted in every spot throughout his dominions, to the disgrace and lasting and loudly expressed sorrow of all the people in the south, who daily longed more and more for the hoped-for return of their ancient rulers, rather than the present tyranny of these people.'

On the evidence of his writing the Croyland chronicler was a querulous, elderly cleric, much given to metaphorical hand-wringing. For him the times were out of joint and his narrative is peppered with exclamations of abhorrence: *O Deus* (Oh God!) and *Quid plura?* (Why go on?). What is to be drawn from his chronicle in Richard's favour lies mostly in the omissions.

For example, the quarrel between Richard and Clarence over Richard's marriage to Warwick's younger daughter and the division of the Warwick estates is recounted in detail, but the accusation made in Tudor times (and still made even today) that Richard had a hand in Clarence's death is not made by this critical contemporary chronicler. Instead there is even a tribute to Richard's ability.

'Such violent dissensions arose between the brothers, and so many arguments were, with the greatest acuteness, put forward on either side, in the king's presence, who sat in judgment in the council-chamber, that all present, and the lawyers even, were quite surprised that these princes should find arguments in such abundance by means of which to support their respective causes. In fact, these three brothers, the king and the two dukes, were possessed of such surpassing talents that, if they had been able to live without dissensions, such a three-fold cord could never have been broken without the utmost difficulty.'

But the quarrel which led to Clarence's execution was between him and his elder brother alone: 'The circumstances that happened in the ensuing Parliament my mind quite shudders to enlarge upon, for then was to be witnessed a sad strife carried on before these two brethren of such high estate. For not a single person uttered a word against the duke except the king; not one individual made answer to the king except the duke.' When another duke became involved, it was not Gloucester: 'Parliament, being of opinion that the informations which they had heard were established, passed sentence upon him of condemnation, the same being pronounced by the mouth of Henry, Duke of Buckingham, who was appointed Seneschal of England for the occasion.'

When he reaches the encounter 'near the abbey of Mirival', later known as the battle of Bosworth, the chronicler does not withhold another rare passage of praise: 'For while fighting, and not in the act of flight, the said King Richard was pierced with numerous deadly wounds, and fell in the field like a brave and most valiant prince.'

Some days after the battle a number of Richard's adherents, who had fought loyally for the king of the realm, were killed in cold blood. According to the chronicler, 'there were also taken prisoner William Catesby, who occupied a distinguished place among all the advisers of the late king, and whose head was cut off at Leicester as a last reward for his excellent offices. Two gentlemen also, of the western parts of the kingdom, father and son, known by the name of Brecher, who after the battle had fallen into the hands of the conquerors, were hanged.' Yet this is followed by no passage bewailing the shedding of innocent blood or the lack of justice and a proper trial from Henry Tudor. Instead the new prince is said to have shown clemency to all and 'began to receive the praises of all, as though he had been an angel sent down from heaven, through whom God had deigned to visit His people, and to deliver it from the evils with which it had hitherto, beyond measure, been afflicted.'

The author of the final continuation of the chronicle, which briefly takes the story further, is a different person and one less certain of Henry VII's claims to clemency and angelic status, not to mention the throne: 'After the coronation of King Henry had been solemnly performed on the day above-mentioned, a parliament was held at Westminster, on which so many matters were treated of (I wish I could say "all *ably* treated of") that the compendious nature of this narrative cannot aspire to comprise an account of the whole of them. Among other things, proscriptions or, as they are more commonly called, "attainders" were voted against thirty persons; a step which, though bespeaking far greater moderation than was ever witnessed under similar circumstances in the time of King Richard or King Edward, was not taken without considerable discussion, or indeed, to speak more truly, considerable censure, of the measures so adopted. Oh God! what assurance from this time forth are our kings to have that, in the day of battle, they will not be deprived of the assistance of even their own subjects, when summoned at the dread mandate of their sovereign? For, a thing that has been too often witnessed, it is far from improbable that, deserted by their adherents, they may find themselves bereft of inheritance, possessions, and even life itself.'

In assessing Richard's record in the light of the Croyland chronicler's strictures it is relevant that another author in the same period should subject a living king to the same kind of moralising and Oh Gods! as that which the second continuator had heaped on the dead Richard. Indeed Henry's offence against a well-ordered society was even greater than Richard's because he cynically dated his reign from the day before the battle of Bosworth. This enabled him to have an act of attainder passed against King Richard for committing treason against Henry Tudor, even though parliament in the end frustrated the royal will in the matter of back-dating. With a king convicted of treason and the estates of his loyal followers forfeited because they were deemed to be traitors, the fabric of society was indeed in tatters.

The third continuator's criticism of Henry even verges on a charge of usurpation. 'In this parliament the sovereignty was confirmed to our lord the king, as being his due, not by one, but by many titles: so that we are to believe that he rules most rightfully over the English people, and that not so much by right of blood as of conquest and victory in warfare. There were some persons, however, who were of opinion that words to that effect might have been more wisely passed over in silence than inserted in our statutes; the more especially because, in the very same parliament, a discussion took place, and that too with the king's consent, relative to his marriage with the Lady Elizabeth, the eldest daughter of King Edward; in whose person it appeared to all that every requisite might be supplied which was wanting to make good the title of the king himself.'

The most noticeable feature of the second continuation of the Croyland Chronicle is the absence of any direct accusation that Richard III murdered his nephews or, indeed, of any suggestion that they were known to be dead. The Chancellor of England or a close associate of his might seem better placed than almost anyone else to learn the truth about their disappearance or, at the very least, to have suspicions sufficiently well founded to be recorded in the privacy of a secluded monastery eight months after Richard's death. The motive of the author in writing his chronicle must have been to set down for posterity a record of events of which he had personal knowledge. He was severely critical of Richard: possibly embittered by dismissal from the chancellorship. If well-informed circles in 1486 believed that the princes had suffered death at the hands of their uncle, what possible reason could he have had for failing to ensure that this crucial fact was unequivocally recorded and the murderer roundly condemned for such an infamous crime?

Yet all he reports is that after Richard's coronation the two sons of Edward IV remained in the Tower of London and that 'in order to deliver them from this captivity, the people of the southern and western parts of the kingdom began to murmur greatly, and to form meetings and confederacies'. When those in the southern counties with grievances decided to rebel, a public proclamation was made that Buckingham would head the rebellion, 'while a rumour was spread that the sons of King Edward before-named had died a violent death, but it was uncertain how'. The context makes plain the chronicler's belief that the rumour was spread as part of a calculated campaign to foment disaffection. There is no suggestion that it was true; the implication is rather the reverse.

In his *Richard III* Charles Ross writes of this chronicler: 'Although he was probably in a position to know about the fate of the princes, he states no clear opinion thereon, preferring instead to cite some verses by "a certain poet" on the three Richards who had ruled England which clearly condemn Richard for his nephews' death.' Not surprisingly, Professor Ross has no explanation for this extraordinary procedure whereby the chronicler tucks away his most vital item of information in some lines of doggerel attributed to no higher authority than *quidam metrista*.

And do the verses 'clearly condemn Richard'? In introducing them the chronicler states that the battle at Bosworth avenged the *cause* of the princes – not their *death*. The 'clearly condemning' Latin phrase translated as 'must destroy his brother's progeny' is *nisi fratris opprimeret proles*. But *opprimere* (to suppress) is as likely to mean 'put down the cause of' as 'kill'; and the princes were certainly destroyed politically and as royal persons by the loss of their inheritance. If this is to be interpreted as the chronicler's sole record of a sensational murder committed by the Richard he so detested, it is strangely oblique.

The explanation may be that, for all his exceptional knowledge of administration and public events during Richard's reign, the author was not privy to the king's own thoughts and deeds, so that his account of Richard's actions and the motivation behind them is often no more than guesswork, inspired by a dislike which extends even to mis-statements of fact. One example of the latter is his denunciation of Richard's taxation as a reversion to the 'benevolences' which Richard had made such a point of abolishing, although, as we learn from another source, the taxes raised by Richard were loans, repayable on a specified date, quite different in kind from the forced payments levied by Edward IV as benevolences. Another example, as we have seen, concerns the famous last charge at Bosworth, where the chronicler solemnly records for posterity that it was Henry who charged Richard.

John Russell's appointment as chancellor dated from May 1483, when he succeeded Archbishop Rotherham, the disgraced adherent of the Woodvilles. It therefore seems likely that he was appointed by Edward V's council as a whole rather than by Richard, the newly appointed Protector, personally. In the interests of a balance of power, one consideration in his appointment might have been that he was *not* Richard's man. If this theory is correct, Russell and his associates would have managed the administration of the realm, but never belonged to the intimate circle of Richard's friends and advisers. In Professor Charles Wood's words (in an unpublished article), Russell would have been 'deliberately excluded from the inner circle of government where options were explored and all important decisions made', and that alone might have engendered or nourished malice and a jaundiced view. It would also have meant that if Richard did have his nephews surreptitiously put to death – or conveyed to Yorkshire out of harm's way – Russell would not have been a party to the secret and was as ignorant of the truth as everyone else who has written on the subject.

However that may be, the Croyland Chronicle does indeed lend some support to the antiRichards with indisputable evidence of hostility towards Richard antedating the Tudor saga. What it does not do is to provide supporting evidence for any of his alleged crimes, and in this respect the silences of the disgruntled second continuator speak louder than the words of those who came after him.

Foreign Observers

Richard features unflatteringly too in the machiavellian *Memoirs* of Philippe de Commynes. This eye-witness account of high politics in Western Europe during the second half of the fifteenth century was written by a politician and diplomat who abandoned his allegiance as a chamberlain and close adviser to Charles the Rash of Burgundy in the struggle against Louis XI of France, to become a chamberlain and even closer adviser to Louis XI of France in the struggle against Charles the Rash of Burgundy. As, in effect, prime minister to the French king between 1472 and 1477, he moved among the great, leading an embassy to Florence, where he negotiated with Lorenzo de Medici, and playing a leading role in the treaty of Picquigny (1475), where he met and talked with Edward IV. Another acquaintance was Henry Tudor during his period of exile in France.

Commynes's *Memoirs* were dictated in about 1490 after his retirement, ostensibly for the benefit of Angelo Cato, Archbishop of Vienne, who intended to write a life of Louis XI. More pertinently, they were a much needed apologia for his career. A master of deceit and double dealing, he has been incautiously represented as a witness of truth by historians dazzled by his inside knowledge and their own good fortune in the legacy of such a rich primary source. But, as his most recent editor, Michael Jones, observes: 'Far from providing a dispassionate survey of the events of Louis's career, approximating as closely to the truth as he claimed. . . Commynes's account has been skilfully constructed to gloss over certain discreditable incidents in his own life, to hide facts about the changing nature of his relationship with Louis XI and the essential failure of his career. A case can be made for arguing that Commynes, in his *Memoirs*, was getting his own back on his numerous enemies. Far from being the simple, honest account of a faithful servant, it is the work of an extremely embittered, devious politician and the conventional textbook view . . . that Commynes "had a detachment which gives his pages the very highest authority" . . . is very wide of the mark.'

In 1966 Commynes achieved the rare distinction of having a complete book devoted to exploding his errors (*La Destruction des Mythes dans les Mémoires de Philippe de Comines* by Jean Dufournet). Yet in 1974 a history teacher and former headmaster of Eton, Sir Robert Birley, bent on persuading readers of *The Times* that Henry VI was a victim of Richard III, rested his case solely on the authority of Commynes, whom he found it necessary to describe as 'a very reputable' historian.

Although he paid several visits to the English possession of Calais, there is no evidence that Commynes ever visited England itself. If he had, he would no doubt have recorded the occasion in the *Memoirs*. When therefore he reports as an unqualified statement of fact that Edward IV's sons had been murdered by the 'wicked' and 'cruel' King Richard, there is no reason to suppose that he is imparting any information obtained at first hand. He was repeating what was no doubt a widespread belief in France. When accusing Richard of the murder of Henry VI, however, he slips in a qualifying phrase: 'King Henry was a very ignorant and almost simple man and, unless I have been deceived, immediately after the battle the Duke of Gloucester, Edward's brother, who later became King Richard, killed this good man with his own hand or at least had him killed in his presence in some obscure place.' Of the death of Richard's wife he records: 'Some said he had her killed.'

Despite the qualifications, Commynes's reports that Richard killed Henry VI and Queen Anne Nevill detract somewhat from his value as evidence for the murder of the princes. So too does the statement later in the *Memoirs* that Buckingham was responsible: 'King Richard did not last long; nor did the Duke of Buckingham, who had put the two children to death.'

Commynes was Lancastrian in sympathy, believing that

Henry VI was the rightful king of England, but admiring Edward IV for his good looks and courage. Edward was the handsomest prince Commynes had ever seen. He had won nine victories, always fighting on foot to share the danger with his common soldiers and show them that he would not ride off and escape if the battle went against them. After a victory it was his policy to spare the lives of those who had fought against him, with the exception of a few prominent rebels among the nobility. But since the *annus mirabilis* of 1471 Edward had abandoned military exploits to practise his equally outstanding sexual prowess.

Commynes's judgment on the conflict between France and England was that, while the English might win the battles, the French won the treaties. At Picquigny Edward, at the head of a formidable invading force but grown fat through self-indulgence, dishonourably allowed himself to be bought off. England and Burgundy had agreed to combine forces and overwhelm France, but Charles of Burgundy failed to keep a rendezvous and Edward then decided to accept money not to fight. The English described the annual payments as tribute; the French called them pensions. Whatever they were, they saved France from the danger of a heavy defeat and the humiliation became Edward's.

Richard took part in the expedition and was notably absent when the two kings reached their amicable agreement. Commynes records his open disapproval: 'The Duke of Gloucester, the King of England's brother, and several others, who were not pleased by this peace, were not present at this conference.' According to Commynes, Richard was persuaded afterwards to visit the French king in Amiens and accept some plate and horses as good-will gifts. But he did not join his brother and others (including Hastings and John Howard) in becoming a pensioner of the French.

To the rulers of France every king of England in the fifteenth century was a natural enemy, for even when the long war had ended and the English were left with nothing in France except Calais the Plantagenets obstinately maintained their claim to the French crown. Richard's behaviour at Picquigny would not have been forgotten and when he became king the French would have been only too ready to believe the worst of him. In

1471 they had equipped and shipped Lancastrians to England in an attempt to topple Edward, and in 1485 they performed the same self-interested service, more successfully, for Henry Tudor. According to Commynes, the King of France gave 'a little money' and 'some three thousand of the most unruly men that could be found and enlisted in Normandy' to this 'enemy of King Richard who had neither money, nor rights, so I believe, to the crown of England'.

Angelo Cato, the man for whom the *Memoirs* were written, was *philosophus et medicus*, holding a professorship at the university of Naples before becoming court physician to, successively, the Neapolitan king, Ferrante, and Louis XI. Also an author, editor and publisher, he was one of the earliest patrons of printing. Deeply interested too in politics and history, he achieved an unlikely but lasting fame as an astrologer with an uncanny knack for accurate predictions.

He won Louis XI's confidence by bringing him back to consciousness after a stroke and is said to have reinforced his influence by announcing to the king in Tours the death of Charles the Rash at the very moment when it was occurring in Nancy. One of his books dealt with poisons and their antidotes. A man who could prolong life, could provide important information regardless of the barriers of time and distance and knew about poisons was irresistible to Louis. In another age Cato might have found himself in trouble for witchcraft. Instead he was rewarded, in 1482, with the archbishopric of Vienne, an elevation readily approved by Pope Sixtus IV, his former tutor.

Cato was almost certainly responsible for the visit to England of Dominic Mancini, a fellow Italian resident in France, and thus for a second contemporary witness of Richard's time. Mancini, a monk and man of letters, the author of moral and theological works in Latin verse, probably crossed the Channel early in 1483 as a member of a French mission to the English court. It seems that his role, like that of many a diplomat, was to act as an intelligence agent. He was to inform Cato, and possibly through him the French court, on events in England. His presence in London coincided with the three crucial months between the death of Edward IV and the coronation of Richard III, after which Cato recalled him to France. His report, which was completed at Beaugency (in the vicinity of the French court) on 1 December 1483, was lost for centuries and discovered by C. A. J. Armstrong, an Oxford historian, in the municipal library at Lille in 1934.

Unlike Commynes, Mancini was a man of integrity and an honest reporter, but the value of his work is limited by his ignorance of England and, indeed, of the English language. It is relatively free of the moralising favoured by Commynes and More, but Mancini's objectivity is seriously qualified by the assumption – unproven and far from certain – that Richard was aiming for the crown from the moment he learned of his brother's death. He seems not to have had even a glimpse of Richard (who was in the north until May 1483) and we are therefore missing the pen portrait which could have saved so much controversy over Richard's personal appearance. As Mr Armstrong states: 'The otherwise unaccountable decision to exclude even a sketch of Richard becomes intelligible only if Mancini had no opportunity to observe him sufficiently. It is noticeable that the narrative grows less detailed as it approaches Richard's final occupation of the throne on 26 June 1483; and there are grounds for supposing that while Mancini had sources of information regarding Edward IV and Edward V he never secured a reliable informant to tell him about Richard III.'

It may have been partly or wholly on Mancini's evidence that the Chancellor of France, in a speech to the States-General in January 1484, accused Richard of murdering his nephews, thus contrasting civilised France, where a regency governed on behalf of a boy king, with the notorious misconduct of the English, who were depicted as specialists in regicide. According to the French chancellor the unruly English had mounted no fewer than twenty-six rebellions against their kings since the time of William the Conqueror. This speech, often cited as evidence of Richard's guilt, has more the flavour of a routine exercise in Anglophobia.

What, then, did Mancini actually report about the fate of Edward V and his brother? He wrote (in Mr Armstrong's translation) as follows: 'But after Hastings was removed, all the attendants who had waited upon the king were debarred access to him. He and his brother were withdrawn into the inner

RICHARD III
Portrait formerly belonging to the Paston family, c.1516.
Artist unknown (*Society of Antiquaries*)

RICHARD III
Portrait c.1590. Artist unknown (*National Portrait Gallery*)

HENRY VII

Portrait by Michael Sittow, 1505 (*National Portrait Gallery*)

EDWARD V

Engraving from a painting by George Vertue. Slaughtered lambs below

LAURENCE OLIVIER AS RICHARD III
in his film of Shakespeare's play (*London Films*, 1955)

SIR THOMAS MORE
Statue outside Chelsea Old Church, London (L. Cubitt Bevis, 1969)

HORACE WALPOLE
Engraving from a painting by J. G. Eccardt, with Strawberry Hill in background

MIDDLEHAM CASTLE

Warwick the Kingmaker's and later Richard III's home in Yorkshire

apartments of the Tower proper, and day by day began to be seen more rarely behind the bars and windows, till at length they ceased to appear altogether. The physician Argentine, the last of his attendants whose services the king enjoyed, reported that the young king, like a victim prepared for sacrifice, sought remission of his sins by daily confession and penance, because he believed that death was facing him.'

This reveals little more than that after the Hastings conspiracy (which Mancini believed to have been invented by Richard as an excuse to be rid of him) Richard was taking precautions against the boys being used in another plot, and that the elder boy (who needed the services of a physician) was, naturally, frightened. There was nothing sinister about their residence in the Tower, where kings traditionally stayed before their coronation, and Mancini's account is not inconsistent with their being removed from there to somewhere more appropriate after Richard's coronation: Sheriff Hutton castle in Yorkshire, for example.

In one of his few purple passages Mancini provides what he obviously felt was an obligatory eulogy for a deposed innocent: 'This context seems to require that I should not pass over in silence the talent of the youth. In word and deed he gave so many proofs of his liberal education, of polite, nay rather scholarly, attainments far beyond his age; all of these should be recounted, but require such labour, that I shall lawfully excuse myself the effort. There is one thing I shall not omit, and that is, his special knowledge of literature, which enabled him to discourse elegantly, to understand fully, and to declaim most excellently from any work whether in verse or prose that came into his hands, unless it were from among the more abstruse authors. He had such dignity in his whole person, and in his face such charm, that however much they might gaze he never wearied the eyes of beholders. I have seen many men burst forth into tears and lamentations when mention was made of him after his removal from men's sight; and already there was a suspicion that he had been done away with.'

John Argentine, a royal physician fearful for his charge, was presumably a source for this heavily loaded passage. Eighteen years later, coincidentally or not, Dr Argentine was to receive the appointment of Provost of King's College, Cambridge at the very time when Henry VII's implausible account of the boys' death was first made public. Mancini, however, with strict regard for truth, concludes this passage with a categorical disclaimer: 'Whether, however, he has been done away with, and by what manner of death, so far I have not at all discovered.' Nor did he subsequently; leaving England too soon to report on Richard's reign.

Mancini confirms the general acceptance by those hostile to Richard that he was indeed named as Protector in his brother's will, which has not survived. He recounts how Edward IV's marriage with Elizabeth Woodville affronted members of the royal family and alienated the nobility. He places the responsibility for Clarence's death squarely on the queen, who believed that her offspring would never come to the throne while he was alive. When Clarence was openly venting his wrath against the Woodvilles, Richard 'being better at concealing his thoughts and besides younger and therefore less influential, neither did nor said anything that could be brought against him'. When Clarence had been put to death, 'Richard, Duke of Gloucester was so overcome with grief for his brother, that he could not dissimulate so well, but that he was overheard to say that he would one day avenge his brother's death. Thenceforth he came very rarely to court. He kept himself within his own lands and set out to acquire the loyalty of his people through favours and justice. The good reputation of his private life and public activities powerfully attracted the esteem of strangers. Such was his renown in warfare that, whenever a difficult and dangerous policy had to be undertaken, it would be entrusted to his discretion and his generalship. By these arts Richard acquired the favour of the people, and avoided the jealousy of the queen, from whom he lived far separated.'

The full title of Mancini's work, which was written in Latin, is *Dominicus Mancinus Ad Angelum Catonem: De Occupatione Regni Anglie Per Riccardum Tercium Libellus*. Mr Armstrong has chosen to translate this as *The Usurpation of Richard the Third*, and this is the title by which it is generally known. Yet, if Mancini had intended 'Usurpation' he would surely have written *usurpatione* not *occupatione*. *Usurpare* is a word which he uses in the text in a different context, and when he uses *occupatione* on another occasion Mr Armstrong interprets it, more exactly, as 'took possession of'. In Mr Armstrong's translation '*occupato iam regno ab Henrico*' becomes simply 'the occupation of the realm by Henry', while '*Riccardus regnum occupavit*' becomes 'Richard usurped the kingdom'. The difference between *usurpatio* and *occupatio* is the difference between seizing wrongfully and seizing (rightly or wrongly) and, whatever the drift of his reporting, the scholarly Mancini nowhere uses the word *usurpatio* in relation to Richard's seizure of the crown.

Indeed, whatever his own beliefs, he sets out fairly enough the argument why the *occupatio* might not be regarded as *usurpatio*. Buckingham 'argued that it would be unjust to crown this lad, who was illegitimate' because his father, when he married his mother, was legally contracted to another wife. This reference is to Bona of Savoy: 'Indeed on Edward's authority' Warwick 'had espoused the other lady by proxy – as it is called – on the continent. Besides, Elizabeth herself had been married to another, and had been ravished rather than espoused by Edward, with the result that their entire offspring was unworthy of the kingship. As for the son of the Duke of Clarence, he had been rendered ineligible for the crown by the felony of his father: since his father after conviction for treason had forfeited not only his own but also his sons' right of succession. The only survivor of the royal stock was Richard, Duke of Gloucester, who was legally entitled to the crown, and could bear its responsibilities thanks to his proficiency. His previous career and blameless morals would be a sure guarantee of his good government.'

Another judgmental translation by Mr Armstrong should perhaps be noted. Referring to Richard and the protectorship, Mancini writes '*qui paulo post, Eduardi liberis oppressis, regnum sibi vindicavit*': literally, 'who shortly afterwards, when Edward's children had been set aside, claimed the throne for himself'. '*Oppressis*' carries the meaning of 'suppression', being overthrown or subdued. Mr Armstrong opts for the strongest sense – destruction – and rejigs the sentence so that Richard is the destroyer, an accusation specifically not made by Mancini. Thus the phrase in translation becomes 'who shortly after destroyed Edward's children and then claimed for himself the throne'.

Like the examination of the alleged bones of the two young

princes in Westminster Abbey during the previous year, Mr Armstrong's discovery of Mancini's manuscript received wide publicity and was generally taken for confirmation of Richard's villainy. A damning article in *The Times* appeared under bold, funereal headlines: *The Crimes of Richard III. Murder of the Two Princes. New Evidence of Guilt.* In this article Mr Armstrong writes that before the disappearance of the princes 'Richard was the hero of the crowd'. But 'like the Great Chronicle of London, the Lille manuscript leaves no doubt that the princes were murdered in the Tower by order of Richard' and this cost him his popularity. Those who have read for themselves what Mancini wrote will take this statement with a large pinch of salt. There is a likelihood that the princes were still alive when Mancini left England, whatever may have happened to them subsequently, and of their fate he specifically avows his ignorance.

Commynes is untrustworthy and Mancini has been condemned as strong on gossip and personal motivation but weak on the intricacies of English politics. Like the Croyland chronicler, they offer indisputable evidence that some of the accusations made against Richard in Tudor times were current in his own lifetime. But in view of the circumstances of his accession and the disappearance of the princes this is scarcely a matter for surprise or a significant pointer towards the truth. Again like the Croyland chronicler, what neither of Angelo's witnesses provides, despite what is so confidently asserted or persuasively suggested by later historians, is any real evidence of Richard's guilt.

10

Rumour and Record

Most chroniclers in the fifteenth and earlier centuries were ill-informed and notoriously unreliable. Either they were simply passing on gossip, the spicier the better, or they were purposefully establishing rights, authenticating claims or currying favour. Polydore Vergil dismisses their work as 'sparse, haphazard, artless and untrue'. The various near-contemporary chronicles of Richard's time do little more than repeat rumours and slanders circulating among the establishment of the new regime. 'Much of the fascination of the history of Richard III,' writes Alison Hanham, 'derives from the need to make an individual decision about the relative weight to be allotted to one somewhat untrustworthy chronicler rather than another.' The creaky platform for the Great Debate is riddled with dry rot, and that is why the argument has never been convincingly won nor irrecoverably lost.

Dr Hanham has done much in her *Richard III and His Early Historians 1483–1535* to disentangle contemporary sources from the propaganda which dates from the succeeding century, and to demonstrate the fallibility of both: 'The idea that any person who lived at the time of the events he reports is necessarily a reliable witness to them would not be entertained by any historian who gave the matter due thought, and a journalist, lawyer or policeman would assure him that even actual eye-witnesses seldom agree about the details of what they saw. But all the same it is often taken for granted that Rous and Fabyan knew what they were talking about because they lived at the period concerned.'

John Rous (1411–1491) has the distinction of being the most despised of the chroniclers. He was a Warwickshire chantry priest and antiquarian whose only first-hand report of events in London was zoological: 'In the days of this king [Edward IV] an elephant was brought to England, which I saw at London, but it soon declined.' In the best time-serving manner he wrote (in *The Rous Roll*) a fulsome eulogy of Richard during Richard's reign and after his death a thorough-going attack on him (in his *History of the Kings of England*) to ingratiate himself with the new king. Both have survived, so that we have rival pen portraits of Richard as model prince and monster written by the same hand. Rous (writes Charles Ross in his Historical Introduction to *The Rous Roll*, 1980) 'was wholly uncritical and undiscriminating in his approach to evidence, willing to purvey as history a whole fantasy world of myth and miracles.'

It is Rous who first made the startling revelation that Richard spent two years in his mother's womb and emerged with a full set of teeth and shoulder-length hair. It is Rous who pins on Richard responsibility for the murder of Henry VI ('as many think . . . by his own hands') and for that of his own wife, Anne Nevill, whom he allegedly poisoned. Yet even in his History he agrees with all other sources in conceding Richard's bravery at Bosworth: 'He bore himself like a noble soldier and, despite his little body and feeble strength, honourably defended himself to his last breath, shouting again and again that he was betrayed, and crying "Treason! Treason! Treason!"' This is the origin of all those anguished cries which have thrilled so many generations of theatre audiences.

Amid all his abuse Rous has another significant passage in praise of Richard: 'This King Richard was praiseworthy for his building, as at Westminster, Nottingham, Warwick, York and Middleham, and many other places, which can be viewed. He founded a noble chantry for a hundred priests in the cathedral of York and another college at Middleham. He founded another in the church of St Mary of Barking, by the Tower of London, and endowed the Queens' College at Cambridge with 500 marks annual rent. The money which was offered him by the peoples of London, Gloucester and Worcester he declined with thanks, affirming that he would rather have their love than their treasure.'

Interestingly, even Rous does not directly accuse Richard of murdering the princes. According to the History he 'ascended the throne of the slaughtered children': the manner of their death, said to be known to very few, is not stated. This contrasts with the unqualified allegations of other murders committed by Richard, including the beheading of Hastings (strongly encouraged by Buckingham).

In the roll which he wrote during Richard's lifetime and failed to destroy, Rous portrays a Richard who 'ruled his subjects in his realm full commendably, punishing offenders of his laws, specially extortioners and oppressors of his commons, and cherishing those that were virtuous, by the which discreet guiding he got great thanks of God and love of all his subjects, rich and poor, and great laud of the people of all other lands about him'.

John Rous is not alone in being caught out as two-faced. During Richard's reign Pietro Carmeliano (a man of letters from Brescia) wrote a poem dedicated to Sir Robert Brackenbury, with a fawning preface in honour of the king: 'If we look first of all for religious devotion, which of our Princes shows a more genuine piety? If for justice, who can we reckon above him throughout the world? If we contemplate the prudence of his service, both in peace and in waging war, who shall we judge his equal? If we look for truth of soul, for wisdom, for loftiness of mind united with modesty, who stands before our King Richard? What Emperor or Prince can be compared with him in good works, or in munificence?' After Richard's death Carmeliano became a secretary to Henry VII and wrote another poem in which Richard features villainously as the murderer of Henry VI and the princes.

Similarly, the University of Oxford is on record as experiencing after Richard's suppression of Buckingham's rebellion 'unbelievable pleasure, o most distinguished king, because of your triumphs over your foes' and no less unbelievable pleasure after Bosworth in an address of congratulation to Henry on his victory over Richard. Obsequiousness is a prudent and time-honoured institutional attitude, as necessary to survival as the servility of courtiers, but both tarnish the lustre of primary sources.

For Richard's early life there are only two sources which were not written during the reign of his successor. *The History of the*

Arrivall of King Edward IV is a Yorkist propaganda account of Edward's recapture of the crown in 1471, in which Richard is scarcely mentioned: at Tewkesbury Edward of Lancaster is slain in the field and Henry VI dies of natural causes. A less partial witness is Dr John Warkworth, Master of St Peter's College, Cambridge from 1473 to 1498. His chronicle, which ends in 1473, provides the best evidence that the Lancastrian heir to the throne was killed during the fighting at Tewkesbury, a fact on which all contemporary sources agree. Later accounts of his murder after the battle are no more than fanciful story-telling by anti-Yorkist chroniclers, but to those determined to find Richard guilty of all possible crimes they have proved too tempting to relinquish. James Gairdner, for example, writing of Richard's alleged complicity in this non-event four hundred years later, exemplifies the antiRichard mentality in these words: 'It is possible that the circumstances of the case were preserved only by tradition, till the days of Polydore Vergil and of Hall the Chronicler; but they are not on that account unworthy of credit.'

Robert Fabyan, a learned draper and alderman of the city of London, is a tantalising contemporary witness. A prosperous pillar of the city establishment who served as sheriff in 1493, he should have been able to tell us so much but cautiously reveals so little. In what time he could spare from money-making and civic duties he fathered sixteen children and wrote an ambitious history, *The New Chronicles of England and France*, which was published shortly after his death in 1513. His account of Richard III's reign is inevitably influenced by the climate of Henry VII's and the necessity not to give offence in high places, but it is without the animus of Henry's apologists and More's essay on villainy.

Fabyan has the Lancastrian Prince of Wales killed after the battle at Tewkesbury, but by the king's servants, with no mention of Richard. He accuses Richard of 'long covert dissimulation' and has Hastings beheaded on a log of wood without trial, but there is no nonsense about witchcraft or withered arms. In Dr Shaw's sermon the illegitimacy of Edward IV's children is alleged, but there is no mention of an allegation that Edward IV himself was illegitimate. Fabyan records, not that the city of London accepted Richard reluctantly, but that Buckingham's eloquence carried the day. The mayor and other city dignitaries were convinced of the Protector's right and title to the crown by 'sugared words of exhortation' from Buckingham and other lords.

As for the princes, they 'were put under sure keeping within the Tower, in such wise that they never came abroad after', and later, 'as the common fame went', they suffered a secret death. Had news of what More set down with such relish not travelled the few yards between Tower and City, or did Fabyan know and not choose to record the story? The answer presumably depends on whether he was writing before or after 1502, when the story was probably invented. It is impossible to deduce whether he himself believed the common fame or whether he is merely recording the orthodoxy of the day and using this phrase to signal his own disbelief. Gairdner rightly complained of Fabyan that his information is 'meagre in the extreme'.

The Elizabethan antiquarian, John Stow, who owned the manuscript, was convinced that the author of *The Great Chronicle of London*, an anonymous two-part work covering events from 1439 to 1496 and 1496 to 1512, was also Fabyan, but this is not a generally accepted attribution. There are variations between this chronicle and his own; although that may be because the relevant passages were written at different dates – those in *The Great Chronicle* in or around 1512; in the *New Chronicles* ten or twenty years earlier.

The city outlook is certainly similar. From the *New Chronicles* we learn that Richard spent his brother's great treasure and had to borrow from the citizens of London, but he gave 'good and sufficient pledges'. *The Great Chronicle* treats us to an eye-witness account of the arrival of Edward V and his uncle in London on 4 May 1483. The mayor and his brethren in scarlet and five hundred commoners in violet robes, all well horsed and well apparelled, rode out from the city to Hornsey park to receive the new king, who was in blue velvet, while the Duke of Gloucester wore a mourning apparel of coarse black cloth, and all their servants were in black too. The king was escorted to the bishop's palace in St Paul's churchyard and the Duke of Gloucester to Crosby place in Bishopsgate Street. It was after the duke had been proclaimed Protector of the Realm that the king moved to the Tower.

The Great Chronicle does not accuse Richard of any responsibility for the death of the Lancastrian Prince of Wales (Edward
IV, it is reported, smote him on the face with the back of his
gauntlet and the king's servants despatched him) or for that of
his brother, Clarence. Nor is the charge made that he was
aiming for the crown at that time or later. On Henry VI's
death, however, 'the common fame then went that the Duke of
Gloucester was not all guiltless', and Hastings was 'a noble
man murdered for his truth and fidelity which he firmly bare to
his master' (presumably Edward IV). As in all near-
contemporary accounts, no plausible explanation is offered for
Richard's sudden move against Hastings, possibly because the
plot against his life involved the mother of Henry VII's queen
and was therefore unmentionable.

According to *The Great Chronicle*, although it is not too clear
on the matter, Dr Shaw's famous sermon referred to both
illegitimacies: the children of King Edward were alleged to be
not 'rightful inheritors' of the crown and, anyway, Edward
himself was a bastard. In his meeting with the city fathers
Buckingham spoke for a good half hour on Richard's behalf and
was not only eloquent but assumed 'an angelic countenance'.
But by this account the city assented 'more for fear than for
love'. In the end *The Great Chronicle*'s judgment on Richard III
differs markedly from that of the Tudor court circle living so
comfortably off the fruits of treason against him. It is regretful
and humane: he 'should have been honourably lauded over all
if he had continued as Protector and suffered the children to
have prospered. But God forgive him his misdeeds!'

This chronicle is best known in the Ricardian controversy for
its report of the last sighting of the princes, but it records no
more than rumours about their death. Another London chronicle, the compilation known as Vitellius A XVI, appears to
have shared a common original with *The Great Chronicle* and
Fabyan's *New Chronicles*. It is, however, alone in openly asserting that Richard 'put to death the two children of King
Edward, for which cause he lost the hearts of the people'. These
words date from the early part of Henry VII's reign, and it is of
some interest that they are not repeated in the other chronicles,
which were written later.

For formal city records with a bearing on Richard III's

reputation we have to look to the north, where much has been made of the city of York's 'great heaviness' at Richard III's death and the danger and defiance of officially recording its sorrow after Henry Tudor's victory. The antiRichard editor of *York Civic Records* (1939) is at some pains to dissociate the city from the taint of such misguided loyalty. Although the city council obeyed Richard, sent him soldiers on request and gave him presents, he finds (in the abbreviated minutes of council meetings) no evidence that they loved him. Indeed, he speculates, they may even have deliberately delayed sending their contingent to Bosworth, and as for the citizens at large, there are some indications – from disturbances and tavern gossip – that Richard was unpopular among them.

In assessing Richard's character and reputation, deductions of that kind seem of little value. Like the nobility, citizens and city fathers in the fifteenth century, as in other centuries, were motivated by self-interest. If their lord granted them protection and privileges on good terms he would have been popular; if the protection and privileges were inadequate or the price too high, he would have been unpopular. Those approving of his nominees for mayor and recorder would have judged him a good lord; those with a grievance or supporting other candidates would not.

'I wish we could have Wrangwish for our mayor, as the Duke of Gloucester will do things for him,' says one bar-fly in a pub in Goodmangate in the 1470's. Another replies: 'If the Duke of Gloucester is for Wrangwish, then we don't want him for mayor.' On another occasion the question 'What might the Duke of Gloucester do for our city?' receives the reply: 'Nothing but grin at us.' These are real exchanges between real men talking about Richard while he was still alive, but it is hard to follow a modern editor when he cites them as significant pieces of evidence. Richard is recorded as the 'special good lord of York' and Wrangwish was twice elected mayor.

The famous minute of the council meeting held on the morrow of Bosworth is worth quoting in full (freed, in the words of one Victorian editor, from 'the repulsive and uncouth orthography of that period'):

Tuesday, Vigil of Saint Bartholomew, 23 August.

Were assembled in the council chamber, where and when it
was shewed by divers persons, especially by John Spooner
sent unto the field of Redmore to bring tidings from the same
to the city, that King Richard, late mercifully reigning over
us, was through the great treason of the Duke of Norfolk and
many others that turned against him, with many other lords
and nobility of these northern parts piteously slain and
murdered, to the great heaviness of this city, the names of
whom follow hereafter.

Wherefore it was determined, for so much as it was that the
Earl of Northumberland was coming to Wressel, that a letter
should be conveyed unto the said earl, beseeching him to give
unto them his best advice how to dispose them at this woeful
season, both to his honour and worship, and the weal and
profit of this city. The tenor whereof followeth.

From this it is plain that, in the view of the city fathers, York
had lost in Richard a good and merciful lord. His death and
that of members of the northern nobility had left them unpro-
tected and panic-stricken. In desperate need of a new patron,
they turned naturally to the now most powerful man in the
region. The ensuing letter to the Earl of Northumberland
offered him their faithful hearts and true service and besought
him to be their right good and tender lord for the wellbeing,
profit and safeguarding of the city.

The city's approach underlines the advantage which Northumberland had gained from standing aloof at Bosworth while
Richard went down fighting. In naming the Duke of Norfolk as
a traitor John Spooner must have returned so hastily that he
failed to obtain accurate information, or else the council was
making a deliberate mistake. The real traitors were the Stanleys, powerful in the north, and Northumberland, even more so
and the city's best hope for protection. To record that these men
were guilty of treason might have been far more risky than a
formal expression of sorrow at the passing of their good lord, the
dead king.

Further rich evidence on the background of the period may
be gleaned from surviving collections of family correspondence:

Plumpton (Yorkshire), Cely (London wool merchants), Stonor (southern land-owners) and, most especially, Paston (East Anglia). They too provide posterity with glimpses of the real world, supplementing and balancing the stylised moralising and literary exercises of the Tudor apologists. Two important Stallworth letters touching on events in London during June 1483 come from the Stonor collection, while the Pastons are often participants and sometimes victims in the national struggle for power. A vivid impression of the mustering of Richard's army before Bosworth may be gained from a summons by the Duke of Norfolk: 'to my well beloved friend John Paston be this bill delivered in haste'.

'Well beloved friend, I commend me to you, letting you to understand that the king's enemies be a land, and that the king would have set forth as upon Monday but only for our Lady day, but for certain he goeth forward as upon Tuesday, for a servant of mine brought to me the certainty. Wherefore I pray you that ye meet me at Bury, for by the grace of God I purpose to lie at Bury as upon Tuesday night, and that ye bring with you such company of tall men as ye may goodly make at my cost and charge, besides that ye have promised the king, and I pray you ordain them jackets of my livery, and I shall content you at your meeting with me. Your lover, J. Norfolk.' The haste and haphazardness of the muster is underlined by the fact that there is no record of John Paston at Bosworth. But whether his non-attendance was due to disloyalty, discretion, tardiness or absence from home when the summons arrived is not known.

Hard facts are available in still surviving official documents. The Rolls of Parliament set out not only the Act of Settlement (otherwise Titulus Regius) passed in January 1484 but the proceedings and legislation of that parliament which suggest that Richard was what would today be called a socially aware and caring king. They are recorded in English: a breach with precedent which heralded the adoption of English as the official language, displacing Latin and Norman French.

In the Calendar of Charter Rolls may be found the date of the creation of John Howard as Duke of Norfolk and William, Viscount Berkeley as Earl of Nottingham. Those were titles bestowed by Edward IV on his younger son, Richard, Duke of York. They belonged to Anne Mowbray, the boy's child bride, and were retained by him after her death. Their transfer to others by Richard III has often been adduced as proof that the younger of the princes in the Tower was dead; but, in fact, Richard was reversing a controversial and probably illegal and much resented decision by his brother to satisfy those with a better claim to the Mowbray titles and estates. The date of the new creations was in each case 28 June 1483, only two days after Richard had formally assumed the crown and more than a week before his coronation – some time before it has been supposed that either of the princes was dead.

In the Calendar of Patent Rolls we can still follow Richard's appointments. John Howard was granted the office of Earl Marshal immediately before his creation as Duke of Norfolk. On 15 July Henry, Duke of Buckingham was granted the office of Constable of England and much else. On 17 July Bracken-bury was appointed Constable of the Tower of London and Master of the Mint throughout the realm, including Calais, and John Kendale, already a loyal retainer of Richard, formally became the king's servant and secretary. A week later Henry, Earl of Northumberland was appointed Warden General of the Marches (east and middle), but for one year only. On 30 November, after Buckingham's rebellion, Northumberland became Great Chamberlain, and on 16 December Buckingham's office of Constable of England was granted to Thomas Stanley Knight, Lord of Stanley. Bare in themselves, these entries provide important evidence of an unwise concentration of power in few hands.

The Calendar of Close Rolls contains information which reflects on the story of Dr Ralph Shaw being put up by Richard to make a public announcement of the illegitimacy of his brother to whom he had been so loyal. The slur on his mother is all the more extraordinary because the widowed Duchess of York was still alive at the time, and Baynards Castle, her London home, was only a short walking distance from St Paul's cross where the accusation was made. The grand dames of the fifteenth century were not the subservient females of Victorian tradition, as the careers of Margaret of Anjou, Elizabeth Woodville and Margaret Beaufort testify. 'Proud Cis', born a Nevill and mother of the King of England for more than twenty years, is likely to have been quite as formidable as that trio of viragos. Yet the Close Rolls record that on 27 June, a few days after Dr Shaw's sermon, the ceremony of delivering the Great Seal 'in a bag of white leather' to the newly appointed Chancellor of England, John, Bishop of Lincoln, took place 'within the chapel in the hospice of Cicely, Duchess of York called Baynards Castle'. If the story of the announcement is true, it seems improbable that Richard himself was responsible, for he appears to have remained on good and dutiful terms with his mother. Perhaps Buckingham was making more mischief.

Richard's reign is flickeringly illuminated by a uniquely valuable manuscript compilation in the Harleian collection in the British Library. This ragbag register of 2,378 items of documentation from the king's signet office, catalogued as Harley MS 433, is the medieval equivalent of the file copies of his private secretary's correspondence, although what has survived is not the complete archive. The Plantagenet rulers in the fifteenth century were diligently served by a departmentalised bureaucracy of clerks who scribbled from reign to reign little affected by the changing colour of the ruler's rose. In the case of grants, for example, the royal assent was normally transmitted by a warrant from his signet office (usually in English) to the office of the privy seal, which in turn authorised the office of the great seal (usually in Norman French) to draw up the necessary documents for signature (usually in Latin). In 1619 a disastrous fire at the banqueting house in Whitehall destroyed all the medieval signet office and privy seal archives except for this collection from the reigns of Edward V and Richard III, which had gone missing after attracting the interest of Elizabeth I's minister, William Cecil, Lord Burghley, from among whose possessions it is said to have been later recovered.

Royal patronage (grants of titles, offices and estates; lists of fees and wages), finance (records and accounts) and diplomacy (letters to other rulers) form the main subject matter of this collection. 'Of no other king,' declares Gairdner, 'have we so minute a record.' The reason for Richard's political failure may be read in detail in the items which record his exercise of patronage. 'From the summer of 1484,' writes Rosemary Horrox in her Introduction to the edition published in 1979, 'the king was faced by a series of minor risings, as well as by the threat of invasion from abroad. As a result he was driven to rely upon a narrowing circle of associates. The closing pages of the register demonstrate very clearly that major grants, at least, were almost all going to men who had already benefited from royal patronage. In other words, the grants were not securing new support for the king but strengthening the influence of his existing affinity.' Inevitably to the resentment of others.

In financial matters the manuscript clarifies the distinction between the loans which Richard raised and the benevolences of Edward IV which he had condemned in parliament. Benevolences were not repaid, whereas repayment of the loans (by June 1486) was guaranteed. 'Legally,' writes Dr Horrox, 'Richard was completely within his rights. The Croyland chronicler is wrong in insisting that the loans were benevolences under another name and that Richard was thus breaking his own word.'

The human face of government is sometimes glimpsed in the pages of Harley 433. Florence Cheney, the widow of a traitor, is taken under Richard's protection, and he issues orders that she is to be allowed 'to live in rest and quiet' and enjoy her lands, goods and chattels without vexation. Edmond Filpot of Twickenham loses his house, tenements and all his goods in a fire, and the king gives him a letter which effectively allows him the status of a charitable foundation, enabling him to solicit for funds to rebuild his house. A similar letter is addressed to 'all abbots, priors, deans, curates, vicars and other ministers of holy Church and to all mayors, sheriffs, bailiffs, constables and other our officers, true liegemen and subjects' on behalf of John Legh of West Retford, whose two barns full of corn and other goods were burned to the ground during his absence in Dunbar, Scotland on the king's service.

These are small matters concerning unimportant people, but they serve to illustrate that during his lifetime Richard the monster was not much in evidence and why to near-contemporary chroniclers he was not a demon king. Indeed he appears to have undertaken the daily chores of sovereignty with exemplary conscientiousness in the best tradition of a feudal lord recognising obligations as well as rights.

11

The First Historian

Like Mancini, Polydore Vergil was an Italian cleric, scholar and author who came to England on an official mission: in his case as chamberlain to Pope Alexander VI and sub-collector of the tribute, Peter's pence. Born in 1470, a native of Urbino and a graduate of Padua university, he arrived in 1502, seventeen years after Richard III's death, and unlike Mancini chose to remain, becoming a naturalised Englishman eight years later.

As a friend of Erasmus, he was made welcome in the intellectual circles of the day and struck up friendships with men of the New Learning – Fisher, Latimer, Linacre, Tunstall, Warham and, most pertinently, Thomas More. Royal favour brought him rich pickings, and he became an archdeacon of Wells and a prebendary of Hereford and St Paul's. After Henry VII's death he was used as an intermediary in Wolsey's lobbying for a cardinal's hat and (probably for working surreptitiously against Wolsey) spent some months in prison, to the indignation of the Pope, before being restored to favour.

Polydore Vergil was not, as revisionists sometimes claim, imported as a tame historian with an urgent assignment to add a much needed veneer of respectability to Tudor claims and pretensions. It was not until some five years after his arrival in the country that Henry VII commissioned him to write a History of England, and he took at least six over the first draft. It was twenty-six years in all before the twenty-six books contained in his *Anglica Historia* were completed (in August 1533), and the work was first published (in Basle) in 1534. In 1551 he returned to spend his old age in Italy, where he died four years later, still in possession of his clerical preferments in England.

This diligent scholar shares with More the distinction of having enriched history with the legend of a monster king, but while More's contribution was probably intended for the private amusement of himself and his friends and written mostly tongue in cheek, Polydore Vergil brought to the legend the authority of a real historian and one, moreover, who has a fair claim to be considered the father of English history. Vergil's Richard III is contemporaneous with More's and unmistakably derived from the same sources.

It is ironic that Vergil should have upset English susceptibilities and brought a storm of criticism on himself by dismissing early and cherished parts of the nation's story as fable rather than fact. A later historian (John Nichols) felt obliged to defend him against the charge that 'he pitcheth somewhat smartly upon the antiquity of Britain': 'It is well observed by many of great reading and judgment that Geoffrey of Monmouth had somewhat hyperbolically extolled the praise and antiquity of the Britons, and interlaced many passages of his own device, and drawn down a series of descents, but with what truth the just and true chronology of time, upon good examination, will soon discover; so that Polydore doth not upon the matter impeach the antiquity of Britain, but the fabulous inventions of the said Geoffrey.'

What then are the fabulous inventions of the said Polydore? It is overstating the case to assert that he rewrote English history to the glorification of Henry Tudor, but clearly he had to balance his integrity as a scholar with the sharp necessity of currying favour. What he published about recent events could have deprived him of the comfortable unearned income derived from his church appointments and landed him in prison, of which he had already had one disagreeable taste. His dilemma was similar to that of a modern historian commissioned to write the history of a public company (where criticism of the current board of directors can scarcely be overt or even implied), but the reward and punishment are to be measured on a rather different scale. In Charles Ross's judgment, Vergil 'was no official hack. Equally, he could not afford to be wholly detached and impartial'.

His editor in Victorian times claimed that few writers of the English story had met with such harsh treatment as Vergil. Down the years he has been charged not only with partiality and deficiency in judgment but even with gross falsehood, although these charges relate mostly to the early parts of his work. He is said, too, to have made sure that his sources would not be available to others. Not only did he fail to return books to the Bodleian library, so that the University of Oxford would not lend him any more until cowed by a direct command from the king, but it is said that he pillaged libraries at his pleasure and even dispatched a whole ship-load of manuscripts to Rome. The most serious charge was made as early as 1574 by John Caius, of Cambridge, who vouched for the fact – which he boldly claimed to be a matter of certain truth – that Polydore Vergil had committed to the flames as many ancient manuscripts as would have filled a wagon, in order that the faults in his history might not be discovered.

No doubt there are both hyperbole and xenophobia in all this, and perhaps the great European scholar was simply absent-minded in returning what he had borrowed or found it necessary to retain documents for an inordinate length of time during his twenty-six-year stretch. On the other hand, the destruction of copies of the Titulus Regius is evidence that Henry VII would not have scrupled to contrive the suppression of any inconvenient truth, and it is not inconceivable that his chosen historian stooped to abetting him and his equally unscrupulous son.

Artistic licence and poetic justice feature prominently in Vergil's method of writing history. Events are embroidered and made into good stories in order to please the reader and put some flesh on bare bones. In the manner of More, characters have speeches made up for them and put into their mouths as set pieces on important occasions. Morals are always being pointed, and calamity is represented as divine retribution. Thus the murder of the innocent princes is seen as a visiting of the sins of the father upon the children. If only Edward IV had not committed perjury (by swearing to the citizens of York in 1471 that he had returned to claim only his dukedom of York and not the crown) and had not had his brother Clarence put to death, it seems that all would have gone well for his sons.

Similarly with Hastings. Although contemporary sources are unanimous is reporting that the Lancastrian Prince of Wales was killed during the fighting at Tewkesbury, Vergil finds it more dramatic to have him brought before Edward IV as a prisoner after the battle to bandy words with him so boldly that the king angrily pushes him towards his retinue, who are not slow to take the hint and kill him on the spot. Those who commit the murder are named as Clarence, Gloucester and Hastings. Gloucester is Vergil's villain, but why Clarence and Hastings? Both suffer a violent death later and the moral is that they are thereby punished for committing a similar crime themselves. Those surprised at finding the name of Hastings included will come across this explanation when they reach Hastings' own death: 'He was one of the smiters of Prince Edward, King Henry VI's son, who [i.e. Hastings] was finally quit with like manner of death'.

It was Vergil who tentatively set in motion the highly implausible tale that Richard III executed Henry VI personally, but he is far from categorical about what later it became fashionable to accept as an established fact: 'The continual report is that Richard Duke of Gloucester killed him with a sword. . . But whosoever were the killer of that holy man. . .'

Another story still commonly believed is that Richard was in some way responsible for the death of his brother Clarence. But if even Polydore Vergil does not level this charge against his villain, other antiRichards should surely think again. In his account of Clarence's grisly end in a butt of malmsey he makes no mention at all of Richard and speculates on two possible reasons why Edward put his brother George to death: the report of a prophecy that someone beginning with G would succeed him as king and their quarrel over George's wish to marry Mary, the heiress of Burgundy. However, 'as touching the cause of his death, though I have enquired of many who were not of least authority among the king's council at that time, yet have I no certainty thereof to leave in memory'.

This is a revealing passage. On the one hand, it gives credence to the proposition that Polydore Vergil's account of Richard III is to be trusted because he had access to the best of primary sources – eye-witnesses of the events of the 1470s and 1480s. On the other hand, those eye-witnesses were also participants in those events and alive and thriving under a Tudor monarch: they therefore had no incentive whatever to tell the whole truth and nothing but the truth, especially to the king's favoured historian. Is it credible that surviving councillors from that period did not know why Clarence was executed? According to the Croyland chronicler, Edward IV came from Windsor to Westminster for the specific purpose of mounting a public confrontation with Clarence and accused him of breaking the law in the presence of the mayor and aldermen of the city of London, the matter being subsequently debated in parliament before sentence was passed. It was a strange lapse of memory if leading councillors really could not remember what was said at that time. Some have supposed that this otherwise unaccountable lacuna conceals the truth that Clarence had made a bid for recognition as the heir presumptive because of the illegality of his brother's marriage, thus casting an embarrassing doubt on the legitimacy of, amongst others, Edward IV's daughter Elizabeth (who was to become Henry VII's wife and Henry VIII's mother) and endorsing the validity of the grounds on which Richard later claimed the crown.

Queen Anne Nevill is reported by Polydore Vergil to have died of either sorrow or poison after Richard, her husband, had forborne from lying with her because of her unfruitfulness and then spread rumours that she was dead. In fact, like her elder sister, who also died young, Anne probably suffered from chronic ill health and may have died of consumption or tuberculosis, but Vergil's smear about Richard enabled later Tudor chroniclers to move on to an unequivocal accusation of murder. As recently as 1981, on the eve of the wedding of the Prince of Wales, *The Times* informed its readers that Anne Nevill had died 'possibly at her husband's hand', so Vergil did not smear in vain. He also reports 'a great rumour' that Edward IV too died from poison, and there seems little reason to doubt that this would have become another of Richard's spectacular crimes by the reckoning of the Tudor chroniclers but for the accident of incontrovertible evidence that he was at a distance of several hundred miles at the time.

To Vergil as to Mancini (both raised amid the pitiless politics of the Italian city states) it was a natural supposition that, on his brother's death, Richard should have determined to seize the crown for himself. 'When Richard had intelligence hereof, he began to be kindled with an ardent desire of sovereignty.' How, one wonders, can Vergil possibly have known, but this unqualified statement is central to his theme, for it follows that all Richard's actions thereafter can be condemned as deceit and hypocrisy, however proper on the surface. There is no safer method of libelling the dead than by an attribution of insincerity. At York 'he commanded all men to swear obedience unto Prince Edward', but not out of loyalty, an earnest of good intentions, as might have been supposed. 'Himself was the first that took the oath, which soon after he was the first to violate.' Derogatory nouns and adjectives abound whenever Richard holds the centre of Vergil's narrative. Translated samples from just two sentences include: spiteful practice, subtlety, sleight, malice, graceless, fraud, wicked, mischievous, frantic and mad.

When Richard reaches London, Vergil has him deliver a speech which promises that he will care for his nephews and govern well and honourably in the young king's name. Significantly, his audience, not enjoying the benefit of the author's inside knowledge of Richard's mind, is reported as believing him. 'When he had spoken these words all men, who suspected no subtlety, thought Duke Richard's advice both meet and honest.'

Although loaded and moralistic, Vergil's history is generally free of the grosser absurdities of Rous and More, but he finds it hard to resist the best stories. The reader is not to be denied the tale of the withered arm. In the scene at the Tower when Hastings is arraigned for plotting with the Woodvilles against the Protector's life, Richard displays his arm as evidence that the sorceress ex-queen had been practising her witchcraft on him. This is such an obvious instance of myth masquerading as history that it must cause even the most credulous reader to wonder what else might, less obviously, fall into that category. What should one suppose to be the real state of Richard's arm? That it was healthy until the day in question and withered thereafter (an unrecorded handicap when he cut down Henry Tudor's standard-bearer at Bosworth); that everyone could see that there was nothing wrong with it and Richard was only pretending; or that the spell was miraculously lifted after some unrecorded counter-incantation and the withering therefore no more than temporary?

Selectivity is another of Vergil's weapons: whatever places Richard in a favourable light is omitted. For example, he carefully avoids mentioning that the council appointed Richard Protector, as Edward IV had willed. The reader is therefore left in ignorance of the fact that Hastings and his fellow conspirators owed allegiance to Richard. He also omits details of the plot, which are likely to have been known to his sources and which would have explained why Richard acted as he did. Even more untruthfully, he explicitly denies that the illegitimacy of Edward IV's children provided the grounds for Richard's claim to the throne. Instead he mentions only the much less plausible bastardy of Edward IV himself. In this he has been caught out by the unexpected survival of a copy of the Titulus Regius and the accounts of Mancini and the chroniclers.

Polydore Vergil's version of the death of the princes is less of a fairy story than More's. At Gloucester, after his coronation, the heinous guilt of Richard's wicked conscience so fretted him that he sent a warrant for his nephews' death to Brackenbury, the lieutenant of the Tower, because so long as they lived he could never feel secure. When Brackenbury procrastinated, Tyrell was sent to do the deed, riding sorrowfully but obediently to London, 'but with what kind of death these sely [innocent] children were executed it is not certainly known'. This is important evidence in exploding the most enduring of the myths about Richard. If his friend More, writing at about the same time, had learned all about Black Will Slaughter and the smothering with pillows, how could Vergil not have known? Its scorning by Vergil, who also loved a good story, is a damning indictment of More's tale.

In Vergil's version Richard, delivered from his care and fear, permitted the rumour of the princes' death to be circulated. His purpose was not concealment, but to give publicity to the crime so that, with the extinction of their claim, his own kingship would become accepted. He miscalculated, however: 'When the fame of this notable foul fact was dispersed through the realm, so great grief struck generally to the hearts of all men that the same, subduing all fear, wept everywhere, and when they could weep no more they cried out: "Is there truly any man living so far at enmity with God, with all that holy is and religious, so utter enemy to man, who would not have abhorred the mischief of so foul a murder?"' Their mother, the ex-queen (soon to effect a reconciliation with Richard, as Vergil does not inform his readers), swooned at the news, lay lifeless, and on recovering made the house ring with her shrieks, beat her breast, tore her hair and prayed for her own death, like a character out of a Greek tragedy.

When all the fuss has died down, Vergil's Richard decides to turn over a new leaf or, at any rate, to make everyone think that he has. He presents the show and countenance of a good man and makes a determined effort to merit God's pardon and procure popularity by good works, such as the founding of a college for a hundred priests at York.

Vergil follows the Croyland chronicler in reporting the dramatically appropriate bad dreams suffered by Richard on the eve of Bosworth. According to the chronicle he imagines himself surrounded by a multitude of demons; in Vergil's version, presumably from the same source, he is haunted by the horrible images of evil spirits who will not let him rest. A sceptic might inquire how the nightmare of a man who was killed a few hours later came to be known. Both accounts meet this point in the only possible way by declaring that Richard himself announced it in the morning: 'to many' according to Vergil. What then, a sceptic might inquire further, is the likelihood of an experienced commander when marshalling his forces for a decisive battle choosing to make a public announcement of terrible ill omens for the day.

In the moralistic manner Richard's end is seen by Vergil as an example to other would-be evil-doers. What happened to Richard is what is wont to happen to all who offend against the laws of God and man: 'it is divine justice that the wicked provoke the punishment they deserve'. The obituary which concludes his *History of Richard the Third* is sprinkled with details of personal information designed to convey and establish authenticity: 'He was little of stature, deformed of body, the one shoulder being higher than the other, a short and sour countenance, which seemed to savour of mischief, and utter evidently craft and deceit. The while he was thinking of any matter, he did continually bite his nether lip, as though that cruel nature of his did so rage against itself in that little carcase. Also he was wont to be ever with his right hand pulling out of the sheath to the middest, and putting in again, the dagger which he did always wear. Truly he had a sharp wit, provident and subtle, apt to both counterfeit and dissemble; his courage also high and fierce, which failed him not in the very death which, when his men forsook him, he rather yielded to take with the sword than by foul flight to prolong his life, uncertain what death perchance soon after by sickness or other violence to suffer.'

What fodder Vergil and More gathered from Richard's enemies for Shakespeare's genius to feed on! In the case of Vergil the chief enemy after Henry himself may have been that most notorious of treacherous trimmers, Thomas Lord Stanley. He was still alive when Vergil arrived in England, had been a councillor when Clarence was put to death, was a member of the Hastings conspiracy, and had turned traitor at Bosworth. As Alison Hanham has pointed out, there are in Vergil's History three mentions of him which conflict with other evidence for the same occasions, and the Stanley family is on record elsewhere as misrepresenting facts to protect family reputations (in a curious ballad known as *The Song of the Lady Bessy*). Denis Hay, on the other hand, points the finger at some of Richard's other enemies: 'Morton, Bray and Urswick would seem, from the internal evidence of the *Anglica Historia*, to have been Vergil's most useful sources of information.'

Scholars of the early sixteenth century were obsessed with the question of morality as it affected rulers. Must the same Christian ethic which established what was right and good in the case of private individuals be applied to the actions of those in charge of government? 'Yes' was the answer of the consensus, and the accounts of Richard III given by Polydore Vergil and Thomas More, writing in or about the same year (1513), are essays on this theme. Dead and disgraced, Richard was convenient for portrayal as an awful example of the wicked prince, living (and more wicked) princes being unmentionable. The theme was pursued a few years later by More in his *Utopia* and Erasmus in his book of precepts for a Christian prince, but most notoriously in another work written in 1513, although not published until many years later: Machiavelli's *Il Principe* (*The Prince*), which gave birth to the word 'machiavellian' to describe rulers like the Medicis, Borgias and Gonzagas and the Richard depicted by Vergil and More.

Machiavelli's exposition and advocacy of the philosophy of political expediency was a shocking attack on the pious precepts of the consensus: 'Everyone admits how praiseworthy it is in a prince to keep faith, and to live with integrity and not with craft. Nevertheless our experience has been that those princes who have done great things have held good faith of little account. . . A wise lord cannot, nor ought he to, keep faith when such observance may be turned against him. . . It is necessary to . . . be a great pretender and dissembler. . . It is unnecessary for a prince to have all the good qualities I have enumerated, but it is very necessary to appear to have them. And I shall dare to say this also, that to have them and always to observe them is injurious, and that to appear to have them is useful: to appear merciful, faithful, humane, religious, upright, and to be so, but with a mind so framed that should you require not to be so, you may be able and know how to change to the opposite. . . A prince ought to take care that he never lets anything slip from his lips that is not replete with the above-named five qualities. . . One prince of the present time whom it is not well to name [Machiavelli has Ferdinand of Aragon in mind] never preaches anything else but peace and good faith, and to both he is most hostile, and either, if he had kept it, would have deprived him of reputation and kingdom many a time.'

This is the political and ethical context in which what was written about Richard in the early sixteenth century must be placed. It was an age when none but ruthless rulers survived (and Richard, be it noted, did not survive). In their own countries they could not be openly condemned except when dead and unpopular with their successors. Richard was thus one of the few recently living candidates available as a subject for sermonising (and others could be obliquely criticised in his name). Wolsey, the great chancellor, became another: it proved a disaster for his reputation too that he fell from favour and died just in time to become another of Polydore Vergil's victims.

The *Anglica Historia* has been described (by Denis Hay) as one of the most influential of all histories of England: 'From the wicked uncle to the grasping prelate, Vergil's story has become part of the national myth.' It is a myth born of political and moral theorising, the requirements of Tudor self-justification and the apologias of traitors circulating at a time when the real Richard had been dead and buried for nearly thirty years.

12

More Myth-Making

Sir Thomas More, Chancellor of England 1529–1532, had no
first-hand acquaintance with affairs of state during Richard's
reign. Born in 1478, he was still a child when Bosworth was
fought. His *History of King Richard III* is not a history, but a
literary exercise in the dramatic representation of villainy. A
third of it is in imaginary dialogue, and the remainder contains
factual inaccuracies and palpable absurdities. The flavour and
authenticity may be judged from its reporting of Richard's
monstrous birth, as alleged in Rous's ridiculous canard.

This virulent piece of character assassination directed
against the last Plantagenet king by someone later put to death
by Henry Tudor's son and, later still (in 1935), canonised as a
saint, has always been a paradox and a puzzle. The most
plausible explanation was put forward only in 1975 by Alison
Hanham, who drew attention to the fact that More was famous
as an intellectual joker and suggested that his account of
Richard III is to a great extent ironical, a parody of history, a
jest at the expense of Polydore Vergil and the unlikely tales with
which he and his like expected to gull the public. More never
completed or sought to publish this work, but what was written
largely in irony was published after his death and has been read
straight ever since.

A surviving letter from Erasmus to Polydore Vergil reveals
that the historian believed that he had offended More, and
parody may have been More's revenge. In his *History* More's
particularly outrageous statements and anecdotes are slyly
qualified by phrases such as 'some wise men think', 'they that

thus deem', 'it is for truth reported' and 'as the fame runs'. These seem to be signals to the reader that what is being reported is no more than worthless tittle-tattle of the kind which historians are in the habit of passing off as historical facts. Subtle leg-pulling of this sort appears the likeliest explanation for passages which lack all credibility.

Uses of dramatic irony are hard to fathom at a distance of time, but a later example of More's sarcasm is all but explicit. In an epitaph on himself sent to Erasmus after his resignation of the chancellorship, he referred to Henry VIII as one who 'alone of all kings worthily deserved both with sword and pen to be called Defender of the Faith, a glory afore not heard of'. Here the context of the occasion and the backhandedness of the compliment unmistakably indicate that the reader should insert for himself the word 'least' between 'kings' and 'worthily'. The sharp sting of derision is evident in the last six words.

More's set-piece description of the subject of his *History* runs as follows: ' . . . little of stature, ill-featured of limbs, crook-backed, his left shoulder much higher than his right, hard-favoured of visage and such as is in princes called warlike, in other men otherwise. He was malicious, wrathful, envious, and, from before his birth, ever froward. It is for truth reported that the duchess his mother had so much ado in her travail that she could not be delivered of him uncut, and that he came into the world with the feet forward – as men be borne out of it – and (as the fame runs) also not untoothed: either men out of hatred report above the truth or else nature changed her course in his beginning who in the course of his life many things unnaturally committed.' Later in the text Richard is awarded, for good measure, a 'shrivelled withered arm and small', previously overlooked.

More is here setting down, with some relish and in finely turned prose, nonsense which 'men out of hatred report' and some knaves pretend and idiots believe to be true. As we learn from Erasmus, having one shoulder visibly higher than the other was a characteristic of More's own personal appearance, so that there are private jokes here too. (Of More Erasmus wrote to Ulrich von Hutten: 'The right shoulder appears slightly more elevated than his left, and this trait, most readily apparent in his walk. . .') Perhaps More also had a reputation for being 'hard-favoured of visage'. Certainly he was short, dark-haired and pale-faced, like Richard.

The account of Richard's connivance in the death of his brother Clarence and of his aspiration to wear the crown is another passage heavily qualified by implicit disclaimers: 'Some wise men also think that his drift, covertly conveyed, lacked not in helping forth his brother of Clarence to his death, which he resisted openly, howbeit somewhat (as men deemed) more faintly than he that were heartily minded to his welfare. And they that thus deem, think that he long time in King Edward's life forethought to be king in case that the king his brother (whose life he looked that evil diet should shorten) should happen to decease (as indeed he did) while his children were young. And they deem that for this intent he was glad of the death of his brother the Duke of Clarence, whose life must needs have hindered him whether the same Duke of Clarence had kept him true to his nephew, the young king, or enterprised to be king himself. But of all this point is there no certainty, and whoso divines upon conjectures may as well shoot too far as too short.' 'Divining upon conjectures' and 'shooting too far' are apt descriptions of much of what has been written about Richard III over the centuries.

The literary merit of More's work is not in dispute. It endures as a masterpiece, standing head and shoulders above the achievements of other gifted early biographers such as Cavendish's *Life of Wolsey* and Roper's life of More himself. It is not a biography, however. The so-called *History of King Richard III* covers no more than the period between Edward IV's death in the spring of 1483 and Buckingham's rebellion in the autumn of the same year. It pictures an unnatural being and his deeds during that time, as seen through the eyes of his enemies. What has immortalised the work is the legendary tale of the death of the princes in the Tower. As the original source of this heart-wrenching climax to the traditional fable of the Wicked Uncle, it has a fair claim to being one of the most misleading historical works ever written. Had the author intended it to masquerade as a contribution to knowledge, Horace Walpole's verdict would be just. More, he wrote in his most waspish vein, 'is an historian who is capable of employing truth only as cement in a fabric of fiction'.

Where checking is possible, the work is sadly defective in accuracy. It should, for instance, have been common knowledge in More's day that, while Edward IV was secretly marrying Elizabeth Woodville, the Earl of Warwick was at the French court negotiating a marriage for him with Bona of Savoy, the French king's sister-in-law. Yet in the *History* Warwick is said to have been in Spain negotiating for the hand of the King of Spain's daughter. More understandably, like Vergil he substitutes the name of Elizabeth Lucy for that of Eleanor Butler in the matter of the pre-contract.

Most flagrant of all are the opening words of the whole work, suggestive of careful research and detailed learning: 'King Edward, of that name the fourth, after he had lived fifty and three years, seven months and six days ... died at Westminster. . .' Yet Edward, in fact, died nineteen days before his forty-first birthday, and his death at such an early age, with his children so young and the succession unprepared, was the occasion of all that followed. Under such seeming precision the error is so gross as to make one wonder whether More is perpetrating a stunning deliberate mistake and laughing up his sleeve from line one. If the error was genuine, then one must suppose that it and many others would have been corrected had More himself had the work published.

The source from which he and Vergil both drew was a poisoned well. They did not invent the Tudor saga. Their contribution was to embellish and perpetuate the version of Richard current at the court of Henry VII. Through the Ropers More's family was connected by marriage to Morton's, and as a boy he lived for some time in the household of the man who had committed treason against Richard, was the intellect behind Henry's usurpation and had been handsomely rewarded for his services, becoming Chancellor of England, Archbishop of Canterbury and a cardinal. The triumphant Morton was, in Francis Bacon's phrase, 'not without inveterate malice against the house of York'.

In Morton's house More would have met men like Christopher Urswick, who had been Morton's secret messenger between England and Brittany in 1483 and became Henry's chaplain and confessor, and Richard Fox, who had joined Henry in exile in Paris and been rewarded with the see of

Winchester. In this circle More seems to have been a favourite, early recognised as a prodigy, for Morton is reported to have said of him: 'This child here waiting at the table, whosoever shall live to see it, will prove a marvellous man.'

Sir George Buck, Sir Clements Markham and others have believed that, because of its extraordinary virulence against Richard, Morton was the real author of the *History of King Richard III* attributed to More, but that view has been exploded by R. W. Chambers as yet another myth. However strong the influence of Morton, the style of the work is characteristically More's. Its theme has much in common with that of his *Utopia*, and the abuse matches the untruthful tirade of obscenities in his *Answer to Luther*.

More did indeed prove a marvellous man. He became a scholar, author and humanist lawyer, a friend of the great Erasmus and one of the brightest lights in the English Renaissance (but also himself a machiavellian politician and a fanatical persecutor of Protestants, believing the burning of heretics to be 'lawful, necessary and well done'). A member of parliament at the age of twenty-six, he became Speaker of the House of Commons before entering the royal service and succeeding to the chancellorship on the fall of Wolsey – who also was a butt for his invective: 'The great wether which is of late fallen, as you all know, so craftily, so scabbedly, yea and so untruly juggled with the king.'

Soon juggling with the king himself, More resigned as chancellor after only three years and was later executed for high treason for refusing to conform to Henry VIII's Act of Supremacy. The day of his death, 6 July 1535, was the anniversary of Richard's coronation. As a master of the genre, More might have been amused at the further irony that his canonisation in the twentieth century has seemingly sanctified the gross absurdities of what 'men deemed' and 'it was for truth reported' about a fellow victim of the Tudors. His *History* is now published in the Yale edition of the *Complete Works of St Thomas More*, a title suggesting a divinely inspired work as though by a St Teresa of Avila or Lisieux (although the editor is far from holding any such view).

More's motives in writing it and in breaking off from writing it can only be surmised. He was about thirty-five at the time and neither chancellor nor saint, but an up-and-coming young lawyer with strong political principles and a genius for descriptive prose and the vivid expression of ideas. There are versions in both Latin and English, and he must have derived satisfaction from the literary exercise. His classical models were Suetonius and Sallust, but above all Tacitus' *Annals*, which had recently been re-discovered. Thus Edward IV is cast in the role of an Augustus as a counterpart to Richard, portrayed as a modern Tiberius. In composing an historical treatise with a moral purpose he was emulating fellow humanists of his time in Germany and Switzerland. His *History* has been described as 'an attack on the non-moral statecraft of the early sixteenth century, exactly as *Utopia* is'.

The obvious example of a machiavellian prince in More's youth had been, not Richard III, but Henry VII. More's youthful epigrams express hatred of just the kind of tyranny practised by the Tudors, and it was this which was to bring him to the block, where in his execution speech he claimed (improbably) to be the king's good servant, but (truly) God's first. As the Duke of Norfolk had warned him: 'By the mass, Master More, it is perilous striving with princes.'

More had first incurred the royal wrath as early as 1504, when as a newly elected burgess he persuaded parliament not to allow the king the full grant which he was seeking. In revenge Henry VII had More's father imprisoned and fined. When, after five more years of extortionate taxation, the king died unlamented, More's congratulatory verses to Henry VIII on his coronation contained a message of hope that tyranny was dead and even a specific reference to the end of a 'gloomy reign'.

The *History* was probably written four years later (possibly not until 1516/17), and Paul Murray Kendall has pointed to the significance of its abandonment at the very point where Henry Tudor was due to make his entry. In the text so far, Richard may have been partly serving as a substitute target, appropriately endowed with Henry's dissimulating character, and it would have been neither truthful to present Henry as the angel of salvation which the story demanded (and as Grafton and Shakespeare followed Polydore Vergil in rounding it off), nor safe to present him in his true colours. How far More was prepared to go is indicated when he refers to Henry VII's reign in the following discreetly critical terms: ' . . . all things were in late days so covertly managed, one thing pretended and another meant, that there was nothing so plain and openly proved but that yet for the common custom of close and covert dealing men had it ever inwardly suspect, as many well counterfeited jewels make the true mistrusted.'

In Kendall's words (in his Introduction in *Richard III: The Great Debate*, 1965): 'Master More, MP and lawyer, would know that it was impossibly dangerous for him to reveal his feelings about Henry VII, and Thomas More, historian, could perceive that he would be unable to continue his work without doing so. Therefore, abandoning the "middle way" of history, More expressed his political concerns more obliquely in the satiric fantasy *Utopia* (1516) and then more directly by entering the service of the king in 1518'. More's Yale editor, R. S. Sylvester, makes the further point that when the *History* was written Buckingham's son, Edward, the third duke, was heir presumptive to the throne. The English version of the *History* ends after the Buckingham rebellion with Morton inciting Henry to treason, the crime for which Henry's son was to execute Buckingham's son not long after More wrote.

The political delicacy of this aspect of the subject matter is likely to have made publication unthinkable, but it is conceivable that in putting the work aside More was influenced by the knowledge that he had been unjust to Richard. 'More would not object if his *History* were construed as a polemic against tyranny,' writes Professor Sylvester: 'what he could not allow was for it to be used as a piece of sheer political propaganda.' It is yet another irony that the work has been just so used ever since the author's death.

Henry VII deserves consideration not only as More's real target but as himself the king of myth-makers. It is not hard to believe that More had the widely hated Henry at least partly in mind when he wrote this description of Richard: 'He was close and secret, a deep dissembler, lowly of countenance, arrogant of heart, outwardly companionable where he inwardly hated, not hesitating to kiss whom he thought to kill, pitiless and cruel, not for evil will always but oftener for ambition and either for the surety or increase of his position. "Friend" and "foe" were to him indifferent: where his advantage grew, he spared no man's death whose life withstood his purpose.'

Henry's record was indeed a foxy one. Even his name is not above suspicion. His grandfather had been Owen ap Meredith ap Tudor, in English Owen Meredith, and Henry's name was therefore properly Henry Meredith (or, in Welsh, Henry ap Edmund). Before and at Bosworth he styled himself Earl of Richmond, although his family had been deprived of the title and he had no right to use it. The honour of Richmond had been forfeited to the crown under Edward IV, so that at Bosworth the real Earl of Richmond was Richard III.

Henry's Welshness was also not quite what he wished to be believed: through his mother, Margaret Beaufort, he was half English; through his father, one quarter Welsh and one quarter French. He used the Welsh connection to associate himself with the Arthurian legend and the ancient British kings, choosing as his emblem the red dragon of Cadwallader, although he probably sprang from humble stock in Anglesey and it was Richard who, through his Mortimer blood, could more justly claim descent from the Welsh princes.

After his victory Henry cheated so comprehensively by attempting to date his reign from the day before the battle that an outraged parliament legislated to outlaw any such thing for all time. He was slow to fulfil his long-standing promise to marry Elizabeth of York and, when married, reluctant to have her crowned queen in case it should be said that he occupied the throne by right of his wife's inheritance. For her first lying-in he sent her to Winchester so that his son, who was duly named Arthur, might be born in the ancient capital of Wessex. After his marriage he adopted the emblem of the single white and red rose to symbolise his status as the unifier of York and Lancaster, but seems to have revived the use of the red rose for this purpose. The usual Lancastrian emblem was the white swan, while the Yorkists normally displayed the falcon and fetterlock and Edward IV's sun in splendour.

Although Henry claimed the sovereignty in his own right, Richard's proclamation of 23 June 1485 denouncing him was wholly accurate in declaring: 'One Henry Tudor . . . usurpeth upon himself the name and title of royal estate of this realm of England, whereunto he hath no manner of interest, right, title or colour, as every man well knoweth.' If, constitutionally, Richard's claim to the throne was debatable, Henry's was not even that: he occupied the throne by divine right (it was said) because God had granted him victory in battle. Yet there are historians who seek to demolish any suggestion of legitimacy in Richard's case while stalwartly making the best case they can for Henry, who was king simply because he said he was and no one was in a position to argue. While 'the usurpation of Richard III' is on every historian's lips, 'the usurpation of Henry VII' is scarcely a familiar phrase.

Indeed, such is the magic of myth that continuing forbearance in criticism of the record of this favoured dynasty is commonplace. When, for example, Henry VIII arbitrarily executes a handful of Plantagenets we are told (by Professor Mortimer Levine) that in the circumstances he 'could not be expected to be tolerant'. Yet when Richard III arbitrarily executes Hastings cries of 'tyrant' and 'reign of terror' rend the pages of history books. Anyone foolhardy enough to suggest that Richard could not be expected to be tolerant of Hastings plotting against his life could expect his reputation as a scholar to be submerged under a barrage of academic anathemas. The double standards of some historians of the Tudor period are not edifying.

Those who preserve and propagate Tudor image-making seldom acknowledge that the true Lancastrian heirs were the Portuguese and Spanish royal families – through John of Gaunt's marriages to Blanche of Lancaster and Constance of Castille. Constance's daughter married Henry III of Castille, grandfather of Isabella, who became the wife of Ferdinand of Aragon and mother of Catherine of Aragon. Thus a true union of the red and white roses occurred when Catherine (red) married successively Prince Arthur and Prince Henry (white through their mother). Queen Mary, the unhappy offspring of the second marriage, was the only monarch whose rose was legitimately double-coloured (and in Philip II of Spain she married another Lancastrian heir).

It is a measure of Henry Tudor's success as a myth-maker that both the hollowness of his pretensions and the oppressiveness of his rule compared with Richard's are so little recognised even today. Under his and his chancellor's tax system, known as Morton's Fork, the rich were assessed on the basis that they could obviously afford to pay, and the poor on the basis that they were concealing what they had and could also afford to pay. Henry's justice was exemplified by Star Chamber trials, and his avarice led him even into the mortal sin of simony (selling church offices), to which the Yorkists never stooped: for the deanery of York, for example, his asking price was one thousand marks. The attainders in his last parliament (1504) numbered fifty-one, the highest on record – a greater number even than his first, when Richard and his supporters were attainted.

'To the day of his death,' believes a modern revisionist (V. B. Lamb in *The Betrayal of Richard III*), 'Henry's hatred of his predecessors was undiminished. Richard had possessed two things which Henry never had – a sound title to the throne and the love of his subjects. Few people can forgive those they have injured and Henry was not a forgiving man.'

Since Henry would have been known to More for what he was, how many of the jewels in More's splendid antiRichard prose did he himself realise to be counterfeited and how many did he believe to be true? Probably he did not much care. What he was presenting, for his own amusement and that of his family and friends, was an elegant essay illustrating the evils of absolute power, whether wielded by Plantagenet or Tudor. Richard is the pretext but not always the centrepiece. Despite its brevity the *History* includes much matter extraneous to his character and actions. There are long arguments about the principles of sanctuary and the validity of Edward IV's marriage to Elizabeth Woodville, an attempted justification of Morton's career, and a great deal about that alluringly 'vile and abominable strumpet', Shore's wife.

His portrait of Richard III and account of events leading to Richard's assumption of the crown must be regarded as More's version of the prevailing orthodoxy among the victorious survivors of that reign, concerned to justify their past treasons and present respectability. But would he not also have received information from less partial quarters – his father, John More, and his father-in-law, John Roper? More's family may have viewed Richard with indifference or disfavour, perhaps judging him to have been little different from other kings since his short-term sovereignty bequeathed no lasting benefits, and More himself was, in principle, a parliamentarian to whom all absolute monarchs were tyrants. The real Richard was irrelevant to his purpose: he was loosing off a political salvo and the bogey-man of the dynasty from whom he might expect advancement lay conveniently in the line of fire.

In 1543, eight years after his death, More's *History* was published by Richard Grafton in a version which was 'corrupt and altered in words and whole sentences'. Grafton printed it as a continuation of Hardyng's *Chronicle*, completing it himself until Richard 'the wretch' was dead and buried 'without any solemnity', and his version was reprinted in 1548 as part of Hall's *Chronicle*. Grafton was a rich London merchant who became a publisher in the Protestant cause and, in the line of duty as the king's printer when Edward VI died, had the misfortune to print the proclamation of Lady Jane Grey as queen.

In 1557 More's nephew, William Rastell, also a printer, published a folio of More's works which included an authentic *History*, taken from a copy in More's own handwriting. Since that date it has remained a prime source for the indictment of Richard III for unparalleled villainy. Shakespeare may be fiction, it is argued, but More is fact. He was a near-contemporary who spoke to those who had been alive in Richard's time. Despite all the inaccuracies, exaggerations and ironies, there must be a solid substructure of truth, for More – now a saint – would never have written as he did about Richard if he had believed him to be an honourable man and a good ruler.

The time-honoured method of judging More's work, according to Kendall, 'is to concede all that can be demonstrated to be false or unsatisfactory but to insist that the story is fundamentally true because *every* detail has not been proved inaccurate. It is a method foreign to logical analysis and to law, and it apparently springs from a rooted predeliction for the Tudor tradition.'

Myth-making is the creation of fiction more enduring than fact. To be sucessful it requires exceptional skill and luck. Henry Tudor, John Morton and Thomas More were all remarkably clever men. The luck has lain partly in the political sagacity and charismatic heroism of Henry's grand-daughter, Elizabeth I, who has infected historians and laymen alike with a chronic attack of Tudorphilia. Mostly, however, it was to be found in the accident of William Shakespeare's genius.

But before considering why and how Shakespeare bestowed the kiss of immortality on Henry Tudor's version of history it will be appropriate to examine More's account of the death of the princes in the Tower, transmuted by Shakespeare into folk-lore, and the truth about Richard's personal appearance and character, so vividly misrepresented by these writers. For the combined pens of More and Shakespeare have proved deadlier by far than the swords of the king's enemies at Bosworth.

13

The Princes: A Dolorous End

The fate of Edward IV's sons was a mystery at the time and has remained so ever since. They disappeared without explanation while under their uncle Richard's protection and in his power. Most historians have therefore followed the lead of his enemies in convicting him of the crime of murdering them, and this conviction has served to establish his eligibility as the murderer of his wife, his brother and the last Lancastrian king and prince. Yet there is no real evidence that the princes in the Tower were murdered by Richard or indeed by anyone else. To repeat Professor Jacob: 'it is unlikely that the circumstances of their death will be known'.

According to *The Great Chronicle of London* (c. 1512), they were seen shooting and playing in the garden of the Tower on various occasions during the mayoralty of Sir Edward (or Edmund) Shaw (or Shaa), which ran from 29 October 1482 to 28 October 1483. A quiet winter followed, but after Easter 1484 there was 'much whispering among the people' that the princes were dead and that Richard had poisoned his wife so that he could marry their sister, Elizabeth. New rumours came later that year. The princes were said to have been smothered, poisoned or drowned in malmsey wine. By whatever means, they were certainly dead, the chronicler believed, and either Sir James Tyrell or an old servant of King Richard (name left blank in the manuscript) was reported to have done the deed.

In his *History of King Richard III* (1513 or possibly later) More confirms that differing versions of the manner of the princes' death were circulating at that time. 'I shall rehearse you the dolorous end of those babes, not after every way that I have heard, but after that way I have so heard by such men and by such means as methinks it were hard but it should be true.'

According to the version of the dolorous end favoured by More, Richard, on his way to Gloucester after his coronation, is overcome by misgiving about his nephews. 'Whereupon he sent one John Green, whom he specially trusted, unto Sir Robert Brackenbury, Constable of the Tower, with a letter and credentials also that the same Sir Robert should in any wise put the two children to death. This John Green did his errand unto Brackenbury, kneeling before Our Lady in the Tower, who plainly answered that he would never put them to death, though he should die therefor; with which answer John Green returning, recounted the same to King Richard at Warwick, yet on his progress.' Richard is displeased and muses: 'Ah, whom shall a man trust?' 'Sir James Tyrell,' replies the page on duty in the royal convenience: 'for this communication had he sitting on the stool – a fitting carpet for such a counsel.'

Meanwhile, back at the Tower, the boys are shut up and deprived of servants except for the ominously named William Slaughter, also known as Black Will. At this the elder boy is so plunged into melancholy that he 'never tied his laces nor in any way cared for himself. . . Sir James Tyrell devised that they should be murdered in their beds. To the execution whereof he appointed Miles Forest . . . a fellow fleshed in murder before time. To him he joined one John Dighton, his own horsekeeper, a big broad strong knave. Then all the others being removed from them, this Miles Forest and John Dighton about midnight (the innocent children lying in their beds) came into the chamber, and suddenly lapped them up among the bedclothes – so bewrapped them and entangled them, keeping down by force the featherbed and pillows hard unto their mouths, that within a while, smothered and stifled, their breath failing, they gave up to God their innocent souls into the joys of heaven, leaving to the tormentors their bodies dead in bed.

'After the wretches perceived them – first by the struggling with the pains of death and after, long lying still – to be thoroughly dead, they laid the bodies naked out upon the bed and fetched Sir James to see them. Who, upon the sight of them, caused those murderers to bury them at the stair-foot, meetly deep in the ground under a great heap of stones.' Richard, however, is not lost to all sense of *comme il faut* and will not permit his nephews to be buried 'in so vile a corner, saying that he would have them buried in a better place because they were a king's sons'. This happily suits More's penchant for sarcasm: 'Lo, the honourable heart of a king!'

It also provides a convenient answer to a critical question. Why, after Bosworth, was Henry VII not able to trace the bodies and expose them to public view as undeniable proof of Richard's guilt, thus strengthening his weak claim to the throne and ridding himself of the threat posed by a succession of pretenders claiming to be the younger prince? 'Whereupon,' More obligingly continues, 'they say that a priest of Sir Robert Brackenbury took up the bodies again and secretly interred them in such place as, by the occasion of his death – for he alone knew it – could never since come to light. Very truth is it and well known that at such time as Sir James Tyrell was in the Tower, for treason committed against the most famous prince, King Henry the Seventh, both Dighton and he were examined, and confessed the murder in manner above written, but whither the bodies were removed they could nothing tell.'

The alleged confession to this sequence of events is bolstered by a reference to disinterested, but unnamed, sources and by some ringing cadences in More's most seductive prose: 'And thus, as I have learned of them that much knew and little cause had to lie, were these two noble princes, these innocent tender children – born of most royal blood, brought up in great prosperity, likely long to live to reign and rule in the realm – by traitorous tyranny taken, deprived of their state, shortly shut up in prison, and privily slain and murdered, their bodies cast God knows where, by the cruel ambition of their unnatural uncle and his pitiless tormentors.' But is 'little cause had to lie' yet another of More's sly ironies?

In all morality tales the wicked have to suffer. Vengeful gods or goddesses like Jehovah or Nemesis, or their agents, such as the Eumenides, strike them down in divine retribution. The archperpetrator of this atrocity, Richard, was 'slain in the field, hacked and hewed by his enemies' hands, haled on horseback dead, his hair contemptuously torn out and pulled like a cur dog'. 'Sir James Tyrell died at Tower Hill, beheaded for treason.' Miles Forest, less dramatically, 'at St Martin's piecemeal rotted away' – alongside the virtuous, one must presume, who also rot piecemeal in graveyards. Oddly then, it would seem that Forest was not convicted of any crime and died in his bed. And as for his fellow smotherer, 'Dighton indeed yet walks alive'. This is so astonishing and lame a conclusion that More immediately adds: 'in good possibility to be hanged ere he die' (which, so far as is known, he never was).

If Dighton was not only living but a free man, as the phrase 'walks alive' implies, why did More not talk to him and obtain evidence at first hand? He could then have clinched the authenticity of his story by naming him as a direct source. And what are we to make of a known assassin of a king walking free ('set at liberty', in Bacon's phrase) thirty years after the murder? One report has Dighton given a pension and packed off to Calais. But even if he had turned king's evidence, would he have escaped so comfortably, and would his story not have received such wide publicity as to put an end to all rumours and uncertainty? Those who cannot believe that the Tudor kings would have granted a free pardon to a regicide (the murderer of Henry VII's brothers-in-law and Henry VIII's uncles) must presume that Dighton's real role was to bear witness to a falsehood so transparent that it could not be safely publicised.

Brackenbury's role in the alleged affair is almost as unlikely. According to More, he refused the king's command to put the two children to death, 'though he should die therefor'. But he did not demur at handing over the keys of the Tower to Tyrell for one night so that someone else could commit the crime. After this brief spell of compassionate absence without leave (which would surely have been noticed and set tongues wagging) he returned to resume his duties to the king whose command he had disobeyed on a matter of supreme importance, and the king retained such confidence in him that he remained in command at the Tower until, two years later, he led the London contingent to Bosworth where he was killed fighting for Richard.

What, too, of the central character in the drama? A close associate of Richard, Sir James Tyrell, survived Bosworth because he was abroad at the time, in command of one of the fortresses guarding Calais. Henry gave him two pardons, called him his 'faithful councillor' and left him as captain of Guisnes for a further seventeen years, employing him also on military and diplomatic missions in Europe.

In 1502, after an attempt to arrest him, Tyrell was lured aboard a man-o-war in Calais harbour on the king's most solemn promise of a safe conduct, promptly clapped in irons, shipped to the Tower and beheaded for associating with the Yorkist pretender on the continent, the Earl of Suffolk (another of Richard's nephews). The indictment contained no mention of the princes and, despite the customary practice, there is no record of a speech from the scaffold. Only when Tyrell was safely executed for quite another reason was it announced that he had confessed to murdering the princes on Richard's orders. Even had that been true, the truthfulness of the confession might be doubted. Tyrell's purpose in making it would have been to save the life of his son, who had been arrested with him, and rescue his family from the penury which would follow an act of attainder. His son's life was spared and there was no act of attainder, so it remains another mystery that no confession by Tyrell was ever published: perhaps because there were some still alive who would have known it to be untrue.

The time-lag is significant. Henry had been king and master of the Tower since 1485. It had taken him seventeen years to produce a story of any kind and even then it was one not backed by a shred of proper evidence. What caused him to rattle the undiscovered bones of the vanished princes in 1502 was probably the death of his eldest son and heir. Arthur died on 2 April and Tyrell was executed on 6 May. Edmund, the youngest prince, had not survived infancy, and Henry himself had been ill since the previous year. With a sick king, unpopular with his subjects, and only one remaining prince, the survival of the upstart Tudors was not highly rated in Europe, and it is likely that the King of Spain made the elucidation of the mystery surrounding Edward IV's sons and confirmation of their death a condition of his consenting to the hand of his daughter being transferred from Arthur to the new heir. This would have accorded with the precedent of 1499 when two other 'princes in the Tower' (the Earl of Warwick, yet another nephew of Richard, and Perkin Warbeck, the *soi-disant* Duke of York) were judicially murdered by Henry VII to clear the way for the

Spanish princess to marry Arthur. (Alternatively or additionally, Henry may have feared that Arthur's death would cause a resurgence of Yorkist activity, and this was a pre-emptive strike against a possible new wave of White Rose aspirants.)

If Henry was acting under diplomatic or political pressure, the need for haste might account for some lack of plausibility in his story as recounted by More. But the time may also have seemed propitious at last, for some eminent servants of church and state who might have had an inkling of the truth had recently died, including Archbishops Morton and Rotherham (Hastings' fellow conspirators) and John Alcock, tutor to Edward V when Prince of Wales and successively Bishop of Rochester, Worcester and Ely. Most relevant may have been Thomas Langton, successively Provost of the Queen's College, Oxford and Bishop of St Davids, Salisbury and Winchester, who died of the plague in 1501 after his nomination to succeed Morton at Canterbury. Unlike the others, Langton, a northerner, had been in favour with Richard III and one of his immediate entourage. His was the effusive praise of Richard: 'He contents the people where he goes best that ever did prince, for many a poor man that hath suffered wrong many days have been relieved and helped by him and his commands now in his progress. And in many great cities and towns were great sums of money given him which all he hath refused. On my truth I never liked the conditions of any prince so well as his.' Langton must have trimmed his sails to Henry's wind, but he had a Yorkist background, had not been guilty of treason, and might have proved a witness to the truth.

The likely untruth of the Henry/More story does not, of course, prove Richard's innocence. One of his most stalwart defenders, Sir Clements Markham, proved this innocence to his own satisfaction by accepting the tale as substantially true, except in one important respect. The murder took place in 1486, not 1483, and the culprit was Henry, not Richard. Markham points out that Tyrell received his first general pardon from Henry on 16 June 1486 and his second on 16 July 1486: 'This would be very singular under ordinary circumstances. . . But it is not so singular when we reflect on what probably took place in the interval.' 'Probably' is certainly overstating the case, and Markham has been heavily condemned for defending one king against unproven accusations of infanticide by levelling a similar charge against another. Nevertheless, there is a suspicious parallel between antedating a murder so that one's enemy becomes the murderer and antedating one's reign so that one's enemy becomes the traitor, as Henry attempted after Bosworth.

There is no evidence whatever that the princes were still alive at the time of Bosworth, but only rumours that they were dead. Markham discovered two references which he took as proof that Edward V had survived some of the rumours of his death, but these have since been discounted. If they did outlive Richard, the boys would probably have been in Yorkshire with their sisters and Clarence cousins and certainly prime targets for seizure by Henry after his victory. No doubt an escape plan would have been prepared, and this has suggested another possibility: a fatal shipwreck on the dangerous journey across the North Sea towards the haven of Burgundian territory, where their aunt, Margaret of York, was dowager duchess.

The behaviour of Elizabeth Woodville, mother of the princes, is often cited as suggesting that the princes may have fallen fatally into Henry's grasp. In 1484 she became reconciled to Richard, putting herself and her daughters into his hands and writing to her son, the Marquess of Dorset, urging him to abandon the Tudor cause. Despite the *quid pro quo* of Richard's oath to protect them, sworn in public, it is hard to believe that this reconciliation was with someone who had recently murdered her sons, but much more plausible if she had evidence that they were alive (or knew them to be dead by accident or another hand). By contrast, shortly after her daughter had become Henry VII's queen a violent and unexplained breach occurred between Henry and Elizabeth Woodville, after which she spent the rest of her life in Bermondsey abbey.

Yet with Henry, as with Richard, there is no real evidence and one must suspect that if he had killed the princes himself he would quickly have produced the corpses and an ingeniously appropriate story implicating Richard. His frantic search of the Tower where he had 'all places open and digged' may have been a deception, but his conduct suggests that he never discovered what had happened to the princes. An uneasy belief that they might still be alive is apparent in his fear that

Warbeck could indeed have been the younger prince, and it is a significant pointer in his favour that Warbeck and his backers never put forward the claim which would have suited them best: that Henry was responsible for the death of the elder boy.

Even if Henry is eliminated from the list of suspects, there remains a respectable case for a verdict of 'not guilty' against Richard and a cast-iron one for 'non proven'. But since (in the comment of Sharon Turner) 'almost all murders, from their privacy, are defective in direct evidence', even some of those who believe that history is guilty of a serious misjudgment of this king accept the view that he may have had his nephews put to death. In their opinion this crime should be judged in the context of the morality of the time and the perspective of crimes committed by other rulers for reasons of state or 'the good of the realm'. Attention has been focused on this particular accusation by Richard's enemies for reasons which have little to do with a balanced historical judgment. In an age when a Duke of Burgundy ordered the assassination of a Duke of Orleans, and a Dauphin of France had a Duke of Burgundy murdered in his presence, there is no need to look beyond the Alps at the Borgias or the Pyrenees at Ferdinand of Aragon to gauge standards.

By this line of reasoning Richard's possible guilt is regarded as a serious blemish on his career and one to be deeply deplored and condemned. But his virtues as a man of probity and courage, and the many benefits which he brought to those whom he ruled as viceroy and king, weigh the balance heavily in his favour notwithstanding. No ruler in any period of history can avoid acts which would be considered immoral in a private individual. Normally these are assessed in the light of his record as a whole; success, particularly success in battle, being a favoured criterion. Richard's successes are to be found in the quality of his administration in the north before he became king, in his saving the country from another outburst of civil war after his brother's untimely death, in his patronage of the church and of learning, and in the enlightened legislation of his reign. All these have been undervalued, unjustly overshadowed through his failure at Bosworth and by the suspicion that he committed one act of consummate wickedness.

Most Ricardians, however, argue fiercely against a natural presumption of Richard's guilt. They contend that once the boys had ceased to be legitimate they no longer represented a threat to him – at the relevant time they were not the princes but the bastards in the Tower. But, while it is true that any incentive to have them put to death after their claim had been formally and constitutionally nullified would have been reduced, their bastardising, even if well founded, was a political act and readily reversible. And it was in fact reversed later, to bolster Henry Tudor's claim to the throne through his marriage with the boys' sister. To maintain that the boys no longer posed any danger to Richard's cause is an exaggeration.

In Richard's favour is the fact that he had another nephew in a not dissimilar position and there is no mystery about what happened to him. Clarence's son would have had a better claim to the throne than Richard if his father's attainder had not disqualified him, and in the fifteenth century this form of forfeiture of rights and estates was more often than not reversed with a change of regime or when the punishment had served its purpose. Although no longer of the blood royal and disabled from succeeding to his father's dukedom and other titles, Clarence's son had been allowed by Edward IV to use the title of the earldom of Warwick belonging to his mother, the King-maker's elder daughter. The young Edward therefore might have become of greater importance in the power game than his cousins, degraded to Lord Bastards.

If the fate of this nephew provides a clue to the fate of the others the finger of suspicion points back to Henry. Edward, Earl of Warwick was well treated by Richard, who after the death of his own son even seems to have considered making him his heir. He and probably his sister and Edward IV's daughters lived during Richard's reign in a royal nursery at Sheriff Hutton, and one of Henry's first acts after the battle of Bosworth was to secure the persons of these children. Edward, aged ten, was taken to the Tower of London, imprisoned there for the rest of his life for the crime of being Clarence's son, and finally killed by Henry for political reasons.

Other arguments for exonerating Richard are neither conclusive nor negligible. In character he was obsessively loyal, and faithful above all to his brother Edward, who bequeathed his sons to Richard's care. Pious and puritan, fatally lacking in the ruthlessness necessary to keep his crown, he lived in an age when men believed in an after-world of eternity in Heaven or Hell. After the general support for him at his coronation he may even have felt an interest in keeping the princes alive, since Henry Tudor's claim was flawed with bastardies too and theirs was therefore still superior to his. By this consideration, killing his nephews would have been not only sinful and criminal but foolish as well.

Among contemporary writings hostile to him nothing is more noticeable than the absence of any confirming evidence to substantiate the belief that Richard had the princes put to death. After Bosworth Henry failed to produce either bodies or evidence, when he badly needed both. On this subject his Act of Attainder directed against Richard is curiously reticent. Here one would have expected this terrible deed, pre-eminent among the catalogue of the dead and defenceless king's alleged crimes, to have been spelled out with uncompromising clarity for universal condemnation. Yet there is no mention of it all; only a general accusation such as lawyers resort to when they wish to make sure of excluding no possible charge. In a catch-all phrase Richard is arraigned for 'the shedding of infants' blood'.

It may be that the use of this phrase simply denotes uncertainty how to refer to Edward V, reflecting a view that his kingship was not to be acknowledged, his existence best forgotten, because Henry could in no way claim to be his heir. If so, it was an uncharacteristic miscalculation on Henry's part. The vanishing act could not be concluded with a wave of his magic wand: dead or alive, the princes were not to be consigned to oblivion. Many people believed (or pretended to believe) that one at least of them had been smuggled abroad and that Perkin Warbeck was indeed Richard, Duke of York. Among them were Sir William Stanley (of Bosworth fame), executed for supporting Warbeck, and the King of Scotland, who gave Warbeck his cousin to marry. True or not, the claim proved convincing enough to be endorsed by Richard's sister, Margaret of Burgundy, and accepted at other European courts.

The strange silence of the Archbishop of Canterbury also speaks in Richard's favour. Descended, like the Duke of Buckingham, from Edward III's youngest son, Cardinal Bourchier was Primate of All England for more than thirty years (1454–1487), during which time he served Lancastrians and Yorkists alike. About to crown Edward V, he found himself crowning Richard instead and, two years later, Henry Tudor. He had cried off Edward IV's funeral, pleading old age and retiring to Knole, and according to Mancini crowned Richard unwillingly, not attending the banquet afterwards. It was he who negotiated with the boy's mother the release of the younger prince from sanctuary at Westminster to join his brother in the state apartments in the Tower. He pledged his honour for the boy's safety. If the boy had been harmed, would he not have spoken out? If he was too afraid while Richard lived, what would have stopped him after Richard was dead? His was precisely the voice whose public testimony Henry would have valued most and most demanded.

Despite the legend, Richard's record does not reveal an unprincipled and blood-thirsty tyrant. He spared traitors like Morton and Stanley after a conspiracy which could have cost him his life. He even spared Stanley's son, Lord Strange, a hostage for his father's good behaviour, when Stanley betrayed him at Bosworth (the legend, of course, has Strange's execution ordered but postponed). This does not suggest the kind of man who would kill the young sons of a brother to whom he had been so unswervingly loyal. It was Henry Tudor who spared no one. It is Henry's record which suggests that he could have killed the princes without hesitation or compunction, as he killed their cousin Edward and as he and his son put others to death for the crime of being Plantagenets.

But if the princes were still alive when rumoured to be dead, why did Richard not choose to put the matter beyond doubt by allowing them to be seen in public? Why, if they were alive, did he consistently behave as though they were dead? These are the most pertinent questions addressed to revisionists, and no answer can be other than speculative.

Perhaps Richard was not worried by the rumours; perhaps he thought taking notice of them was beneath him or would be interpreted as a sign of weakness; perhaps he simply did not want to draw attention to Edward. Perhaps, knowing that he would be blamed if they died, he was too concerned for the safety of the boys on security grounds, for they stood in the path of Henry Tudor, who was supported by the French king, and there were important people at the English court in the pay of

France – Hastings and Morton had been among them. If Vergil is to be believed, Richard actually encouraged the rumours, himself wishing to cast doubt on the princes' fate and whereabouts. Uncertainty might have served his purpose in keeping the opposition factions – Lancastrians and Woodvilles, Edwardians and Buckinghamites – disunited. He 'suffered the intelligence of their death to be published, that he might disconcert their plans and awaken the fears of his enemies' (Lingard).

The boys may have been dead, but not killed. Edward V is thought to have suffered from a jaw infection and could have died of natural causes. Some support for this supposition is to be found in the curious fact that none of the pretenders who plagued Henry VII tried to pass themselves off as Edward. If the deposed king had died naturally while in the care or custody of the man who had taken the throne from him and there was no announcement because it would not have been believed, what then would have become of the younger boy? He might have lived to become Perkin Warbeck, or be hidden incognito behind monastery walls. Even Polydore Vergil reports the possibility of his being taken abroad.

Another possibility is an accident in a bungled attempt to smuggle them out of Richard's control: a drowning in the Thames when their boat overturned or shipwreck at sea on their way to the continent. That would at least explain one of the most puzzling aspects of the princes' disappearance: that no one at all, however well placed, seems to have had certain knowledge of their end. The well-informed contemporary Croyland chronicler did not know, and even Richard's own silence may be accounted for by ignorance.

Might the princes have been killed by someone acting without Richard's knowledge, either misguidedly in his interests or in Henry Tudor's or in some other? The problem of access narrows the field, and it is difficult to imagine who might qualify under the first heading. John Howard in gratitude for his dukedom of Norfolk? The faithful Brackenbury? Both might have had sufficient authority within the Tower, but they are unlikely to have been so rash and foolish. The names of Catesby and Ratcliffe have been proposed, but they were without the power to act on their own initiative.

Under the second heading Margaret Beaufort is the obvious
candidate. A strong-minded conspirator, she was in London at
the centre of power as the wife of Lord Stanley (Steward of
Richard's household) despite her Lancastrian blood and Tudor
son, and there seem few scruples she would not have set aside to
advance her son's passage to the throne. The death of the
princes was doubly beneficial to her cause as kingmaker: it
removed rival claimants to the throne and, by throwing suspicion on Richard, weakened his position too.

But in the search for solutions the most favoured candidate
for murderer after Richard himself is Henry Stafford, Duke of
Buckingham, acting in no one's interest but his own. Buckingham was a descendant of Thomas of Woodstock, Edward III's
youngest son, as well as of John of Gaunt through the Beaufort
line. He was the only living Plantagenet who could challenge
Richard; the premier peer of England; an immensely wealthy
and powerful aspirant to the crown, and a man of volatile and
unstable character.

As Constable of England, Buckingham had the power to
dispose of the princes if he could circumvent the royal will. In
Richard's absence on his royal progress through the country at
the time of the princes' disappearance he had the opportunity.
It is doubtful whether anyone could have denied him access to
the Tower. Fired with an ambition which was to lead him into
armed revolt, he had a strong motive. The secret death of the
princes was likely to help him as much as Henry Tudor, by
removing competition for the crown and blackening Richard's
name.

A letter written by Richard from Minster Lovell during his
progress, telling of a misdeed of great gravity perpetrated by
person or persons unknown, might refer to Buckingham killing
the princes. Richard's reaction to his rebellion was unusually
sharp and bitter. When it failed and Buckingham begged for a
private audience with the king before his execution, Richard
refused, describing him as 'the most untrue creature who ever
lived'. If Buckingham had intended to bargain for his life with a
confession, the solution to the mystery died with him in the
market square at Salisbury. Lack of proof and knowing that he
himself would be blamed would explain why Richard never
proclaimed Buckingham's guilt.

An unauthorised act of murder by Buckingham would account for Elizabeth Woodville's reconciliation with Richard. Most of what is regarded as evidence against Richard – the rumours and the bones in Westminster Abbey for instance – could be applied just as aptly to an indictment of Buckingham, the evil genius, whose name recurs in reports on the seizure of Rivers and the execution of Hastings as well as the death of the princes. A chronicle compiled by an unknown London citizen and discovered in the library of the College of Arms as recently as 1980 states that the princes were put to death on the advice of Buckingham, and other mentions of his involvement in their death occur in a manuscript dating from about 1490, owned by Humphrey Lloyd (d. 1568), and – for what they are worth – in Commynes and Molinet.

But casting Buckingham in the role of principal assassin does not necessarily lead to Richard's acquittal. Historians are agreed that Buckingham would never have dared to act without Richard's complicity or, at least, connivance. To believe that he would have committed the crime without a direct command from the king is 'little short of fantasy', declares Professor Ross sternly, citing the assassination of Becket as an isolated example of an unsanctioned political murder. Modern near-fantasists, however, may find significance in identifying Buckingham – without whose intervention Richard of Gloucester might never have become king – as one of their number. He inhabited a borderland between reality and fantasy for six meteoric months, and they may find the example of Becket's murder pertinent, noting More's echo of Henry II's 'Who will rid me of this turbulent priest?' with Richard III's 'Ah, whom shall a man trust?'

'The available evidence admits of no decisive solution,' concludes Professor Kendall. 'Richard may well have committed the crime, or been ultimately responsible for its commission. The Duke of Buckingham may well have committed the crime, or persuaded Richard to allow its commission. What is inaccurate, misleading and merely tiresome is for modern writers to declare flatly that Richard is guilty or to retail as fact the outworn tale of Thomas More.'

14

The Posthumous Hunchback

Few statements about Richard III go unchallenged. Most have to be qualified by a 'probably' or a prudent 'it is not implausible to suppose that'. But there is sufficient evidence to justify the categorical assertion that he suffered from no physical deformity. Shakespeare can plead dramatic licence, untutored groundlings may cry 'Give us more hump!', but there can be no excuse for the inventions of the Tudor chroniclers or for those historians who have followed them so gleefully and made themselves accomplices in an act of monstrification (Ruskin's word to describe 'many forms of so-called decoration').

Hostile contemporary commentators were certainly in the business of 'decorating' their accounts of this king and would scarcely have failed to draw attention to a hunchback or a withered arm when writing after his death, as Rous and the Croyland chronicler were, or abroad like Mancini and Commynes. Yet none does so, although all were addressing readers likely to be unsympathetic to Richard and any suggestion of physical deformity would have been a tasty tidbit.

It was Rous who invented Richard's monstrous birth, retold by More and Shakespeare: two years in the womb and entry into the world long-haired and fully toothed. Yet, despite his anxiety to ingratiate himself with the new regime after Richard's death, this time-server makes no worse an aspersion on the dead king's physique than that 'he was small of stature, with a short face and unequal shoulders, the right higher and the left lower'. (The Latin words for 'right' and 'left' are written into the manuscript later, and More has them the other way round.) Rous was a dependant of the Warwick family, into which Richard married. During the progress after his coronation the king spent a week at Warwick, and Rous supplies a list of the leading courtiers accompanying him (headed by five bishops and the King of Scotland's brother). It seems likely that he saw Richard on that occasion. But many others will have seen him too. Rous could make up what tale he pleased about Richard's birth without too much fear of contradiction, but at the time when he wrote there were plenty of people alive who knew what Richard looked like as an adult.

The Croyland chronicler would have been among them. As a member of Edward IV's council, he must have been familiar with Richard's personal appearance. But again, although he has biting comments to make on the king's activities and is at no pains to conceal his dislike of him, there is no reference to any physical peculiarity. All the reader learns is that Richard's face was thin and his complexion pale.

Mancini's silence on this point, too, is eloquent. He was in London in 1483 and would have moved in circles where Richard's appearance was known. In the account of his visit, written in France towards the end of the year and probably used by the French chancellor in denouncing Richard for the murder of his nephews, any report of physical abnormality would have been particularly well received and recorded in the French court and parliament.

Two other writers who had seen Richard with their own eyes and recorded nothing unusual are Fabyan, the London chronicler, who wrote after Richard's death, and Commynes, who as a chronicler took a special interest in the personal appearance of princes. When in the case of Edward IV there is something striking to report, a description even occurs twice. But although he gives an account of Richard's conduct at Picquigny, where the two men met, Commynes finds nothing remarkable to report about his appearance. Nor is there any such reference in the Paston letters, Warkworth's chronicle, *The Arrivall of Edward IV* or other contemporary writing.

It would be odd, moreover, if a physical deformity had not been noted on the occasion of Richard's death. According to Fabyan, his body was carried naked and 'unreverently' to the Greyfriars monastery in Leicester, where it was exposed to the public view for three days before being buried. According to *The Great Chronicle*, even the king's privy member was on public exhibition. What an opportunity for the public to enjoy a long uninterrupted view of the famous hunchback and withered arm! Someone would surely have satisfied the general curiosity with anatomical details.

In his sermon urging Richard's claim to the crown, delivered at St Paul's cross to the citizens of London in June 1483, Ralph Shaw made a special point of drawing attention to Richard's appearance, likening him to his father as evidence that his legitimacy, unlike his brothers', was above suspicion. The audience he was addressing would have known very well what Richard looked like, and some would have remembered his father. Edward was blond and tall, Clarence blond and of average height; so this evidence points to Richard and his father being dark-haired and short. 'Of bodily shape comely enough, only of low stature' is the description given by John Stow, the Elizabethan antiquarian, reporting what he had learned from speaking to old men who remembered Richard. 'Below medium height' seems the most accurate assessment, and this would hardly have been unusual: his father was probably stocky, and Henry Tudor (so we are told by Hall) 'was a man of no great stature'. If Richard's had been exceptionally low we may be sure that the Tudor chroniclers would have given him the full Quasimodo treatment and posterity would have come to know him as a dwarf as well as a hunchback.

There is further evidence to be found in the reminiscences of a Silesian visitor to England. Nicolas von Poppelau was an itinerant knight who travelled Europe in search of adventure and the means of making a living. His diary breathes the spirit of long-dead chivalry and records diplomatic assignments. According to his own boast, he took with him on his travels a lance which was so heavy that no one else could lift it. On 1 May 1484 he had a private audience with Richard at Pontefract castle, where he presented letters of introduction from the Emperor Frederick III.

Richard seems to have been captivated by von Poppelau, who regaled him with a description of the King of Hungary's victory over the Turks the previous year. 'I wish that my kingdom lay upon the confines of Turkey,' Richard replied.

'With my own people alone and without the help of other princes I should like to drive away not only the Turks, but all my foes.' This reads like an authentic expression of Richard's true character: a bold romantic. These are the words of the man who was to engage the enemy at Bosworth without waiting for his whole army to assemble, and to lead his last charge 'with his own people alone'.

Nicolas von Poppelau tells us that Richard was taller than himself by three fingers (about two inches), but much leaner: 'he had delicate arms and legs, also a great heart'. This lends support to the suggestion of Richard's frailty as an infant ('Richard liveth yet') and does not necessarily contradict other evidence about his height – the Silesian noted for his prodigious feats of strength may have been a squat, thickset muscle man. This seems altogether more likely than Mr Armstrong's conclusion that Richard was tall, weedy and drooping.

The words of diplomats are not always to be taken at face value, but it is worth noting the sentiments expressed by Archibald Whitelaw, a member of the King of Scotland's council and an envoy to the English court, in an oration to Richard in September 1484. He declaims, in a Latin quotation, that never has so much spirit or greater virtue reigned in such a small body. The compliment is formal, but a reference to the king's *corpore* as *minori* and *exiguo* would scarcely have been made if Richard had been large or tall. Whitelaw was in England to negotiate the marriage of Prince James, the heir to the Scottish throne, with Anne de la Pole, a niece of King Richard, not for an exchange of diplomatic insults.

'Shame on the hang-lipped Saracen for slaying angels of Christ,' wrote a Welsh versifier greeting Henry Tudor's accession to the throne. Richard is the Saracen, and this is the only reference to any unseemliness about his lips, but there may be less hwyl and more truth in the comment from the same source that 'little R' was 'pale and sad'. More flattering than 'hang-lipped Saracen', but scarcely more credible, is the boast of an elderly Countess of Desmond (as reported by Horace Walpole) that she had danced with Richard and 'he was the handsomest man in the room, except his brother'. The countess died in 1604 at the reputed age of 140, Sir Walter Ralegh credulously vouching for her having been born during Edward IV's reign.

The records of the city of York contain an account of a drunken squabble in the year 1490 during which one party abused the Earl of Northumberland for betraying King Richard at Bosworth 'with much other unfitting language concerning the said earl' and the other attacked King Richard as a hypocrite and a 'crouchback', rightly buried in a dyke like a dog. The parties then came to blows.

This is the only recorded contemporary or near-contemporary use of the word 'crouchback' in connection with Richard's appearance. If not mere drunken abuse, it may indicate that, like many people then and now, he was round-shouldered or walked with a slight stoop. If that constitutes deformity, those similarly deformed in the twentieth century must be numbered in millions. They include athletes such as Bjorn Borg, walking hunchbacked between rallies from one side of the tennis court to the other, and statesmen like Sir Winston Churchill (on the clear evidence of his statue in Parliament Square, London, erected at a time when many who knew him were still alive).

The painting of Richard III now in Windsor Castle is the prototype of many similar portrayals of the king. Like the rather different picture once belonging to the Paston family and now to the Society of Antiquaries (dated by the tree-ring method to between 1512 and 1520 and showing no trace of physical deformity), it was painted some thirty years after his death and is not a royal icon, like earlier Plantagenet portraits and their images on coins, but the picture of a real person, copied presumably from a likeness taken during his lifetime. As X-raying has recently revealed, one shoulder was later doctored to suggest deformity, but not the face, which is that of an earnest, anxious, not ill-looking man, giving no credence or credibility to the Tudor demonology and comparing favourably with the crafty features of Henry Tudor which hang beside a later version of the same painting in the National Portrait Gallery. It is salutary to visit the gallery and take Hamlet's advice: 'Look here, upon this picture, and on this.'

In Josephine Tey's novel, *The Daughter of Time*, in which Inspector Grant sets out to solve the mystery of the murder of the princes in the Tower, this picture of Richard, exhibiting no sign of villainy, is taken as *prima facie* evidence of his innocence.

Later copies of the painting, of which there are plenty still to be seen in country houses (at Arundel, Charlecote, Hatfield, Longleat, Montacute, Wimpole and elsewhere), tend to show a less prepossessing face. In the version which hangs in the hall of King's College, Cambridge (in belated recognition of his contribution to the building of the chapel) not only is the unevenness of the shoulders exaggerated but the King displays a haggard and ravaged countenance.

Richard's hunchback and withered arm were the figments of Thomas More's fertile imagination. They represented a distortion apposite to the burden of his homily and were perhaps not intended to be understood as historical truth. Their *raison d'être* was the common superstition of the period that a warped body signified an evil character. Deformity was a sign of the devil's own or at least the mark of God's disfavour. From More and for this reason Shakespeare developed his famous lump of foul deformity, and the tradition continued to develop under its own impetus. By 1643, in Baker's *Chronicles of the Kings of England*, Richard has become splay-footed and goggle-eyed: 'born a monster in nature . . . and just such were the qualities of his mind'.

This lingering medieval superstition was no pagan belief, but derived from Christian doctrine, backed by biblical authority. In the book of Leviticus (chapter 21) the Lord issues His instructions to Moses concerning the priesthood. Moses was ordered to speak to Aaron, saying 'Whoever he be of thy seed in their generations that hath any blemish, let him not approach to offer the bread of God'. Among the blemished, such as the blind and the lame, specifically barred from coming near the altar in case they profane the sanctuaries of the Lord, are the crook-backed.

Some of those who have been at pains to explode the myth of Richard's deformity have identified themselves with him physically. Horace Walpole, who was frail, may have done so. Arthur Noel Kincaid, the modern editor of Buck, writes: 'Men who are short and slight but nevertheless possess unusual strength and stamina are by no means a physiological phenomenon (I cite myself as an example).' Paul Murray Kendall, a recent biographer who was himself bodily robust, argues for a similar robustness in Richard: 'In inuring his slight frame to bear easily the weight of armour, in practising assiduously when still a boy with the sword arm, in forcing his frail body to become strong, Richard probably developed an unusually powerful right shoulder and a torso ribbed with muscle, which, in contrast to his thin arms and legs and a less prominent left shoulder, produced a vague, general suggestion of lack of bodily proportion or symmetry.' That such asymmetry has been noted in cavalry regiments in more recent times lends some support to Kendall's theory.

This obsessively personal aspect of Ricardian studies is neatly summarised in the dead-pan words of the most re-nowned Englishman of the twentieth century, notable for his own hunched shoulders and formidable scowl. In his *History of the English Speaking People* (first published in 1956, but written in the late 1930s) Sir Winston Churchill writes: 'Not only is every possible crime attributed by More to Richard, and some impossible ones, but he is presented as a physical monster, crookbacked and withered of arm. No one in his lifetime seems to have remarked these deformities, but they are now very familiar to us through Shakespeare's play.'

Richard's character is less easy to determine than his phy-sique. The Plantagenets maintained themselves for 350 years as seasoned autocrats in a brutal world, but Richard, in mind as in body, was probably less seasoned than most; hence the brevity of his reign and life. He seems to have been brave and resolute, honest and generous, benevolent and well-intentioned, patri-otic and incorruptible, but of limited ability and intelligence and fatally impulsive. Pious, charitable and cultivated, he was a munificent patron of the church and of music and scholarship: his 'bountiful and gracious charity' and 'large and abundant alms' were bestowed on the University of Cambridge among many other beneficiaries. But in the business of government he was a poor judge of character, allowing himself to be deceived not only by the magnates – Buckingham, Northumberland and the Stanleys – but by lesser traitors whom he should have known better than to trust. Loyal himself, he seems to have been un-able to inspire loyalty in others, outside the intimate circle of his own household. Was he too trusting, or too suspicious of the wrong people.

Confidence in his goodness and mercy he did inspire, as the

wills of Edward IV and Earl Rivers testify, and his treatment of the widows of Rivers, Hastings and Buckingham was exceptionally humane. Yet – reserved, introvert, lacking in charisma – in the person of a king he may have given the impression of never quite measuring up to the job. Professor Charles Wood has cited him as an example of the Peter principle, a man promoted beyond his abilities: the paragon of a divisional commander and viceroy incapable of succeeding as commander-in-chief and king. Certainly from the moment of his brother's death until his own he is seen to be struggling against the odds which were to overwhelm him: never quite in control, the victim not the master of events. Yet it must be acknowledged that he faced circumstances which would have taxed the guile and resolution of the cleverest and most hardened of men. If reports of his 'sharp wit' (Vergil) and skill in debate with Clarence (Croyland chronicler) are accurate, wisdom might have grown on him with experience.

That he was a religious man there is little doubt. 'The personal quality of Richard III's piety is well documented by his surviving books,' writes Dr Pamela Tudor-Craig in the catalogue to the exhibition on Richard III mounted by the National Portrait Gallery in 1973. 'Not only did he own the Wycliffe New Testament but parts, if not the whole, of an Old Testament in English. In neither case were they grand presentation books made for him. . . The fact that none of Richard's surviving books except his Book of Hours is in Latin suggests that he could not read Latin except liturgically; it also argues that he wanted to read the books himself.' This is precious evidence which has miraculously escaped destruction or loss. The Wycliffe New Testament has been in the possession of the New York Public Library since 1884, when it was acquired from J. J. Astor, while Richard's Books of Hours, containing a personal prayer in Latin added for him in a rough hand, may be seen in Lambeth Palace Library.

This prayer is a small revelation. Through the crack it opens, perhaps on the months between his wife's death and his own, we catch a poignant glimpse of a man tormented by grief and hostility. In it he begs Christ to defend him *ab omni malo atque ab hoste maligno*: 'from all evil and an evil enemy'. Another ominous passage reads (in translation): 'deign to free me, thy servant

King Richard, from all the tribulation, grief and anguish in which I am held, and from all the snares of my enemies, and deign to send Michael the archangel to my aid against them'.

Ambitious to do well and to do good, Richard III was far from abnormal. A fleeting, unfledged, tortured king, dead at thirty-two, he should have died thereafter.

15

Shakespeare and his Lump of Foul Deformity

When the first Duke of Marlborough remarked that all the history he knew came from Shakespeare, he spoke for many before and since, including (by their own confessions) the elder Pitt and the poet Southey. Indeed the whole youth of England, it was once said, took their theology from Milton and their history from Shakespeare. From whom then, it is a matter of some interest to inquire, did the bard himself take his history: in particular his history of the last Plantagenet.

Shakespeare made the worst of Richard III, and Richard III brought out the best in Shakespeare. Shakespeare's *Richard III* has a claim to being the finest melodrama ever written, and in the bard's own canon of thirty-six plays probably only *Hamlet* stands higher in popular esteem. The title role of Richard III has proved more attractive to leading actors of succeeding generations than any except the prince of Denmark himself. Thomas More had left Richard's reputation groggy, and Shakespeare, best of poets and most intelligent of Englishmen, delivered the *coup de grâce*. In the Great Debate he occupies the centre of the stage, as befits our leading actor/playwright. It is his Richard III who has lived in the public consciousness for nearly four hundred years, and it is his undying caricature of a human being which has provoked the revisionist movement. His is the genius which has embalmed and mummified Richard as the archetypal villain. In transmuting pinchbeck historical absurdities into the gold of legend, Shakespeare is both the inspiration of the antiRichards and the founding father of the Ricardian cause.

Like Richard's, Shakespeare's own life and character are
enigmas as yet unresolved. To his contemporaries he was
'gentle' Shakespeare, a good-natured, even-tempered colleague who took no part in literary feuds or thespian back-
biting. Among Ben Jonson's acquaintances he was almost
alone in avoiding a public quarrel with that cantankerous
author; from whom he even won (qualified) admiration. Unlike
the literary stereotype, Shakespeare wrote fluently and with
little revision. He was careful with money, becoming a share-
holder in the Globe theatre and saving to invest in property in
his home town. He was bent on enhancing his own and his
family's social status and devoted time and money to achieving
formal recognition as a gentleman.

In the search for material for his dramas Shakespeare was
undiscriminating, often lifting from others. He was influenced
by the chronicle plays and morality plays of his time and by the
tragedies of the living Marlowe and long dead Seneca, but
research did not interest him and he tended to be careless about
facts. Jonson, the painstaking scholar, was critical of that sea
coast in Bohemia, a country generally known to lie at a
distance from any ocean. But, geography not being important to him and not bothering to check, Shakespeare had simply
copied from a work of fiction by Robert Greene, who publicly
accused him of plagiarism on other counts. Similarly his
Richard III harks straight back to More and Polydore Vergil –
later Tudor chroniclers having nothing to add to the traditional
version except embroidery. From More he took Richard's
physical deformity and the murder of the princes; from Vergil
the gnawing conscience and the nightmare of ghosts at Bosworth.

The Tudor imagination, it has been observed, revelled in
Richard III. He was the man they loved to hate. In 1543
Richard Grafton published his continuation of John Hardyng's
Chronicle, which had ended with the reign of Henry VI. Here the
theme is: 'as the report and fame went, the Duke of Gloucester
was suspected' of every piece of skulduggery perpetrated. The
princes are smothered and stifled, long passages of More's
virulence are included, and Richard's higher shoulder becomes
'much' higher. Five years later Grafton published Edward
Hall's chronicle, *The Union of the Two Noble and Illustre Families of*

Lancastre and Yorke, for the most part a translation of Polydore Vergil from Latin into English. Once again, Henry VI is murdered by Richard with a dagger 'as the constant fame ran', but this time an element of doubt is conceded: 'but whosoever was the man-queller of this holy man. . .' (man-queller being man-slayer). The substitution of Elizabeth Lucy for Eleanor Butler is perpetuated. Hall (Eton and King's) was a judge, a member of parliament and an extreme Protestant who may have escaped a burning by dying before Mary Tudor became queen. (She had his book burned instead.)

Ralph or Raphael Holinshed was the next transmitter of the virus, the last link in the chain between Richard's enemies and William Shakespeare, the spell-binder who exercised his magic on the hotch-potch of rumours, gossip and anecdote which passed for history in that unscientific age. Holinshed, probably a Cheshire man, was educated at Cambridge and arrived in London in 1560. Based on Hall, his *Chronicles*, a three-volume compilation which enjoyed a long reign as the standard history of England, were first published in 1577, an enlarged second edition appearing two years later (after his death). He had boasted of keeping 'an especial eye' on the truth, but incorporated his sources uncritically and beat the drum loudly for patriotism and protestantism. Even so, the work was extensively mutilated by the censorship of Elizabeth I's privy council which, it is safe to assume, would have ensured the excision before publication of any passages not sufficiently unfavourable to the last Plantagenet king. It was the second edition of Holinshed which Shakespeare possessed. With Plutarch's *Lives*, on which he based his Roman plays, Holinshed's *Chronicles* must have been amongst the most-thumbed books in his library. From this quarry he excavated the material for his history plays and for *King Lear* and *Macbeth* (witches included), often following the text closely.

'History teaches us what to imitate and what to shun' is the burden of another Shakespearean source, *A Mirror for Magistrates* (first edition 1559), a curious collection of moralising monologues by various hands, in which historical characters such as Clarence, Buckingham and Richard himself make imaginary autobiographical confessions in excruciating verse.

Here is an extract from 'The complaynt of Henrye duke of Buckingham' about Richard and the princes:

> And I most cursed caytief that I was,
> Seeing the state vnstedfast howe it stood,
> His chief complyce to bryng the same to passe,
> Vnhappy wretche consented to theyr blood.

Published for the edification of 'all the nobility and all other in office', in the manner of Boccaccio's *The Fall of Princes* (which had been translated into English by John Lydgate), *A Mirror for Magistrates* proved a popular work, with further editions published in 1563, 1571 and 1574. Its statement of the terms on which loyalty is owed to a bad king may well have influenced Shakespeare among others. 'Whatsoever man, woman or child is by the consent of the whole realm established in the royal seat, so it have not been injuriously procured by rigour of sword and open force, but quietly either of inheritance, succession, lawful bequest, common consent or election, is undoubtedly chosen by God to be his deputy.' That was written with Richard III in mind, but its closer relevance to the victor of Bosworth, the reigning monarch's grandfather, can hardly have escaped the notice of sharp-witted Elizabethans. Early Tudor doctrine had of necessity been the rather different one enunciated by the tyrant Creon in the *Antigone* of Sophocles: whoever is in authority must be obeyed, whatever the circumstances.

The most important single contribution made by this work to the so-called Tudor saga about Richard III is the first unqualified accusation that Richard was to blame for the death of his brother Clarence. Adopted by Shakespeare, this item in the indictment obtained general acceptance thereafter. *A Mirror for Magistrates* is responsible, too, for the still lingering belief that William Collingbourne was 'cruelly executed for making a foolish rhyme' (The Cat, the Rat, and Lovell our Dog/Rule all England under a Hog). In fact, Collingbourne suffered for (in Fabyan's words) 'sundry treasons' and (in Kendall's) for offering 'one Thomas Yate £8 to bear a message to Henry Tudor urging him to land in the south of England in the fall and advising him to tell the French court that the English king would only trifle with their envoys since he meant to make war on France'.

More, the father of the Tudor myth, and Hall, the transmitter of Vergil, were the sources for the Latin verse drama, *Richardus Tertius* (1579), written by Thomas Legge, Master of Caius College, Cambridge. Until Shakespeare, writing tragedies in the Elizabethan period was an occupation for university men, and the modish model was Seneca, who had been tutor to the Emperor Nero, all but ruled the Roman empire in his name, took time off to write nine tragedies and was forced to commit suicide. Legge's Richardus is a Roman tyrant taken from the pages of Senecan drama. There is no evidence that Shakespeare was acquainted with this work, but he almost certainly knew another play, *The True Tragedy of Richard the Third* (author unknown), also based on More and Hall. This was not registered at Stationers Hall until June 1594, but internal evidence suggests that it was written before the year of the Armada (1588). It was staged by the Queen's Majesty's Players, probably in 1592, and critics are divided on what Shakespeare may or may not have borrowed from it. It is here, for instance, that Richard first utters his cry for a horse at Bosworth.

Like Shakespeare's, the Richard of *The True Tragedy* has been ambitious and plotting for the crown long before the death of Edward IV: a treatment which follows naturally from his responsibility for Clarence's death.

> Have I removed such logs out of my sight as my brother
> Clarence
> And King Henry the Sixth, to suffer a child to shadow me,
> Nay, more, my nephew to disinherit me.

This is a bloodier play than Shakespeare's and the princes are smothered on stage in full view of the audience, following discussion among the hired assassins whether they should be shot by pistols, have their throats cut, or be taken by the heels and have their brains beaten out against the walls.

Richard makes his Shakespearean debut in an earlier play in the first tetralogy of historical dramas. In the last act of *Henry VI part II* he bandies insults with Clifford, who describes him as

'heap of wrath, foul indigested lump, As crooked in thy man-
ners as thy shape', and with Young Clifford, who addresses him
as 'foul stigmatic'. He then proceeds to kill the Duke of
Somerset at the first battle of St Albans – historically, a
prodigious feat at the age of two. At the beginning of *Henry VI
part III* he makes a stirring opening by throwing Somerset's
head on to the stage and announcing that he is hoping to do the
same with King Henry's. (Severed heads were popular with the
groundlings and every Elizabethan props department carried a
good selection.) Later in the play he resists Clarence's blandishments and remains loyal to Edward IV, 'not for the love of
Edward, but the crown'. After the battle of Tewkesbury the
three brothers take turns at stabbing Henry VI's son and
Richard even offers to kill Queen Margaret as well. Then he
hastens to the Tower where, after enduring twenty-four lines of
abuse from King Henry, he stabs him too. In a gloating and
triumphant soliloquy over the royal corpse ('I that have neither
pity, love, nor fear. . .') he prepares the audience for the next
instalment:

King Henry and the prince his son are gone:
Clarence, thy turn is next, and then the rest.

Richard III itself opens with Shakespeare in dazzling form. It
is difficult to believe that better poetic drama has ever been
written than the soliloquy in which the deformed Richard
introduces himself to the audience and announces his own
villainy. This is followed by encounters with Clarence whose
death he is plotting, with Hastings whom he is to kill, and with
Anne whose husband and father he has killed and whom he
woos over the coffin of her father-in-law, yet another victim. At
the palace he then meets Rivers, Grey and Buckingham, three
more of his victims, and the first act ends with the murder of
Clarence before King Edward's countermanding order can
reach the Tower.

It is a mark of good fiction when a character runs away with
the author, and the lump of foul deformity seems to have taken
over as Shakespeare was writing. This Richard positively
delights in the invective and name-calling hurled at him by the
other characters: hog, dog, toad, hedgehog, spider, swine. His

humour is wry and sardonic, he woos the audience with winks and displays superhuman energy. Into a black tragedy Shakespeare injects comedy, in defiance of the rules of classical drama. The discussion on conscience between Clarence's murderers is written for laughs. Richard is an engaging card, laughing at himself. Magically, Anne succumbs to his advances in the most unpropitious of circumstances for courtship, and his sexual attraction reaches out to women in the audience. He overcomes his physical disability to prove as irresistible as Don Giovanni, heading in the end for the same destination.

This is both a play about crime and retribution and a psychological study of villainy and self-love ('Richard loves Richard'). No fewer than eleven ghosts visit him and his enemy on the eve of Bosworth, uttering a melancholy 'despair and die' to Richard and an encouraging 'live and flourish' to Henry. The parade of victims musters Prince Edward of Lancaster; King Henry VI; Clarence; Rivers, Grey and Vaughan (a triple act); Hastings; the two princes; Queen Anne; and Buckingham. This concluding reminder of his wholesale butchery temporarily unnerves our anti-hero, but he recovers and is game to the end, going down fighting in a burst of defiance and panache.

Did Shakespeare himself believe in the eleven murders, the hunchback and the withered arm? He is inscrutable, but the text may contain a clue or two. In Act 3, Scene 1 Edward V inquires whether Julius Caesar built the Tower and Buckingham tells him that it was begun by Caesar. 'Is it upon record,' demands the precocious prince, 'or else reported successively from age to age?' Upon record, he is told. But supposing there were no record, he persists, 'methinks the truth should live from age to age'. The contrast between what is recorded and what is passed down by word of mouth and becomes tradition is pointed but left hanging, Richard merely commenting in a wicked aside: 'So wise so young, they say, do never live long'.

But if the young Edward is presented as priggish, his brother is brattish and even less endearing. It is puzzling that Shakespeare should have chosen to alienate the audience's sympathy with such an unfuriatingly pert little Duke of York, inviting, if not smothering, at least a clip over the ear. Even his own mother is exasperated and calls him 'a parlous boy'. It is odd, too, that their murder, which the audience has paid its hard-earned pence to see, should take place off stage. And their deaths are reported in uncharacteristically emetic verse: 'those tender babes . . . girdling one another Within their innocent alabaster arms: Their lips were four red roses on a stalk. . . A book of prayers on their pillow lay.' Faint suspicions as to which side Shakespeare was really on deepen when concern is expressed for the safety of Clarence's children after his death. These, some of the audience would not have been unaware, became the victims, not of Richard III, but of Henry VII and Henry VIII. Spare my poor children, implores Clarence. Richard did, but the Tudors didn't.

In all his history plays Shakespeare is preoccupied with politics. The history he takes as he finds it in the chronicles: that is not his prime interest. He is a student of the use and abuse of power, exploring the ambiguity of political acts, the impenetrability of political motives and, above all, the connection between political actions and human relationships. The framework of his two English tetralogies (the eight plays running chronologically from *Richard II* to *Richard III*) is constructed to a pattern: prosperity, crime, civil war, prosperity. They were written over a period of about ten years, the second four first, with *Richard III* the finale but central to the overall theme, in which power-seeking is exposed against a background of corruption, the immorality of statecraft set against the norms of justice. The Tudor saga of Richard III provided Shakespeare with a parade ground on which to exercise such themes. The truth about the king is not an item on his agenda.

Thus, although using real names and events, Shakespeare's *Richard III*, described by one critic as 'a gargoyle on the great cathedral of English history', is not essentially a history play at all. Much of the plot, for instance, is interchangeable with that of *Macbeth*. For Richmond in Brittany read Malcolm in England; for the princes in the Tower read Macduff's children; for Bosworth read Dunsinane. Shakespearean drama was close in spirit to the medieval morality plays, less a dramatisation of real historical events than a source of moral lessons. As a mirror in which men could glimpse their likenesses and draw useful deductions as a guide to their own conduct, history was rated below poetry because it showed men behaving as they did, not as they ought. Poetry is golden, said Sir Philip Sidney in Aristotelian vein, history brazen.

The German critic, Lessing, argued that the tragic poet should follow historical truth only if what actually happened forms a well constructed plot. This was the view of Schiller whose *Maria Stuart*, like Shakespeare's *Richard III*, is both a work of art and a travesty of history: it contains a famous non-existent meeting between Elizabeth I and Mary Queen of Scots. Schiller is on record as believing that a dramatist is not a chronicler, that factual accuracy is beside the point, that a play is a work of the imagination not a matter of historical research: there is no reason why a playwright should allow an historian's scruples to cramp his style. 'History,' Schiller believed, 'is only a storehouse for my imagination, and its subjects must put up with what they have become in my hands.' Shakespeare would have agreed with him that inner truth, philosophical truth, the truth of art are general truths more important than the particular truths of history.

Other reasons why Richard III has had to put up with what he became in Shakespeare's hands are more mundane. Shakespeare was a professional entertainer with a living to earn at a time when plays had to be licensed and censorship was so severe that it could put a company of players out of business and into prison. First published in 1597, his *Richard III* was probably written some six years earlier and first performed in 1593 during a period of uncertainty over the succession, deep religious divisions and economic unrest so severe that it led to food riots. The treatment of kings was a particularly delicate and dangerous assignment, and before the end of James I's reign official suspicion of history plays effectively killed the genre. Moreover, the authorities saw danger not only in the sentiments expressed by dramatists but in the very fact of uncontrolled crowds gathering together at theatres. In London the city fathers frowned on theatres as places of crime and prostitution, if not outright sedition. Under James I and Charles I the popular theatre was gradually supplanted by an exclusively court theatre, until in 1642 all theatres were closed.

In these conditions even sticking close to historical orthodoxy as officially licensed for printing in chronicles such as Holinshed's and Hall's did not necessarily protect Shakespeare and his company from prosecution and imprisonment. The treatment was all-important. Any questioning of the villainy of the last Plantagenet might have proved an act of self-destruction, and if he had so questioned, it is unlikely that any record of his folly would have survived. Apart from the constraints upon him, Shakespeare aimed to please his patrons and his audience. It was theatre-loving courtiers who protected the livelihood of actors against the closure threatened by theatre-hating magistrates and puritans. The theatre was therefore, in self-defence, conformist. And the Elizabethan theatre-goer looked for the expected. Often the plot was spelt out for him in advance in a prologue. Not for him the new interpretation or the twist in the tail.

An immediate success and later hailed as the 'showpiece of the Theatre Theatrical', *Richard III* – or some version of it – has been an unflagging favourite among actors and audiences since its first performance, and not only in England and other English-speaking countries but also, in translation, throughout the world. Richard Burbage played the title role until his death in 1619, and such was the play's popularity that even by then the phrase 'a horse, a horse, my kingdom for a horse' had come into common usage. So closely was he identified with the part that shortly after his death a guide pointed out to a party touring the battlefield at Bosworth the very spot where Burbage fell.

Another anecdote is more apocryphal, but seemingly shows Shakespeare in a characteristic role. Before one performance Burbage was overheard by the playwright making an assignation to meet with a lady of his choice after the end of the play. While Burbage was still on stage valiantly fighting the battle of Bosworth, Shakespeare slipped in ahead of him with the lady, so that when the actor reached the house a message was sent to him from the already occupied bedroom. It informed him that William the Conqueror came before Richard III.

Revisionists are still thought by some to be committing 'little less than sacrilege' when they 'impugn the statements of England's mightiest dramatist'. Even today they are not infrequently accused of wishing to put Shakespeare down: 'nothing is more belittling or misleading than to see him as parroting "Tudor propaganda",' complains the editor of the 1981 Arden edition of the play. But the charge is 'immortalising' not 'parroting'. Putting Shakespeare down would be a futile, unattainable objective. What revisionists really seek is wider recognition that Shakespeare was not an historian, was not concerned with historical truth, and in his *Richard III* wrote what later came to be known as historical fiction and, later still, faction or docu-drama. They would like Dukes of Marlborough, prime ministers, poets laureate and the youth of England to learn their history elsewhere. They believe that Shakespeare himself would not disagree with their judgment that his value as a witness to the character, appearance and career of the real King Richard is precisely nil.

16

After the Tudors: Bacon and Buck

When in 1603 the last of the Tudors died no one had told much
of the truth about Richard III for a hundred and eighteen
years, and the mould of his reputation had set. The Richard of
the saga was the child of Tudor self-interest and a humanist
approach to history in which historical reality was less valued
than didacticism and rhetoric. The real Richard had become
shrouded in political and literary fantasy. 'By the end of the
sixteenth century,' writes A. R. Myers, 'the facts of his real
appearance, character and deeds had been buried under a great
mound of tradition. He had become the archetypal tyrant-king,
incarnate and enthroned.'

None of the children of Henry VIII was blessed with an heir,
and in *The History of the World* (1614) Sir Walter Ralegh boldly
extended the crime and punishment cycle of the Hall/
Shakespeare saga to encompass Henry Tudor. He saw the
sterility of Henry's grandchildren as retribution, but not for the
usurpation of Richard's throne; rather – somewhat surprisingly
– for his ingratitude towards Sir William Stanley ('the taking off
of Stanley's head who set the crown on his'). To Ralegh,
Richard was 'this cruel king' and 'the greatest monster in
mischief of all that forewent him', but Henry VIII too was
the very picture and pattern of a merciless prince. Writing in
the reign of James VI and I, Ralegh tactfully saw the union of
the English and Scottish lions (gold and gules) as bringing
more harmony and happiness than the blending of the roses,
white and red. This, however, did not save him from death at
the hands of the 'temperate, revengeless' king.

By nature James was timid and effeminate, a very different person from the militant, masculine Elizabeth I, and it is said that wags in the streets of London hailed his succession with cries of 'The King is dead, long live the Queen'. At court there was a transformation, and the judgment that Ralegh was executed for being left over from the previous reign is not wholly comical. Censorship and the laws of treason continued unchanged, but the climate was generally more encouraging to freedom of thought. James lived in terror of popish plots and assassination, but he did not suffer from the Tudors' morbid sense of dynastic insecurity which had made life so precarious for their better-born subjects.

The Stuarts were no recent upstarts: they had been kings for nearly three hundred years. James himself became a king at the age of thirteen months, and on his accession to the English throne had already reigned in Scotland for more than thirty-five years. According to his own reckoning (in a singularly inapt metaphor imported from France) he was the husband and the whole realm his wife. He was God's personal representative here on earth and not averse to comparing himself with the deity. When warned by his council that his affair with George Villiers was giving him a bad name in the courts of Europe, he responded with memorable blasphemy: 'Christ had his John and I have my George'. James derived his claim to the English crown through a daughter of Henry VII, so the time was hardly ripe for any public rehabilitation of the last Plantagenet, but to a sovereign with such pretensions the Plantagenets were no bogey men menacing the legitimacy of his rule.

Hard on Shakespeare's heels came Bacon, a second chancellor to pronounce a verdict of guilty on Richard. But 'the wisest, brightest, meanest of mankind' (according to Alexander Pope) was too intelligent to swallow the Tudor saga whole and exercised a rather more sophisticated judgment. In the pecking order of Richard's character assassins he takes third place. As Robert Surtees, the early nineteenth-century historian of Durham, has it: 'The magic powers of Shakespeare have struck more terror to the soul of Richard than fifty Mores or Bacons armed in proof.'

Thomas More can scarcely be said to have been armed in proof where Richard was concerned. Francis Bacon, Viscount

St Albans (1561–1626), Lord Chancellor of England, entered the Ricardian controversy a century later with his adulatory but not wholly uncritical biography of Henry VII. The third of the three brightest stars of the English renaissance, his fame has survived in history as a brilliant but unscrupulous politician and lawyer and in literature as the polymath author of works on philosophy and science as well as politics and the law. His *New Atlantis* rivals More's *Utopia*; as a biographical study his *Henry VII* puts More's *Richard III* to shame; and he has even been thought by some to be the only person capable of writing Shakespeare's plays.

Bacon was a loyal monarchist. The manuscript of his *History of the Reign of King Henry the Seventh* was written in 1621 and sent to James I for approval before publication the next year. Following a public confession of bribery and corruption, his career had just ended in disgrace, a fine of £40,000, a sentence of imprisonment in the Tower of London during His Majesty's pleasure, and perpetual disqualification from public office. Coincidentally or not, the manuscript reached the king in October and a general pardon reached the author in November.

Bacon is the originator of the phrase from which Josephine Tey took the title of her Ricardian novel: 'Truth is the daughter of time'. In *Advancement of Learning* and *Novum Organum* he expounds his belief that true knowledge can come only from experience: the voice of authority must not be mistaken for the truth. Thus Bacon's assessment of Richard III has to be seen in the light of his scepticism about the reliability of tradition, but in the shadow of an urgent necessity to ingratiate himself with a royal descendant of Henry Tudor.

He resolves his dilemma by accepting the traditional view of Richard, but hedging it with reservations. Richard was a tyrant 'both in title and regiment', Henry Tudor's victory at Bosworth was greeted with 'great cries of joy', and although Henry 'of his nobleness' ordered an honourable interment for the dead tyrant, the friars at Leicester preferred to bury him obscurely and no man blamed them for it. Nevertheless, Richard was 'a prince in military virtue approved, jealous of the honour of the English nation, and likewise a good law-maker, for the ease and solace of the common people: yet his cruelties and parricides, in the opinion of all men, weighed down his virtues and merits; and, in the opinion of wise men, even those virtues themselves were conceived to be rather fained and affected things to serve his ambition than true qualities ingenerate in his judgment or nature.'

'At Picquigny, as upon all other occasions, Richard, then Duke of Gloucester, stood ever upon the side of honour', but he took this stance to raise his reputation to the disadvantage of his brother, King Edward: even then the tyrant-to-be was aiming for the throne. For Bacon as for others, when Richard acts wickedly it is proof positive of villainy, but when he acts virtuously he is cunningly concealing his wickedness. Yet 'a good law-maker, for the ease and solace of the common people' ('politic and wholesome laws') and 'stood ever upon the side of honour' are Baconian tributes much savoured and quoted by latter-day revisionists.

In the grievous matter of the princes in the Tower Bacon follows the gospel according to St Thomas More, but specifically attributes dissemination of that strangely overdue account of the murder to the serious challenge presented by Perkin Warbeck and his supporters and Henry's need, accordingly, 'to make it manifest to the world that the Duke of York was indeed murdered'. Only four people are said to have had direct knowledge of the boys' death and two of those were dead (Miles Forest and the priest of the Tower, who reburied the bodies). The survivors (Sir James Tyrell and John Dighton) Henry 'caused to be committed to the Tower and examined'. The outcome was not unpredictable, and Bacon inserts a saving clause, in the Moreish manner, to preserve the author's credibility: 'They agreed both in a tale (as the king gave out)'.

Bacon then casts further doubt on the confessions, which were 'delivered abroad': 'But the king nevertheless made no use of them in any of his Declarations; whereby (as it seems) those examinations left the business somewhat perplexed. And as for Sir James Tyrell, he was soon after beheaded in the Tower yard, for other matters of treason. But John Dighton (who it seemeth spake best for the king) was forthwith set at liberty and was the principal means of divulging this tradition. Therefore this kind of proof being left so naked. . .'

As the king gave out! Speaking best for the king! Proof left so naked! Bacon's recapitulation of More falls some way short of unqualified endorsement.

Yet there is no reason to question the sincerity of Bacon's preference for Henry Tudor. Bacon admired success and Richard was a failure. Henry, on the other hand, emerged from apparently hopeless exile to win the crown of England against all probability. He held on to it grimly until the passage of time brought acceptance, dying in his bed and leaving his heir 'a huge mass of money' ('near eighteen hundred thousand pounds sterling'). As a consolation prize, Richard's memory continued to be treasured in the north while Henry's 'great renown throughout Europe and his scarce credible riches and the perpetual constancy of his prosperous successes' were balanced by personal friendlessness and 'the great hatred of his people'. Indeed the root of 'much hatred' against him 'throughout the realm' was 'the discountenancing of the house of York which the general body of the realm still affected' – a decisive verdict by Bacon on the relative popularity of the two kings.

Generally, Ralegh and Bacon were expressing the consensus of their age. Michael Drayton, for example, in his *Poly-Olbion* (1613) presents Richard as 'this Viper, this most vile devourer of his kind', 'who nor God nor human laws respected'. Yet Richard's bravery was never in doubt. In *Bosworth Field*, published posthumously in 1629, another poet, Sir John Beaumont, has the traditionally fearless Richard scorning Catesby's call to flee:

> 'Let cowards trust their horses' nimble feet
> And in their course with new destruction meet,
> Gain thou some hours to draw thy fearful breath:
> To me ignoble flight is worse than death.'

At the same time, and even before Elizabeth I was dead, it seems that the official line on Richard III was being questioned in what may be described as intellectual circles. In 1601 even a performance of Shakespeare's *Richard II* (showing the deposition of a king) was considered seditious, but antiquarianism, not in the public eye, had been developing with little official interference, stimulated by the availability of books and documents of all kinds rescued from the libraries of the monastic houses destroyed by Henry VIII. The Society of Antiquaries was founded in 1586, and among its founder members were Robert Cotton, avid collector of books and manuscripts, William Camden, genealogist and historian, and John Stow, annalist and chronicler.

In his *Britannia* Camden records that Richard 'inhumanly murthered his Nephews, usurp'd the Throne', but also that 'in the opinion of the wise, he is to be reckon'd in the number of bad men, but of good Princes'. Stow affirms that Richard's murder of his nephews was never proved against him. He refers to Richard's 'election' to the throne, not to his 'usurpation', and his denial of Richard's alleged deformity is reported as follows: 'And some say peremptorily that he was not deformed. One of these is the honest John Stow, who could not flatter and speak dishonestly, and who was a man very diligent and much inquisitive to uncover all things concerning the affairs or words or persons of princes.'

The author of these words was a prominent member of this circle of antiquarians. Sir George Buck, educated at Cambridge and the Inns of Court, became a member of parliament and an Esquire of the Body towards the end of Elizabeth I's reign. He undertook diplomatic missions for the crown and wrote numerous works of poetry, drama, history and belles-lettres. Sir George was proud of his lineage, and that is, no doubt, what moved him to write the first anti-traditional history of Richard III.

In the fifteenth and sixteenth centuries the Bucks were adherents of the Howards. Ancestors of Sir George had been members of the household of Edward IV and Richard III, and his great-grandfather (so he believed) held the post of Controller of Richard III's household. No supporting evidence for this has been found, but a John Buck did indeed fight for his king at Bosworth and was considered sufficiently important to be executed afterwards and have his name included in the list of attainders of Richard's supporters.

In the early part of James I's reign Sir George became Master of the Revels. In this office he was responsible for licensing plays and supervising royal performances from 1607 to 1618 – a few years too late to pass judgment on Shakespeare's *Richard III*. His own *The History of King Richard III* was written in

1619. Two years later, in financial straits through the non-pay-
ment of money owed to him by the Exchequer, he was driven to
insanity and died in 1622, leaving the manuscript unedited and
unpublished. Twenty-five years later a much revised and
distorted version was published by a great-nephew of the same
name. Sir George's original text was not published in an
authentic edition until 1979, painstakingly reconstructed and
restored by Arthur Noel Kincaid.

Sir George believed that 'all King Richard's guilt is but
suspicion. And suspicion is in law no more guilt or culpableness
than imagination.' 'Because he hath been accused of great
crimes, and slanderously (as I verily believe),' the opening
Advertisement to the Reader runs, 'I shall make endeavour to
answer for him, and to clear and redeem him from those
improbable imputations and strange and spiteful scandals and
rescue him entirely from those wrongs, and to make truth
(hereby concealed and oppressed and almost utterly sup-
pressed) present herself to the light. . . And these shall also see
the calumniators and false accusers of this prince detected and
convinced of slanders and of lies. And the good and loyal barons
shall be distinguished from the bad and false barons. And
Morton and More and their apes shall be delineated and
painted in their own colours.'

The apes were the chroniclers, who pandered to 'the ignorant
and never-understanding vulgar', the public which took its
history from pamphlets, ballads and plays. They were 'the
trumpeters and echoes of Morton and More' who peddled
'stories and romances'. To scholars like Buck, Shakespeare's
Richard III would have fallen into this category of pulp fiction,
titillating the groundlings with sensational tales of 'orrible
murder and other appetising crimes. Sir William Cornwallis
the younger claimed to read such stuff in the lavatory and use it
for lavatory paper afterwards.

Buck's *History* falls into five parts. Book I gives an account of
Richard III's lineage and of his life up to the suppression of the
Duke of Buckingham's rebellion, at which time the king was 'in
a flourishing and glorious estate, and reigning in peace'. Book
II, covering the remainder of his life, contains long sections on
the illegitimacy of the Beauforts (from whom the Tudor claim
was derived) and the genealogy of the Howards and the Bucks.

Book III sets out to refute, one by one, the various accusations made against the king, including his deformity, and states 'many strong arguments and testimonies for the assertion that Perkin Warbeck was Richard, Duke of York'. The main subjects of Book IV are the bastardy of Edward IV's children and the suggestion of a marriage between the widowed King Richard and his niece, Elizabeth of York. Book V contains an account of the king's virtues and good works and the fate of the remaining Plantagenets after his death.

Buck wrote of Henry Tudor and his supporters in a manner which would have been inconceivable twenty years earlier. 'All they which came with arms against the anointed and sacred king, and with purpose to depose and bereave him of the crown and of his life, who was their sovereign and liege lord and their lawful anointed king, were all rebels, and monstrous great ones.' They were 'Welsh and false knights and esquires' and 'perfidious and rebellious Englishmen'. 'The malice of Dr Morton' and his 'secret and traitorous practices' come in for special castigation.

The king, on the other hand, when the battle was going against him, 'was so resolute, or rather so wilful and so obstinate, and even fatally . . . so jealous of his honour and of the reputation of his valour, and so much scorned and abhorred the imputation and taint of cowardice and of fear, as that he resolved to adventure his fortunes and his life and his crown and all rather than by flight to save himself or to shun and avoid that present and dangerous conflict or battle with his traitorous enemies.'

When it came to the fatal last charge across Redmore Heath 'the king's device and resolution in so desperate a case was commendable and politic and wise and very heroical. For if that had well succeeded, he had made an end of all such quarrels, and he should have enjoyed all peace and prosperity. . . But the king had ill fortune in his enterprise. And ill fortune is accounted a vice in military adventures. . . And for this cause this king is reputed to be vicious and namely to be rash and to be obstinate and to be furious and overweening his own strength and courage.'

Buck's admiration is not blind and he details the faults which lost Richard the crown and his life and, with them, his reputation. The fault of omission was that he treated traitors too leniently. He should have cut off the heads of Morton, Stanley, Dorset and the two Courtenays as he had been forced to do with Hastings and Buckingham. His faults of commission lay in under-rating his enemies through scorn and contempt, and in rashness on the battlefield.

The treatment of Richard's corpse by Henry and his followers, who 'imitating the vultures or wolves, tore and rent his flesh and carcase', is contrasted with the honourable treatment of King Harold's body by William the Conqueror. Even when, after public exposure for three days, the body was finally buried, the malice and the slanders continued. Of the latter Buck writes that they have been 'so many and so gross and false as I have not read or heard of any prince so impudently and foully injured'. But if Buck thought his apologia would put a stop to them he was over-sanguine.

Soon after the publication of the *History*, Bishop Fuller, of *Worthies* fame, was reasserting (in *The Church History of Britain*, 1655) that Richard was 'low in stature, crook-backed, with one shoulder higher than the other, having a prominent gobbertooth, a warlike countenance. . . Yet a modern author, in a book by him lately set forth, eveneth his shoulders, smootheth his back, planeth his teeth, maketh him in all points a comely and beautiful person; nor stoppeth he here, but, proceeding from his naturals to his morals, maketh him as virtuous as handsome . . . concealing most, denying some, defending others of his foulest facts, wherewith in all ages since he standeth charged on record.'

The verdict of Buck's modern editor, Arthur Kincaid, is rather different: 'Buck sees Richard occasionally as a parallel to Christ, but only in that both, having sacred status, were betrayed and vilified. He is far from setting up Richard as a Christlike figure, and in all cases he deals with Richard's reputation by shrewd analysis rather than emotional harangue. Upon dispassionate examination, one finds not a heated emotional defence of a hero but a surprisingly cool examination. Buck's passion appears to be rather for accuracy than for Richard III. He shows the same regard for minor historical inaccuracies as for Richard's reputation. His defence springs not from hero worship but from a concern over the illogical and inaccurate nature of the traditional portrayal. His final assessment of Richard is balanced and judicious: "Although this prince was not so superlative as to assume the name of holy or best, you see him a wise, magnificent, and a valiant man, and a just, bountiful and temperate; and an eloquent and magnanimous and pious prince; and a benefactor to the holy church and to the realm. Yet for all this it hath been his fortune to be aspersed and fouled and to fall into this malice of those who have been ill-affected towards him. . ." '

Sir George Buck has an assured place in Ricardian historiography as the pioneer of revisionism: in particular, he was the first to use the Croyland Chronicle and the Titulus Regius as source material. But he had one (dubious) precursor. Towards the end of Elizabeth I's reign Sir William Cornwallis – the man who used pamphlets as lavatory paper – wrote *A Brief Discourse in Praise of King Richard the Third: or an Apology against the Malicious Slanders and Accusations of his Detracting Adversaries*. Cornwallis was a writer of paradoxes, a form of essay in which rhetoric was used to defend the apparently indefensible and win a difficult argument by skill in debate. His defence of Richard III is therefore suspect. When published in 1616 as *The Encomium of Richard III*, it appeared in a collection of similar essays, which included defences of Julian the Apostate and the French pox. Cornwallis moved in the same circles as Buck, however, and he may have been adroitly circulating genuine opinions in a form which would ensure their protection from official censure.

Thomas Habington (1560–1647) was a rich convert to Roman Catholicism who spent six years imprisoned in the Tower of London for plotting against Elizabeth I on behalf of Mary Queen of Scots and narrowly escaped execution. Incorrigible, he sheltered Henry Garnett, the Jesuit provincial, after the Gunpowder Plot, concealing him in one of the record number of eleven priest holes with which his mansion in Worcestershire was ingeniously riddled. His *Historie of Edward the Fourth, King of England* was published in 1640 by command of Charles I, and this may have been intended as a mark of royal approval for the expression of a mood more sympathetic to the House of York, the last dynasty of the old faith.

The *Historie* is not a hagiography: 'I am only to give you the picture of King Edward, without flattery or detraction; which is rare in history'. Nevertheless, Edward as presented is to be numbered among the best of princes and this does little for Richard, who is cast in his Shakespearean role, full of ambition and deceit and intent upon undermining his brother. Richard 'studied nothing but his own purposes' and was not heard to murmur against Clarence only because he was 'deep in mischief'. On the other hand, it is unbelievable that he should personally have carried out the execution of King Henry (which was 'resolved in King Edward's cabinet council'); and those who ascribe King Edward's death to poison are 'the passionate enemies of Richard, Duke of Gloucester's memory' who 'condemn him for those crimes from which he was, however, actually most innocent'.

Anti-Tudor sentiment in the seventeenth century was not confined to Roman Catholics, and its growth inevitably called into question the orthodoxies of the sixteenth. Sir Henry Spelman, for instance, an influential member of parliament and stalwart Anglican, mounted a fierce attack on the dissolution of the monasteries in *The History and Fate of Sacrilege*, written in the 1630's, although not published until 1698. In *England's Worthies*, published in 1684, William Winstanley handed Buck's revised Richard down to another generation: 'But as Honour is always attended on by Envy, so hath this worthy Prince's fame been blasted by malicious traducers who, like Shakespeare in his play of him, render him dreadfully black in his actions, a monster of nature, rather than a man of admirable parts'.

The revisionist cause, if not yet established, was at least in being and the critics of traditionalist chroniclers were no longer muzzled. But acceptance was another matter, and far from won. The re-telling of Tudor tales – with embellishment – by John Trussell, who in *A Continuation of the Collection of the History of England* (1636) claimed to have 'left no chronicle of this land that purse or prayer could purchase, unperused', was typical of the time. As John Dryden, poet laureate 1670–1689 and the leading literary figure in England during the latter half of the seventeenth century, commented scathingly: 'We find but few historians, of all ages, who have been diligent enough in their search for truth; and it is their common method to take on trust what they deliver to the public, by which means a falsehood once received from a famed writer becomes traditional to posterity.'

The Marriage that Never Was

The most intriguing item in the long calendar of Richard III's alleged crimes is the curious case of the would-be marriage to his niece, Elizabeth of York, eldest daughter of Edward IV. At first blush this would seem yet another of the implausible canards assiduously circulated to discredit him, but it is, in fact, well documented, and Sir George Buck made a singular contibution to the tale of this strange affair.

The death of his only legitimate son in April 1484 left Richard downcast and politically vulnerable. When they received the news, writes the Croyland chronicler, 'you might have seen his father and mother in a state almost bordering on madness, by reason of their sudden grief'.

Richard recognised another son, John of Gloucester, but he was illegitimate and still a child. No attempt was made to have him accepted as heir to the throne, as Henry VIII later attempted with his bastard, Henry, Duke of Richmond, before the birth of a legitimate son. Instead, Richard seems to have turned first to Clarence's son, the young Edward, Earl of Warwick, who was barred from the succession – and a better claim to the throne than Richard's – only by his father's attainder. Warwick, however, was not only a minor but may have been simple-minded: later he was said not to be able to tell a goose from a capon. The final choice therefore fell on another nephew, John, Earl of Lincoln, eldest son of the Duke of Suffolk and Richard's sister Elizabeth.

The designation of Lincoln as heir to the throne would have enjoyed no legal status once Richard was dead, and an heir of his own body remained an urgent political requirement. Since his queen was in ill health and evidently incapable of producing more children, rumours that he was plotting her death were, inevitably, soon in circulation. At the same time there were reports from Brittany that those who had fled overseas after the failure of Buckingham's rebellion had sworn fealty to Henry Tudor as king on the understanding that he would legitimise his claim by marrying Elizabeth of York. The circumstances were now such that Tudor historians could later claim that Richard poisoned his wife in order to marry his niece, thus bolstering his own title to the throne and making her unavailable to his rival. As a matter of record, though, the queen did not die until March 1485 and, when she did, Richard did not marry his niece.

Much has been made of the scandalous story that at the court festivities the previous Christmas the queen and Elizabeth of York wore similar dresses. The authority for this tale is the Croyland chronicler, a contemporary witness who, although unreliable and hostile to Richard, would hardly have invented it. 'During this feast of the Nativity,' he writes, 'far too much attention was given to dancing and gaiety, and vain changes of apparel presented to Queen Anne and the Lady Elizabeth, the eldest daughter of the late king, being of similar colour and shape; a thing that caused the people to murmur and the nobles and prelates greatly to wonder thereat; while it was said by many that the king was bent, either on the anticipated death of the queen taking place, or else, by means of a divorce, for which he supposed he had quite sufficient grounds, on contracting a marriage with the said Elizabeth. For it appeared that in no other way could his kingly power be established, or the hopes of his rival be put an end to. In the course of a few days after this, the queen fell extremely sick, and her illness was supposed to have increased still more and more, because the king entirely shunned her bed, declaring that it was by the advice of his physicians that he did so.'

In view of subsequent embroidery it should be noted that the chronicler does not state that the material was presented by Richard, nor that the dresses were actually worn, nor that the king paid his niece any 'indiscreet attentions'. The key word in the original Latin text is *distributis*: similar items of dress were presented to the two ladies (donor unstated). Yet this has been developed by antiRichard historians into 'Elizabeth appeared in robes exactly similar to those worn by the queen consort' (Lingard) and 'the eldest daughter of King Edward danced at her uncle's court, arrayed like a second queen' (Gairdner).

The next twist to this early example of a royal human interest story reaches us by courtesy of Buck. Writing about 1619, he claimed to have seen a letter written by Elizabeth of York in which she declares her love for Richard. It was addressed to John Howard, Duke of Norfolk and carefully preserved in the cabinet of the Earl of Arundel, head of the house of Howard in Buck's day.

In this letter, dating from February 1485, the princess, who had reached her nineteenth birthday earlier in the month, expresses her impatience that the queen is taking so long to die. She writes to Norfolk as a close friend of her father and prays him, in Buck's words, 'to be a mediator for her in the cause of the marriage to the king, who, as she wrote, was her only joy and maker in this world, and that she was his in heart and in thoughts, in body and in all. And then she intimated that the better half of February was past, and that she feared the queen would never die. And all these be her own words, written with her own hand, and this is the sum of her letter, whereof I have seen the autograph or original draft under her own hand.'

This immodest effusion has overturned so many preconceived notions that most historians have roundly denounced it as an invention of the deranged Sir George, not to mention an unwarrantable slur on English maidenhood. It provides an outstanding instance of historians dismissing evidence which runs contrary to their own theories and prejudices. For Sir George was not insane when he wrote his History; as Master of the Revels he had held an important and responsible public appointment; and it is apparent from Kincaid's edition of his History that he was a genuine scholar. He himself finds the letter somewhat of an embarrassment to explain: 'It may be observed that this young lady was inexpert in wordly affairs.'

Gairdner, the great Victorian antiRichard, wriggled agonisingly over it: the princess must have inwardly abhorred the match, but she was in the tyrant's power. 'That she could have been eager to obtain the hand of her brothers' murderer is too monstrous to be believed'; so perhaps he passed their death off as an unhappy accident or else she just saw no chance of safety except in 'an acceptance of his horrible overtures'. (Not that there is any evidence of overtures on his part.) On balance Gairdner preferred the letter to be non-existent – 'there are grounds for suspicion which may fairly justify incredulity' – or if not non-existent, at least misconstrued. The French chronicler Jean Molinet, by contrast, entertains no doubts, informing his readers that Richard made the princess pregnant and she had a child by him.

Accepting the letter as authentic, revisionists can argue that these are scarcely the words which a girl would use about a physically deformed monster and certainly not about one whom she believed guilty of murdering her brothers. Indeed the letter may be taken as a pointer to Richard's innocence in the matter of his nephews' death. Traditionalists will counter with the argument that the language of love is formal only, signifying no genuine affection, and that the letter is likely to have been dictated by the girl's mother, the ever-scheming Elizabeth Woodville, who was using her daughter as the spearhead of a Woodville return to power.

This last interpretation receives some support from developments after the death of Richard's queen. 'A little before Easter,' in the account of the Croyland chronicler, the mayor and commons of London were summoned to the great hall of the Hospital of St John in Clerkenwell to hear the king make 'in a loud and distinct voice' a formal public denial of his intention to marry his niece. This declaration, seen as a shameful humiliation, was apparently forced upon Richard by his northern supporters, who had gained estates and appointments taken from the Woodvilles on his accession and feared their loss if the Woodvilles were to regain royal favour. The king 'was told to his face' by Ratcliffe and Catesby, 'to whose opinion the king hardly ever dared offer any opposition', that if he did not make this declaration 'all the people of the north . . . would rise in rebellion against him'. This is an odd glimpse of tyrant as puppet. Alternatively, Richard may really have been a willing party to the disclaimer, and Buck right in believing that his wooing was 'counterfeit'.

The marriage of an uncle with a niece, so often cited as yet another instance of Richard's unnaturalness, would have required papal dispensation, but it was not, like marriage between aunt and nephew, expressly forbidden as a prohibited degree under canon law. Abhorred in England, it was not unknown abroad, and the political benefits of such a union would have been considerable. The heiress of York would have been joined to Richard instead of Henry Tudor, and the Woodville interests, still powerful, would have moved over from opposition to become supporters of the crown. Henry's historian, Polydore Vergil, tells us that when news of the proposed marriage reached Brittany, it made Henry Tudor sick in the stomach.

Those who believe that Richard never intended to marry his niece point to the fact that parliament had declared her illegitimate and to have regarded her as otherwise would have invalidated his own claim to the throne. By this argument, it must be supposed that Richard permitted false rumours of his intentions to circulate in order to discomfort Henry Tudor, at the same time drawing the sting from Woodville discontent by encouraging their belief that a comeback might be staged by these means. Elizabeth's letter would be evidence that the Woodvilles were making at least some of the running, and this would have been in character.

Royal favour and hypergamy were the main roads to advancement at that time. Through her marriage to Edward IV Elizabeth Woodville had raised herself higher than any other commoner in English history and then consolidated her position through grants, honours and alliances to her family. Her father, a recently ennobled knight, became Earl Rivers and Treasurer and Constable of England. Sir Thomas Grey, her son by a previous marriage, married the king's niece Anne, heiress to the Duke of Exeter, and became Marquess of Dorset. Her five sisters became married, respectively, to the Duke of Buckingham, the heirs to the earldoms of Arundel, Kent and Essex, and Lord Herbert. One brother, Anthony, married the daughter of the late Lord Scales and assumed that title; another, Lionel, became Bishop of Salisbury; and a third, John, was married at the age of nineteen to the dowager Duchess of Norfolk, aged eighty (*maritagium diabolicum*, moaned one chronicler). In the light of this impressive record it is a reasonable guess that the idea of an alliance between her daughter and King Richard originated with Elizabeth Woodville, not with the intended bride or groom.

If the king himself was not serious about the match, why did he not take the easy course of frustrating Henry Tudor by marrying Elizabeth of York to someone else? Disparagement – frowned upon, but not uncommon – was a convenient method of neutralising heiresses. Marrying Elizabeth to a political nonentity would have removed her from the corridors of power. After his accession Henry Tudor used this method with Elizabeth's sister, Cecily, who, following the death of her first husband, was married off to one Thomas Kyme. But it may be that Richard did not wish to alienate the Woodvilles further; or, more simply, that he liked Elizabeth and did not feel inclined to treat her in that way. The most likely answer is to be found in Harley 433: a solemn oath not to disparage her daughters was part of his settlement with Elizabeth Woodville when she agreed to bring her family out of sanctuary and persuade her son, Dorset, to desert Henry Tudor and return home. Perhaps there were no suitable husbands among the nobility and gentry whom Richard did not regard as a potential threat. One obvious candidate would have been his own illegitimate son, but perhaps Elizabeth Woodville jibbed at that: her first intended groom may even have been Richard's other son, the dead Prince of Wales.

A solution to the mystery of the incestuous marriage that never was, so shocking to historians and apparently confirming their worst suspicions of this most monstrous of monarchs, may lie in the state archives in Lisbon. For there is some evidence that after the death of Anne Nevill a mission (headed by the Yorkist commander, Sir Edward Brampton, a converted Portuguese Jew) was sent from England to Portugal to negotiate a double marriage: that of Richard with Princess Joana and that of Elizabeth of York with the Duke of Beja, a politically safe husband of appropriate rank.

Bosworth intervening, Elizabeth became legitimate again and Queen of England as Henry's bride, not Richard's, but only after parliament had accepted his claim to the throne in his own right and petitioned him to marry her. He then delayed her coronation for nearly two years, until it was pressed on him by his advisers and her own popularity. Bacon, in a chilling phrase, describes him as not uxorious, and Elizabeth is said to have been kept in subjection by her mother-in-law, Margaret Beaufort. After dutifully giving birth to eight children she died in 1503 on her thirty-eighth birthday: 'a very noble woman and much beloved'.

This tale of a non-marriage, presented by the prim Croyland chronicler as an endeavour by Richard to gratify an incestuous passion 'to the extreme abhorrence of the Almighty', has proved too good to be forgotten. It forms, for example, the subject of a melodrama by John Caryl, *The Englishe Princess or The Death of Richard III*, which was found by Pepys (who saw it at the Duke of York's playhouse on 7 March 1667) to be 'a most sad, melancholy play, and pretty good'. In it Richard the monster (played 'excellently well' by Thomas Betterton, the leading tragic actor of the day) attempts to force the princess against her will. She hates him and loves Henry, who invades England to save her life (death, if not a worse fate, awaits her, and the frustrated Richard has employed Miles Forest to strike again). In the final scene Henry kills Richard in single combat and wins the crown for her, not himself.

The Epilogue, which is addressed to the reigning monarch, Charles II, diplomatically makes the point that, however wicked Richard may have been, Cromwell's parliamentarians were even more reprehensible:

Richard is dead; and now begins your reign:
Let not the Tyrant live in you again.
For though one Tyrant be a nation's Curse,
Yet Commonwealths of Tyrants are much worse.
Their Name is Legion; and a Rump (you know)
In Cruelty all Richards does outgo.

18

Walpole's Historic Doubts

Horace Walpole, fourth Earl of Orford, was the most prominent figure in the eighteenth century to enter the lists on Richard
III's behalf. His *Historic Doubts on the Life and Reign of King
Richard the Third* is a classic defence which has enshrined him in
a central niche among the Ricardian venerated: Buck, Halsted,
Markham and Kendall. *Historic Doubts* scores a number of
palpable hits and is still illuminating and pertinent to the
controversy. Many of the arguments in Richard's favour voiced
today are echoes of Walpole. On the other hand, the work
contains a number of palpable mishits also, and these have
been pounced upon by antiRichards to discredit the whole.
Sneers and cries of 'whitewash!' from outraged traditionalists
broke out as soon as it was published and have continued ever
since.

The youngest child of Sir Robert, the prime minster, Horace
Walpole was born in 1717 (and christened Horatio). He was
weak and delicate and thought unlikely to survive infancy, and
this early parallel with Richard III is underlined by a similarity
in elder brothers. While Horace was low of stature, Robert and
Edward Walpole were tall and sturdy, as Edward and George
Plantagenet had been. Unlike Richard, however, Horace was
one of nature's bystanders, living in a less turbulent century
and not to be trapped in the hazards of warfare except on the
printed page. Pale and frail but in persistently good spirits, he
enjoyed his weak constitution for nearly eighty years. Although
a sufferer from gout, he had, as he put it, teeth, eyes and ears till
the end.

When the word 'dilettante' is mentioned, many think first of Walpole, whose many interests embraced literature, painting, architecture, history, antiquarianism and printing as well as the politics and social life of his own time. Living comfortably off sinecures obtained for him by his father (Clerk of the Estreats, Comptroller of the Pipe and Usher of the Exchequer), he was never gainfully employed but occupied his time in far from idle self-indulgence. A victim of verbal diarrhoea, his literary output was vast: the Yale edition of his surviving letters runs to thirty-nine volumes. He was a long-serving member of parliament, representing the Cornish borough of Callington for thirteen years, although (like some fifteenth-century bishops and their dioceses) without ever actually visiting the place. In re-building his Thames-side country house at Twickenham, he invented an architectural style: Strawberry Hill Gothic. In conscious imitation of the patrons of Caxton (the Earl of Worcester and Earl Rivers) he set up his own press at Strawberry Hill and became the pioneer of the English private press.

Walpole was an enemy of injustice and intolerance and a doughty fighter in a good cause. His disinterested efforts to save the unfortunate Admiral Byng resemble those of the later Ricardian, Sir Clements Markham, in his public campaign for the release of an unjustly convicted seaman. Walpole had never met Byng, who was courtmartialled and sentenced to be shot after the loss of Minorca to the French in 1756. The admiral was innocent of cowardice but convicted of negligence. Many recognised that he was a scapegoat for the incompetence of the government, but it was the dilettante Walpole who took action. He lobbied intensively and at short notice instigated an emergency debate in the House of Commons, but to no avail. It was left to Byng himself to prove the injustice by facing a firing squad at Portsmouth with exemplary courage.

Walpole was nearly fifty when, after being troubled for some years by the injustice of historians towards Richard III, he decided to record his *Historic Doubts*. They were published on 1 February 1768. 'Many of the crimes imputed to Richard seemed improbable; and, what was stronger, contrary to his interest,' Walpole writes in the Preface: 'and as it was easy to perceive, under all the glare of encomiums which historians have heaped on the wisdom of Henry the Seventh, that he was a mean and unfeeling tyrant, I suspected that they had blackened his rival, till Henry, by the contrast, should appear in a kind of amiable light.'

Towards historians Walpole affects the aristocratic disdain of the more gifted amateur. They were so incompetent that if the dead were to come to life they would be unable to recognise the events of their own times 'as transmitted to us by ignorance and misrepresentation'. Specifically, the picture which they had drawn of Richard III was 'formed by prejudice and invention'.

As a true Protestant, Walpole places much of the blame for the sorry state of historical studies on the Church of Rome. A 'deluge of error burst upon the world' when 'Christian monks and saints laid truth waste'. 'Virtues and vices were rated by the standard of bigotry; and the militia of the church became the only historians.' In the middle ages 'the public did not enjoy even those fallible vehicles of intelligence, newspapers', and events were little known to the monks who undertook to write the history of them. In the course of his work Walpole claims to have convicted historians of 'partiality, absurdities, contradictions and falsehoods' – accusations which are still music to some Ricardian ears and which continue to be made against historians, most frequently by other historians.

Thomas More's *History of King Richard III* is one of Walpole's special targets and he notes that, however much More must be respected for his later achievements, the author of the *History* was no more than an under-sheriff. Francis Bacon's *Life of Henry VII* comes under heavy fire too. 'And here,' Walpole writes at one point, 'let me lament that two of the greatest men in our annals have prostituted their admirable pens, the one to blacken a great prince, the other to varnish a pitiable tyrant. I mean the two chancellors, Sir Thomas More and Lord Bacon. The most senseless stories of the mob are converted to history by the former; the latter is still more culpable.' In Henry VII Bacon had held up for posterity's admiration a man of 'mean cunning', 'a sanguinary, sordid and trembling usurper', who cheated and oppressed his subjects.

A footnote to this passage extends the line of attack. The Hanoverian Walpole seizes the opportunity for a side-swipe at a Stuart historian: 'It is unfortunate that another great chancellor should have written a history with the same propensity to misrepresentation, I mean Lord Clarendon. It is hoped no more chancellors will write our story, till they can divest themselves of that habit of their profession, apologising for a bad cause.'

Hanoverian and Jacobite were the nearest equivalent to York and Lancaster in Walpole's time. The rebellions of 1715 and 1745 had been put down, and the establishment of the day was still basking in the Glorious Revolution of 1688 and the Protestant succession which it initiated. There were comparisons to be drawn between Richard III and William III, not to the disadvantage of either.

'The great regularity with which the coronation was prepared and conducted, and the extraordinary concourse of the nobility at it, have not at all the air of an unwelcome revolution, accomplished merely by violence. On the contrary, it bore great resemblance to a much later event, which, being the last of the kind, we term The Revolution. The three estates of nobility, clergy and people, which called Richard to the crown, and whose act was confirmed by the subsequent parliament, trod the same steps as the convention did which elected the Prince of Orange: both setting aside an illegal pretender, the legitimacy of whose birth was called into question. And though the partisans of the Stuarts may exult at my comparing King William to Richard the Third, it will be no matter of triumph, since it appears that Richard's cause was as good as King William's, and that in both instances it was a free election.'

It was Buck's work which had converted Walpole from acceptance of history's verdict on Richard as 'the great assassin' to leadership in the revisionist cause. Buck had discovered the Titulus Regius in the roll of Richard III's parliament and Walpole uses it and the later published Croyland Chronicle to good effect against More, whose substitution of the courtesan Elizabeth Lucy for the Earl of Shrewsbury's daughter as the lady of Edward IV's pre-contract is seen as abysmal ignorance or a downright lie, so that More's meticulously detailed stories are unlikely to be true when he shows himself ignorant of some 'very material and public facts' of the period. More was writing 'to amuse his leisure and exercise his fancy' and his work is pronounced to be 'invention and romance'.

THE PRINCES IN THE TOWER
by Sir John Everett Millais, 1878
(*Royal Holloway College,
Egham, Surrey*)

THE BURIAL OF THE PRINCES
IN THE TOWER
Engraving from a painting
by James Northcote

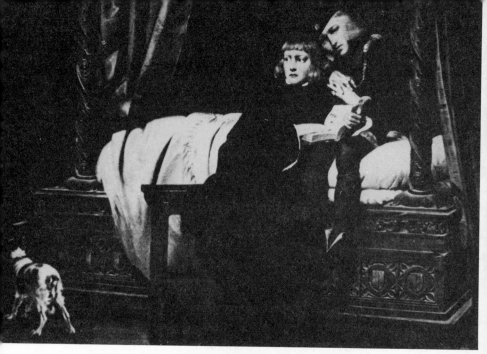

THE SONS OF EDWARD IV
by Paul Delaroche, 1831 (*Wallace Collection, London*)

DAVID GARRICK AS RICHARD III
(on the eve of Bosworth in Shakespeare's play)
by William Hogarth (*Walker Art Gallery, Liverpool*)

CROSBY HALL
Richard III's London home,
built in Bishopsgate Street
in 1466 and removed to
Chelsea Embankment in 1908

CROYLAND ABBEY 716–1539
The ruins of the abbey at
Crowland, Lincolnshire, where
the Croyland Chronicle was
written

FOTHERINGHAY CASTLE

Richard's birth-place in Northamptonshire. Sheep may safely graze . . .

FOTHERINGHAY CHURCH

The mausoleum of the house of York

SIR CLEMENTS MARKHAM
Bust outside the Royal
Geographical Society building
in Kensington Gore, London

MEMORIAL TO
QUEEN ANNE NEVILL
on the sanctuary wall,
Westminster Abbey.
Installed in 1960 to
mark her burial place

ANNE NEVILL
1456-1485
QUEEN OF ENGLAND
YOUNGER DAUGHTER OF RICHARD EARL
OF WARWICK CALLED THE KINGMAKER
WIFE TO THE LAST PLANTAGENET KING
RICHARD III

*In person she was seemly, amiable and
beauteous . . . And according to the
interpretation of her name Anne
full gracious*

REQUIESCAT IN PACE

BOSWORTH
Richard III's battle standard
flying from the crest of
Ambion Hill

Richard, the last
Plantagenet King of
England, was slain here
22nd. August 1485

BOSWORTH
The death stone on the
battlefield (1974)

RICHARD III
KING OF ENGLAND
KILLED AT
BOSWORTH FIELD
IN THIS COUNTY
22ND AUGUST 1485
Buried in the
Church of The Grey Friars
in this Parish

MEMORIAL TO RICHARD III

Memorial stone in the chancel of Leicester Cathedral, dedicated in 1982

At the outset Walpole cautiously denies that he is going to write a vindication of Richard. He was not the man to replace one dogma with another. What he intends to show is that, although Richard may have been as bad as he is painted, 'we have little or no reason to believe so'. The seven Supposed Crimes of Richard the Third are listed: the murders of the Lancastrian Prince of Wales, Henry VI, Clarence, the princes in the Tower and Queen Anne Nevill, and the executions of Rivers, Grey and Vaughan, and of Hastings. He then proceeds to examine the evidence in each case and in that of three other allegations designed to blacken Richard's name: his intended marriage to his niece, the penance of Mistress Shore and his personal deformities. In 150 pages of densely reasoned argument *Historic Doubts* dismisses, to the author's satisfaction, most of the evidence against Richard III on all these counts. Samples of the argument will convey at least the depth of Walpole's immersion in the subject.

Even the Tudor chroniclers, Hall and Holinshed, do not accuse Richard of the murder of Clarence. Richard's lack of haste in setting off for London after Edward IV's death, in particular his stay at York for a memorial service, do not support the supposition that he had already made plans to dispossess his nephew. If he had designs on the crown when he first reached London, would he have assumed the protectorship which he could accept only by acknowledging his nephew's title? The unlikelihood that Richard would have authorised a public declaration that his mother, still alive, had committed adultery is compounded by the fact that, with Edward declared illegitimate, Richard would still have been left with a legitimate elder sister, who had sons with a [possibly] superior claim, so that Dr Shaw's sermon, if correctly reported, would have cleared the path to the throne for the Earl of Lincoln, not Richard himself. On the death of the princes More's words 'some remain yet in doubt whether they were *in his days* destroyed or not' are noted: the italics are Walpole's. Bacon's account of the confessions of Dighton and Tyrell is noted as really Henry VII's: they are '*as the king gave out*'. The strange behaviour of Elizabeth Woodville if Richard had murdered her sons does not escape Walpole's notice. Nor does the silence of the Archbishop of Canterbury: 'As Bourchier survived

Richard, was it not incumbent on him to show that the Duke of York had been assassinated in spite of all his endeavours to save him? What can be argued from this inactivity of Bourchier, but that he did not believe the children were murdered?'

It was unfortunate for Walpole that what occasioned him to take his plunge into the Ricardian controversy was the discovery of a document from Richard's time the import of which he misread. It was a set of Wardrobe accounts which included those for Richard's coronation but other entries too, one of them itemising apparel for the lord Edward, son of the late King Edward. This led him to the conclusion that Edward V probably attended Richard III's coronation and, with the support of other flimsy evidence, to suggest that it was Richard's intention to restore his nephew to the throne 'when young Edward should be of full age'. He also finds Richard innocent of the murder of the younger of the princes by accepting Perkin Warbeck's claim to be genuine, much argument being spent on refuting errors made by Bacon which purported to prove Warbeck an impostor.

'There is,' run the opening lines of *Historic Doubts*, 'a kind of literary superstition, which men are apt to contract from habit, and which makes them look on any attempt towards shaking their belief in any established characters, no matter whether good or bad, as a sort of profanation. They are determined to adhere to their first impressions, and are equally offended at any innovations, whether the person whose character is to be raised or depressed were patriot or tyrant, saint or sinner. No indulgence is granted to those who would ascertain the truth.' Certainly, as he had foreseen, none was granted to Walpole.

Historic Doubts was criticised courteously by Hume and by Gibbon (who praised the author's ingenuity but declared himself unconvinced by the arguments) but less courteously in the *Critical Review* and *London Chronicle* and by the Society of Antiquaries, of which Walpole was a member. F. W. Guidickins, a lawyer of the Middle Temple, wrote a hundred-page Answer in a better forensic manner than Walpole's, making some telling rejoinders, but reducing the debate to its most tedious and sterile. He argued, for example, that although Walpole might be correct in asserting that Richard III was handsome (on the dubious evidence of an aged Countess of

Desmond) that would not necessarily invalidate John Rous's claim that he was two years in the womb (unlikely, concedes F. W. G.) and was born with hair on his shoulders (a good tuft of hair on the shoulders is not incompatible with handsomeness) and with teeth (although F. W. G. cannot vouch for its truth, one historian records that Louis XIV was born with teeth and he was said to be a handsome king).

In a private letter the twenty-year-old Earl of Carlisle, an Etonian friend of Charles James Fox, expressed the traditionalist reaction rather more succinctly and jauntily: 'The Emperor Nero's character wants a little white-washing, and so does Mrs Brownrigg's who was hanged for murdering her apprentices the other day. I hope he will undertake them next, as they seem, next to his hero, to want it the most.'

Stung by the criticisms, Walpole wrote lengthy rejoinders, but these were not published until after his death. In them he made vigorous counter-attacks on Hume, the Dean of Exeter, who had also defended the traditional view ('the most exemplary fathers of the church have not always been the best logicians'), and other much-to-be-derided critics. Meanwhile there was cause for satisfaction too. Sales were so brisk that Dodgson, his publisher, called on the day after publication to ask him to prepare a second edition. From abroad Voltaire wrote flatteringly to beg for a copy.

Despite all its flaws and the attacks made upon it, *Historic Doubts* was immediately influential and has remained so. As a leading representative of the age of reason, Walpole had set out to expose a shadowy historical problem to the searching light of dialectics, and his opponents had at least recognised the seriousness of the attempt and responded in kind. The outcome was bound to be some sharing of his doubts, which many accepted as well-founded even if his conclusions were not.

Walpole's romantic interest and involvement with royalty in general and unfortunate monarchs in particular did not begin or end with Richard III. In 1753 he had risen gallantly but ill-advisedly to the assistance of Theodore, King of Corsica, who was languishing in the King's Bench prison unable to pay his debts. To secure his release, Walpole persuaded Garrick to give a special charity performance of Shakespeare's play about yet another unfortunate monarch, *King Lear*. But the money raised was insufficient and, after accepting it, His Majesty became ungratefully abusive. 'I have done with countenancing kings,' Walpole declared in disgust, but when Theodore died he could not resist composing an elegant epitaph for the royal tombstone, which, surviving the bombing of the church during the second World War, may still be read in the churchyard of St Anne's, Soho.

There is, too, a curious connection between Walpole and the dukedom of Gloucester. The title had not been a fortunate one since Richard's day. The Tudors had no use for it, but it was rescued from extinction by the Stuarts and borne by Charles I's third son, Henry, and Queen Anne's eldest son, William, both of whom died young. In Walpole's day George III's brother, William Henry, was created Duke of Gloucester, and Walpole's niece, Maria, the widowed Lady Waldegrave, became his mistress in a clandestine affair – Walpole being pointedly advised to write some Historic Doubts on the present Duke of Gloucester too. After a secret marriage the couple lived together openly, until the duke's brother, the Duke of Cumberland, announced his marriage to the widowed Mrs Horton, 'the greatest reprobate in England', and precipitated the Royal Marriage Act which forbade, and continues to forbid, the marriage of descendants of George II without the sovereign's consent. After much ado the Gloucester marriage was recognised and Walpole had a royal niece. Her son, William Frederick, succeeded to the title, but although Chancellor of the University of Cambridge his intellect was such that he became more widely known as Silly Billy. After his death in 1834, childless, the title again became extinct until revived in 1928 for Prince Henry (third son of George V), whose son is the present holder of the title.

Walpole's single-handed defence of Richard III may be seen as an expression of his romantic nature as well as a protest against injustice. His motivation was doubtless mixed, hatred of Popery and Tudor tyranny mingling with contempt for historians and indeed, in the light of his writings on its painting and poetry, for the whole of the middle ages. In *The Castle of Otranto* he reveals his enthralment by the grotesque, so that Richard's alleged monstrosity too may have attracted him. Above all, Walpole was a compulsive iconoclast and must have derived amusement from the paradox of shattering an unsaintly image.

Alas for their memory, old men sometimes recant, and Walpole's brief *Postscript to my Historic Doubts*, written in February 1793, might be better described as *Historic Doubts on Historic Doubts*. The terror of the French Revolution, and specifically the complicity of another royal duke in the death of a sovereign, persuaded him that Richard could after all have committed any of the atrocities of which he was accused. If Philip, Duke of Orleans stood revealed as a monster in 'an age called not only civilised but enlightened', why not Richard, Duke of Gloucester in an age of barbarism? Men were not always guided by reason; human nature was not what he had so confidently supposed.

It is a gruesome footnote to Horace Walpole's foray into Ricardianism that the French edition of his *Historic Doubts*, published in 1800, should have appeared in a translation made by none other than the guillotined king himself. This had been Louis XVI's occupation in the Bastille while awaiting execution. Presumably he found consolation in demonstrating that kings who become the victims of historical misjudgment may hope for an eventual resurrection of their good name.

19

Other Eighteenth-Century Views

The climate of opinion in which Walpole's *Historic Doubts* met with such a stony reception is best exemplified in the views of David Hume, the most highly regarded Scottish philosopher since Duns Scotus and one of the foremost intellects in the Europe of the eighteenth century. Born in Edinburgh in 1711 and made famous by his *Treatise on Human Nature* written at the age of twenty-six, Hume was a philosophical iconoclast with a reputation for the critical destruction of accepted ideas – a sceptic in religion and much else, but not in the matter of Richard III's reputation, where he swallowed More and the Tudor saga without question. Hume had in common with Walpole a rationalist approach to history and a scorn for monkish chronicles, but they led him in the opposite direction.

Some other historians of the period, notably William Guthrie and Thomas Carte, used the arguments of rhetoric to attack the traditional accounts of Richard's murder of his nephews. In Richard's situation after he had been crowned, they argued, only a fool would have brought odium on himself by killing the deposed Edward and his brother, and whatever Richard may have been he was not a fool. Hume, taking the same view of human nature, adopted a different view of Richard III. His reason was blind faith in More's absolute veracity. He believed that Sir Thomas More's 'singular magnanimity, probity and judgment make him an evidence beyond all exception . . . his authority is irresistible and sufficient to overbalance a hundred little doubts and scruples and objections'.

Although little valued today, Hume's *History of England*

enjoyed great popularity in his own century and well into the next. Published in 1762, shortly before *Historic Doubts*, the first two volumes covered the period from the arrival of Julius Caesar to the death of Richard III in nearly nine hundred pages. Hume did not lack stamina, but he used history as an exercise for his literary talents and to bring his moral principles and philosophical convictions to bear on information which others had assembled. He was disinclined to trouble himself with much research, and the use of students as research assistants was not then considered a necessary part of the historian's apparatus.

Thus Hume ignored Buck, the revisionist, and regurgitated More and the whole established tradition for the benefit of his readers. Richard had a 'fierce and savage nature'. He was 'a man who had abandoned all principles of honour and humanity'. 'Never was there an usurpation in any country more flagrant than that of Richard, nor more repugnant to every principle of justice and public interest.' Hume's moral fervour was in the tradition of John Knox, and it carried him beyond the bounds of known truth. Overlooking the existence of the Titulus Regius, as well as the probability that Richard's reforming legislation would have been welcomed by his subjects at large, he asserted that Richard's 'title was never acknowledged by any national assembly, scarce even by the lowest populace to whom he appealed'.

For Hume nothing Richard does can be good, and his physical deformity is not in doubt: he was 'hump-backed and had a very harsh disagreeable visage; so that his body was in every particular no less deformed than his mind'. That being so, his fate was to be lamented because it was too good for him: Richard 'perished by a fate too mild and honourable for his multiplied and detestable enormities'. Hume's own inhumanity in the expression of these sentiments must be excused as rationalist sermonising or judged as failure to resist a tempting opportunity for the composition of fine-sounding prose. The assertion that Richard's body was deformed 'in every particular', echoing the phrase 'to disproportion me in every part', raises the suspicion that Hume was guilty of using Shakespeare as an historical source.

A difficulty for those who have faith both in More and in the

authenticity of some allegedly princely bones unearthed in
the Tower of London during the seventeenth century is that the
bones were discovered in a place from which he specifically
states that they were removed. This is usually side-stepped by
antiRichards, but Hume meets it with a supposition: 'Perhaps
Richard's chaplain had died before he found an opportunity of
executing his master's commands; and the bodies being supposed to be already removed, a diligent search was not made for
them by Henry in the place where they had been interred.' This
is remarkably feeble, for few things are less likely than that
Henry, anxious to convict his predecessor of the crime beyond
all doubt, his very crown threatened by a succession of pretenders claiming to be the younger prince, should have failed to
make the most diligent of searches. Hume is on firmer ground
when, in a long appendix designed to dispel doubts about the
imposture of Warbeck, he points to the fact that the boys were
in Richard's custody: he was answerable for them and gave no
account of them. 'He could not say, with Cain, that he was not
his nephews' keeper.'

Between the black of Hume and the white of Walpole more
balanced views were held. Paul de Rapin-Thoyras was the first
French historian to tackle English history on a grand scale:
Volume VI of his *History of England*, covering the relevant
period, had appeared in an English translation in 1728. His
impartiality as a Great Debater is manifest not because he
occupies a grey middle ground but because he embraces both
points of view in succession.

Rapin (as he is usually known) came to England first as a
Huguenot refugee and then, after a period in Holland, as a
soldier in William of Orange's unopposed expeditionary force
in 1688. Afterwards he fought with distinction as an ensign at
the siege of Carrickfergus and a lieutenant at the battle of the
Boyne. When he turned to writing, he proved equally successful. A pioneer version of history according to the Whigs, his
History of England, written primarily for foreigners, ran to six
editions in French and seven in English translation, becoming
the standard work until superseded by Hume's.

At first Rapin sees Richard III to be aiming at the throne as
early as 1477 and therefore an accomplice in the despatch of
Clarence: 'All the historians agree that from this time forward

the Duke of Gloucester had thoughts of securing the crown after the death of the king and that therefore the Duke of Clarence could not but be an eyesore to him.' But some pages later a note of caution is added: 'It is pretty difficult to judge whether before the death of Edward IV the Duke of Gloucester had any thoughts of mounting the throne to the prejudice of his nephews.'

All the other murders traditionally ascribed to Richard are recounted too: the Lancastrian Prince of Wales, Henry VI (the dagger story, but a caution about the truth of it), Hastings (the withered arm story), the princes (smothered) and Queen Anne Nevill. In the case of the queen, 'historians most favourable to Richard say that she died of grief and vexation because he showed an aversion to her; others speak plainer and affirm that he hastened her death'. In either event it was a judgment on her for marrying her first husband's murderer. Interestingly, Rapin airs the possibility of Richard murdering Edward IV too: 'some accuse the Duke of Gloucester of poisoning him'. However, this is said to be an accusation not grounded on proof and 'ought not to be too hastily credited'. Rapin himself ought not to be too hastily credited at times: when, for instance, in a footnote he informs the reader of a Shropshire man, Thomas Parr, who was born in 1483, lived through ten reigns and died in 1635, aged 152.

After the accusations comes Rapin's judgment that 'it would be a hard matter to find in history a prince bad enough to match' Richard, and there the case would appear to rest until the reader is startled to attention by some after-thoughts. He is suddenly required to note that historians writing in the reigns of Henry VII and Henry VIII to please those monarchs have aggravated the heinousness of Richard's actions. Very probably they have ascribed some things to him on no very good ground, for example murdering with his own hand Henry VI and his son. They have overlooked his good qualities: good sense, sound judgment, uncommon valour and his great concern that justice be administered impartially to all his subjects. Perhaps he would have proved a good king if he had been able to fix himself firmly on the throne: there is a parallel here with the Emperor Caesar Augustus. Rapin's translator (an Essex vicar), alluding to Richard's care to check vice and his concern with good government, concludes: 'His enemies seem to own that, excepting his cruelties to gain and keep the crown, one might judge him to be a good king.'

Between Rapin and Hume the major historical work (published between 1747 and 1755) was *A General History of England* by Thomas Carte, who on the title page, in a clear reference to the interloping Whiggish Frenchman, is described in capital letters as 'an ENGLISHMAN' (a boast not open to Hume). Educated at both Oxford and Cambridge, Carte was a nonjuring Jacobite clergyman and a quarrelsome controversialist. On the eve of the Hanoverian succession he published a remarkably untimely defence of Charles I and later had to flee the country and live in France under an assumed name. On his return he determined to write a history of England from original documents, which Rapin had not used. In Richard III he found another unpopular cause to embrace and made good use of Buck, whom Rapin had rejected.

According to Carte, it was Dorset and Hastings who killed the Lancastrian Prince of Wales after the battle of Tewkesbury, with Richard 'not offering his sword to hurt'. In 1477 'the queen and her relations governed all at court' and were responsible for disposing of Clarence, who was 'hot, proud, restless, querulous and grasping', while Richard remained 'the master of his temper' and avoided an open breach with them. Carte does not believe in the truth of the pre-contract, however. 'Pretences are never wanting on such occasions: and they were now furnished by the late king's inordinate passion for the ladies.' Nevertheless, the story, canvassed among the nobility, was accepted by them.

The supposed murder of the princes Carte finds 'a point of mere conjecture', the traditional tale implausible and an evident falsehood. In the prelude to Buckingham's rebellion Margaret Beaufort persuades the duke that her son's claim is superior to his and they agree on Henry marrying Edward IV's eldest daughter, Elizabeth. 'The scheme seemed likely to succeed: and as there was no objection to it, but from the life of Edward V and his brother Richard, Duke of York, then close prisoners in the Tower of London, it was thought necessary to give out that these young princes had been murdered there by their uncle's orders. The English catch eagerly at every thing they hear and believe it implicitly.' In Carte's opinion there was a strong presumption that Edward V died of ill health and that Richard, Duke of York reappeared as Perkin Warbeck.

Carte praises Richard for excellent laws, impartial justice, the establishment of good order and for being 'bold in war and wise in council'. He disallows the hunchback. 'No prince could well have a better character than Richard had gained till he came to be Protector and dethroned his nephew: this action, and the views of the Lancastrian faction, gave birth to the calumnies with which he was loaded.' It was Henry VII ('much more cruel') who was lacking in justice and humanity.

Unfortunately for Richard's reputation, Carte was irredeemably tainted with Jacobitism and his *History* did not enjoy the success of esteem or sales accorded to Rapin's or Hume's. His historical judgment was more balanced than Walpole's, but it was Walpole who achieved fame as the man who took the baton of revisionism from Buck and bore it on towards the next century, still a lap or two behind the traditionalists, but valiantly keeping the contest and the challenge alive. 'Nothing can be a stronger proof how ingenious and agreeable that gentleman's pen is' (wrote Hume) 'than his being able to make an inquiry concerning a remote point of English history an object of general conversation.'

The gathering momentum of scepticism about English history's traditional monster, thus precipitated, was appropriately aided by the most famous non-conformist of the century, a Walpole convert. John Wesley (1703–1791), the evangelist and principal founder of Methodism, was wholly convinced by *Historic Doubts*. In his Journal of 1769 he expresses surprise that 'all our historians should have so readily swallowed' the traditional account of Richard III as an 'amazing monster'. The second volume of his *A Concise History of England* includes a strong defence of Richard by the novel method of repeating all the traditional stories and interspersing them with comments such as 'I doubt many of these facts', 'I doubt this whole account', 'an idle, senseless, improbable tale!' and, of the murder of the princes, 'an absolute falsehood'.

The Scottish historian, Malcolm Laing (1726–1818), was another disciple of Walpole, writing a thorough-going vindication of Richard in his completion of Robert Henry's *History of Great Britain* (1793). The great panjandrum himself, Dr Johnson, on the other hand, was not to be drawn. He greeted *Historic Doubts* with uncustomary moderation and discretion. Walpole, he observed, had 'got together a great many curious things and told them in an elegant manner'. The pronouncement of an even-handed verdict was left to William Hutton, who in *The Battle of Bosworth Field* (1788) set Richard in a wider historical perspective and judged him to be just one of a bad lot, but with redeeming virtues.

'Many of the English princes have been as guilty as Richard, but less blamed, because more successful. The treatment of Duke Robert by his brothers, William Rufus and Henry the First, was infinitely more diabolical than that of Richard to Clarence. King John murdered his nephew and his sovereign, as well as Richard, but this is little noticed by the historian, though Richard was by far the better king. Henry the Fourth stands almost excused, who really murdered Richard the Second, while our hero is condemned for the death of Henry the Sixth, though not guilty. The destruction of Warwick by Henry the Seventh was as vile a murder as that of Edward the Fifth; nay, were it possible to speak in palliation of this worst of crimes, Richard was the least culpable, for he had one temptation Henry had not: Edward the Fifth had an absolute right to the crown, but Warwick only a shadow. And the artful Queen Elizabeth, who by her address was idolised by the subject and immortalised by the historian, basely destroyed a sovereign princess, over whom she exercised power without right, Mary Queen of Scots; and, to augment the cruelty, suffered her to be insulted at the block.

'Richard's crimes originated from ambition, and took their complexion from the boldness of his character. Could he have lawfully claimed a crown, he might have made an excellent monarch; or had a crown been totally out of his reach, he might have been a valuable subject; but, placed between the two, he partook of both and marred the subject to make the monarch. He was a faithful servant, a brave soldier, an admirable legislator; yet one of the vilest of men. Perhaps History cannot produce an instance of such an asssemblage of virtues and defects in one person. In him were united as many excellencies as would furnish several shining characters and as many faults as would damn a troop.'

20

The Nineteenth Century

By the end of the eighteenth century the burial mound of Richard's reputation was criss-crossed with the tunnels of disbelieving explorers, burrowing for truth. Was the poetical superman of the saga really indestructible; was the human victim of systematic misrepresentation beyond all hope of rescue? Buck, Walpole and their followers believed not, and if they had failed to prove Richard innocent, at least they had demonstrated the failure of the Tudor chroniclers to prove him guilty. Under their influence Hutton even transformed his appearance: 'As the prejudice of the Lancastrian writers declined, Richard's misshapen body, like a block of marble under the chisel of an artist, assumed a fairer form and, brightening by degrees, he is incontestably proved, at the end of three centuries, to have been a handsome man.'

In the dawn of an age of romance a similar scepticism about the victors' version of history seems to have been shared by the most eminent writers of genuine fiction. In *Rob Roy* (1818) Walter Scott appears unaware of Richard's 'fairer form': his villain is described by the hero as a 'bandy-legged, bull-necked, limping scoundrel! Richard III in all but his hump-back'. His heroine, on the other hand, claims a Yorkist ancestor who was, so she declares, 'sorely slandered by a sad fellow called Will Shakespeare, whose Lancastrian partialities, and a certain knack of embodying them, has turned history upside down, or rather inside out'.

Describing herself as 'a partial, prejudiced and ignorant Historian', the fifteen-year-old Jane Austen firmly nailed her colours to Richard's mast in *The History of England* (1791): 'The Character of this Prince has been in general very severely treated by Historians, but as he was a York, I am inclined to suppose him a very respectable Man. It has indeed been confidently asserted that he killed his two Nephews and his Wife, but it has also been declared that he did *not* kill his two Nephews, which I am inclined to believe true.' Whether or not she had second thoughts later in life is not recorded.

During the seventeenth century comparisons had been drawn between Cromwell and Richard, the current and archetypal tyrants. During the mid-eighteenth century the unpopular William, Duke of Cumberland ('Butcher' Cumberland), uncle of the boy who was to become George III, was identified as a potential Richard III, but no such parallels were drawn when the teenaged Victoria succeeded to the throne in preference to the then Duke of Cumberland, her uncle Ernest Augustus, who had to be content with Hanover.

John Lingard has been called 'the only considerable historian of this period who clung to the Tudor historical tradition'. To him, Richard was 'a prince of insatiable ambition who could conceal the most bloody projects under the mask of affection and loyalty': 'a monster in human shape', 'no man could pity his death'. There are only three appendices to the third volume of Lingard's *A History of England* (1819), a volume which covers the reigns of nine kings between 1327 and 1509. Note A is an attack on those who believe in Edward IV's pre-contract with Eleanor Butler. Note B is an attack on those who seek to exonerate Richard III from the murder of the princes. Note C is an attack on those who choose to doubt that Perkin Warbeck was an impostor.

This historian's obsession with the iniquity of Richard III sprang from his devotion to Thomas More, the Catholic martyr. A Roman Catholic priest, rewarded for his *History* by doctorates from Pope Pius VII, he was concerned to rehabilitate More as a witness of truth after the strictures of Walpole and his revisionist disciple, Laing, who was not only an historian but also a liberal politician.

Lingard provides only one of several outstanding examples of the enduring influence of More among intellectuals, which has proved scarcely less important in the perpetuation of Richard's traditional reputation than Shakespeare's at a more popular level. It is a nice irony that More's principled stand against the despotism of the Tudors should have so established his bona fides with Hume as to persuade that sceptic into acceptance of traditional authority, and that it should bring Lingard down on the side of the dynasty which separated the church of England from the church of Rome. Their faith in More's veracity was later matched by that of James Gairdner, and those who read More's *History of King Richard III* today can only wonder at such credulity. As has been remarked of Thucydides, a much better historian than More: 'It is astonishing how a solemn manner and a noble style will carry unsupported and unfounded statements without dispute down the ages.'

Richard's reputation was now on a see-saw, and a weighty riposte to Lingard, whose work had been criticised by Protestants and Catholics alike, followed within a few years, written by a Quaker. In *The History of England during the Middle Ages* (1823) it was Sharon Turner's endeavour, so he tells the reader, 'to reduce the obloquy under which Richard III has laboured, to its just proportion; and to distinguish how much of his exaggerated crimes is fairly imputable to himself, and how much to his age and party'. In this he expresses himself greatly indebted to the Harleian manuscript 433 for new light on Richard's reign and conduct. This 'has enabled the author to draw this singular man more in the real shape and features than has yet been done'. His conclusion does little for the reputations of More, Hume and Lingard: 'From an eagerness in the Tudor princes and their partisans to destroy all public sympathy for Richard III and the line of York, which he had headed, and which others after him survived to represent, no part of our history has been more disfigured by passion, prejudice, injustice and inaccuracy than the two reigns of Edward V and Richard III.'

Turning his back on the chroniclers and historians of previous centuries, Turner proclaims a new, dispassionate and scientific approach to historiography. 'Modern criticism, averse alike to fable and to rhetoric, wishes history neither to defame nor to blazon, but to explore and narrate the simple truth, wherever it is penetrable or attainable, unvarnished and untwisted.' In this process Richard's image is greatly improved without being laundered to an improbable whiteness.

It is a virtue of Sharon Turner's work that he sees the king in the context of his time: the 'creature and mirror' of a violent age. Richard 'did not live in an age of modern moral sensibility'. He was representative of the European aristocracy of the time and carried an 'unshrinking temper, fierce selfishness and proud ambition to their worst consequences'. So far from his being a peculiar monstrosity of nature, it is doubtful whether any of his contemporaries 'would, under the same circumstances, dangers, inducements and impulses, have acted differently'.

According to Sharon Turner's interpretation, the great defect in Richard's character was a kind of cowardice. 'Brave to the utmost edge of peril in the martial conflict, he was an intellectual coward and preferred to prevent danger by crime.' Edward IV defied his rivals, but Richard was always afraid of them and was thus led to 'debase himself into wickedness which Edward would have disdained'. He murdered his dethroned nephews through lack of moral courage. He 'acted uniformly afterwards as if they were dead and . . . there seems no just reason for disbelieving their catastrophe. . . Almost all murders, from their privacy, are defective in direct evidence. . . The new facts adduced in this history may be allowed to place Richard's other actions in a light more favourable to his character; but on the murder of his nephews, his memory must remain with all its former stains. It can neither be vindicated nor denied.'

Turner's Richard is a victim of treachery. His legislation promoting justice and law and order and prohibiting the wearing of liveries and cognisances made him unpopular among the great. Hence the *nobilium defectionem* noted by Polydore Vergil. There was no national movement in favour of Henry Tudor. At Bosworth it was 'a perfidious combination of five noblemen which destroyed Richard'. The moral indignation heaped on Richard should be heaped also on Henry I, John, Edward III and Henry IV, but none suffered an early and violent end, and living on and dying in one's bed greatly assists a reputation.

In his account of medieval England Sharon Turner, born of Yorkshire stock, devotes nearly 300 pages to the reigns of the three Yorkist kings, but this substantial work is now little read. Turner is a man in the middle, a moderate revisionist, not to be embraced by either party in the Great Debate. His obsession took a different form to Lingard's, and he was inspired to add to his four works of English history and *The Sacred History of the World* by writing a poem on Richard III. Published in 1845, this contains fifteen books, running to 274 pages; it had taken him nearly fifty years to complete. Even so it covers only the period between Edward IV's last illness and the death of Richard's son, leaving the climax of Bosworth unachieved.

The verse form is iambic pentameters in rhyming couplets. Thus, when Rivers explains to Edward V what it means to be king, the boy exclaims:

> Your lessons such bewildering scenes evince,
> I wish I had not been by birth a prince.

The tale is a moral one. Conscience and ambition struggle within Richard, and ambition wins. The upright Protector turns villain and murders his nephews. Although complaining in his preface of the misrepresentation of Tudor writers and affirming that Richard could not have been 'that mere cruel, malignant and odious ruffian' which Shakespeare portrayed, the author is anxious not to be thought an apologist. All crimes are inexcusable, and explanations and illustrations of real character and motive must not be mistaken for apology or excuse. In the premature death of his own son Richard's wickedness is properly punished. Elizabeth Woodville, the mother of his murdered nephews, exults:

> 'He childless too! There is a RIGHTEOUS God!'
> She said and, trembling, kneel'd upon the sod.

(It is clear from the context that what she knelt on was the ground, not an unnatural Richard prostrated by grief.)

Despite all this and the author's express disclaimer, the Dictionary of National Biography condemns Sharon Turner's poem as a 'dismally long and half-hearted kind of apology' for the king, 'judiciously rejected' by the author's usual publisher. More exactly, it is an exercise in ambivalence, to which the

Richard enigma is prone to condemn many of the bewitched.

Between the Histories of Lingard and Turner the parlous condition of English historical studies was formally recognised by parliament on 24 July 1822, when the House of Commons resolved to present a humble address to George IV, drawing that monarch's attention to the unhappy fact that 'the ancient historians of the realm' were both inaccurate and inadequate. He was begged to authorise the publication of complete editions of manuscript documents in the state archives.

George IV being graciously pleased to comply, much material essential for a scientific approach to the events of the past was made available for the first time. Stacks of medieval parliamentary rolls, patent rolls, charter rolls, close rolls and other chancery records lay inaccessibly preserved in various makeshift stores: in the Wakefield Tower and the chapel in the White Tower of the Tower of London, in the Rolls Chapel and Rolls House, even in the chapter house of Westminster Abbey. By order of His Majesty's Commissioners on the Public Records these were now to be brought out into the light of day, examined, transcribed, printed and published.

Nor was this all. Towards the end of Elizabeth I's reign Sir Thomas Bodley had abandoned a career at court to dedicate himself to the collection of books and manuscripts for the university library at Oxford which still bears his name. His contemporary, Sir Robert Cotton, described by Francis Bacon as 'a worthy preserver and treasurer of rare antiquities', had spent forty years collecting manuscripts for his own satisfaction and the benefit of posterity. By the early part of the nineteenth century his Cottonian library had been deposited in the British Museum, together with the royal library (donated by George III) and other great collections, including that most relevant to Richard III: the Harleian.

The man responsible for this last collection was Robert Harley, who became speaker of the House of Commons in 1700 and, as Earl of Oxford and Mortimer, prime minister in 1711. Yet he found time also to 'rescue from oblivion and destruction such valuable records of our national antiquities as had escaped the diligence of former collectors'. When his son died, there were nearly 8,000 volumes of manuscripts in what became known as the Harleian Miscellany. (His wife being constantly obliged to look elsewhere for company, his numerous children were similarly described.)

The more important items in these collections were now made available in scholarly editions of transcriptions or translations from the Latin by editors such as Sir Harris Nicolas, J. G. Nichols and Sir Henry Ellis, published by the Camden Society, the Antiquarian Society, the Selden Society and similar learned associations formed for that purpose. Ellis edited Fabyan's *Chronicles* (1811) and an English translation of Vergil's *Anglica Historia* (1844). *York Records* (extracts from the municipal records which contained references to Richard III) were published in 1843. The Camden Society published Warkworth's *Chronicle* in 1839, and the first (and only) English version of the *Croyland Chronicle* was published by Bohn's Antiquarian Library in 1854. Family records such as the Paston letters and the Plumpton correspondence were also now published for the first time.

Thus More's much reissued *Richard III* and Shakespeare's, continually reprinted and performed, were at last challenged by some hard facts and a closer acquaintance with more authentic sources. Those so disposed could now embark upon 'a full and impartial examination of original documents', ignoring historians whose work was based on hearsay or traditional evidence. The records which 'have remained in manuscript until within the last few years' were welcomed by Caroline A. Halsted among others as 'far truer guides than those chroniclers who made their elaborate narratives the vehicle of their own prejudices rather than the means of perpetuating the truth'.

Her two-volume biography, *Richard III as Duke of Gloucester and King of England* (1844), has provided latter-day Ricardians with much pleasure and ammunition, while being subjected to a barrage of academic flak and some chauvinistic sneering by male historians. Real romance entered Miss Halsted's life when she married the rector of Middleham, where Richard had lived and whose church was the spiritual centre of his collegiate foundation there, and this has been adduced as confirmation that her heart belonged, not to the Victorian cleric, but to the protagonist in her saga.

Yet Caroline Halsted's standards of scholarship were high,

and throughout a Life stretching across more than a thousand pages the prose remains clear and crisp. Readable today, it was reprinted (by Alan Sutton) in a limited edition in 1977. Her partiality for Richard is founded on research, not sentiment. 'It is time that at least some justice was done to Richard III as a monarch, however opinions may vary as regards the measure of his guilt as a man', but let it not 'be supposed that in entering upon the arena of controversy respecting the alleged acts of Richard III, any desire is entertained of exalting him into a hero of romance. The crimes laid to his charge, whether real or imaginary . . . were many and grievous; and his elevation to the crown was marked by transactions which, to speak in the mildest terms, were open to severe condemnation, unmitigable censure.' And again: 'The purport of this memoir is not unduly to exalt Richard of Gloucester, either in mind or person, still less to invest him with qualifications and personalities more fitted to embellish a romance than to find a place in the plain, unvarnished statements of historical research: its design is simply to rescue his memory from unfounded aspersions.'

Miss Halsted's starting point was recognition of the lack of trustworthy contemporary chroniclers and the violent prejudices and strong antipathies of those who wrote about Richard after his death. 'Shrinking from such corrupt and uncertain authority, history becomes silent; she resigns the doubtful and the mysterious to the poet, whose imagination weaves out of such materials the dark and terrible tragedies by which he seeks to awe and to instruct. Thus it has been with the period of Richard the Third. The historian relates comparatively little, the poet is full to overflowing. . . The genius of Shakespeare seized upon the history of Richard the Third as a vacant possession and peopled it with beings who have indeed historic names, but whose attributed descriptions and actions are, for the most part, the mere imaginings of the bard.' (Or, more often, the mere imaginings of others.)

Not for nothing was Miss Halsted also the author of *Obligations of Literature to the Mothers of England*. Conscientiously she proceeded to examine every document which she could uncover, published or unpublished, and the number of those cited in her footnotes bears witness to her diligence. Most were so inaccessible that 'it is by no means astonishing that they have occasionally escaped the notice of general historians'.

'When brought together and placed in opposition to the statements which have so long and so lamentably passed for history, the results were so convincing that the author felt encouraged to submit them to the public. She was well aware that in so doing she should oppose herself to opinions long and deeply rooted – to a part of our national historical belief, which it is something like heresy to dispute. But, strong in the power of the evidences she has analysed, and in the belief that no prejudice can withstand the truth when fairly and simply displayed, she indulges the hope that, her unwearied research having fortified her with facts, and her own views being supported by those who rank high in literary fame, she may be shielded from the charge either of defective judgment or of presumption in her bold undertaking.'

'The favourable opinion of many literary friends possessed of taste and judgment' is claimed in Miss Halsted's preface, tantalisingly suggesting an early Victorian coterie of Ricardian heretics. The work is dedicated to Viscount Sidmouth, in whom it is said to have excited a warm feeling of interest, but in the politics of his own time Sidmouth was not noted for radical heresies or dissent from traditional views, and he seems an unlikely Ricardian. Starting life as Henry Addington and becoming a friend and associate of William Pitt the younger, he served as prime minister without making much of a mark ('Pitt is to Addington/As London is to Paddington') and then became a staunchly repressive Home Secretary during the Luddite troubles, opposed Catholic emancipation and voted against the 1832 Reform Bill.

Despite her good intentions Miss Halsted's work falls little short of hagiography, as she purposefully rescues King Richard from shallow imputations and weeds from the pages of history the fabulous tales long associated with his memory. She is no admirer of other members of the house of York, seeing no good in Clarence and being severely critical of Edward IV. Their defects are used to highlight Richard's virtues.

Hard-headed modern historians insist that medieval marriages among the aristocracy were strictly business deals: love rarely intruded. Thus Richard and Anne Nevill were good catches for each other in the worldly terms of status and estates. Although they had met in childhood, we have no knowledge of their feelings towards each other. But Caroline Halsted is not to be denied romance: 'Their marriage ultimately, in spite of their separation and the innumerable obstacles that were opposed to it from all quarters, warrants the assumption that Richard at least was early attached to his future bride, and justifies the inference likewise that the attachment was mutual.'

When Clarence, who had married her elder sister, hid Anne to prevent the marriage and the division of the Warwick estates, Richard – if we can believe the Croyland chronicler – 'discovered the maiden in the attire of a kitchen maid in London'. Did this ruthless tyrant of tradition take advantage of her situation and compel her by force or stratagem to become his wife? No; he behaved strictly according to Victorian etiquette, escorting her to sanctuary in St Martin's and then 'openly and honourably' seeking the king's consent to the marriage. 'The most imaginative mind could scarcely have desired a hero of romance to act a nobler and more chivalrous part, one more dignified towards the object of his attachment, one more honourable to himself, more straight-forward, more worthy of his hitherto irreproachable career.' Yet it must be added that his conduct was also sensible and in his own best interests.

Caroline Halsted's hyperbole may be derided, but her premises were well founded and her courage undeniable. Armed with some new but scarcely conclusive evidence and little other support, she launched a full frontal assault on bardolatry in a literary equivalent of Richard's charge against superior forces at Bosworth: 'A few years since it would have been thought little less than sacrilege to impugn the statements of England's mighty dramatist.' Although the spirit of research had weakened the influence of mere tradition, 'yet is the lofty position of the bard of Avon so inseparably interwoven with national pride and national affection that the necessity of making apparent how much his masterly pen was misled by corrupt authorities is a task from which a daring hand might shrink.' But not Miss Halsted's.

Her principles did not permit her to approve Richard's assumption of the crown. On 15 June 1483 'only one short week remained in which to aim at sovereignty or to sink back into the position of a subject. Richard, in an evil hour, yielded to the worldliness of a corrupt age and a pernicious education; and by this dereliction of moral and religious duty he cast from him the glory of being held up to the admiration of posterity as an example of rigid virtue and self-denial, instead of being chronicled as an usurper and the slave of his ungovernable ambition.'

Not that there was any validity in the chroniclers' charge of usurpation. 'For upwards of four centuries he has been designated as an usurper; but has consideration ever been duly bestowed on the literal acceptation of the term or of its application to this monarch?' Once the charge of illegitimacy had led to Edward V's deposition, the throne became vacant and Richard was invited to fill it by due process of law. 'Hereditary succession to the crown at this period of English history was but feebly recognised, and the right of parliament to depose one monarch and elevate another had been admitted, not only in the previous reign of Edward IV . . . but also in the case of Edward III and Henry IV.'

More than fifty pages are devoted to a determined attempt to 'unravel the tangled web of falsehood and deceit' in which the fate of Edward V and his brother is enveloped – a point which had hitherto 'baffled effectually the labours of the antiquary, the historian and the philosopher'. Much is made of Polydore Vergil's statement that it was generally reported and believed that the boys were still alive during Henry VII's reign, secretly conveyed away and 'obscurely concealed in some distant region'. Richard's guilt is emphatically non-proven. Although, sadly, 'the mass of mankind are so prone to suspicion that oft repeated and long received accusations will at length prevail', 'no more substantial basis even for the accusation exists than the envenomed shaft of political malice'.

When Carlyle and Macaulay expressed their disapproval of female historians it was probably another bluestocking they had in mind. In collaboration with her sister Elizabeth, Agnes Strickland (1796–1874) wrote *Historical Tales of Illustrious British Children* (1833), which ran to three editions, and *Tales and Stories from History* (1836), whose popularity was such that a ninth edition was being called for in 1870. But her best-known and most enduring work, still be found in half-morocco sets on the shelves of antiquarian booksellers, is *Lives of the Queens of*

England (1840) in twelve octavo volumes, dedicated by gracious permission to the young Queen Victoria. This was succeeded by *Lives of the Queens of Scotland and English Princesses connected with the Royal Succession of Great Britain* (1859) and *Lives of the Bachelor Kings of England* (1861).

Like Caroline Halsted and unlike the contemporary Ladies of Quality who wrote scandalous fiction, the Misses Strickland were serious writers, painstaking in research, claiming to work from 'official records and other authentic documents, private as well as public'. They were, however, no specialists and not of a mind to discard tradition, which was their stock in trade. The biography of Richard III's queen in *Lives of the Queens of England* was contributed by Elizabeth, the shy sister whose share in the authorship went unacknowledged. To her the long-suffering Anne of Warwick's husband was a venomous hunchback with a temper as disagreeable as his person. More's story of his withered arm 'proves malformation in his figure'.

After the death of her son 'maternal sorrow put an end to the existence of the broken-hearted queen, who expired of a decay slow enough to acquit her husband of the charge of poisoning her'. Her funeral was 'most pompous and magnificent' and 'she lies interred near the altar at Westminster . . . but no memorial marks the spot where the broken heart of the hapless Anne of Warwick found rest from as much sorrow as could possibly be crowded into the brief span of thirty-one years'. But at least the omission of a memorial was to be remedied: by the Richard III Society a hundred and twenty years later.

The growth of an informed middle class, of popular education and of literacy generally, created a wider but shallow awareness of the past and encouraged an uncritical acceptance of the traditional Richard as the arch-villain of English history. For most, history was tales about the past or, as the brothers Goncourt described it, 'a novel that has been lived'. The most enthralling of those tales was the story of the princes in the Tower and their wicked uncle, and a villainous, scheming Richard duly made his appearance in historical novels such as Bulwer Lytton's *The Last of the Barons* (1843) and *The Woodman* by G. P. R. James (1849). By the time of Mark Twain's *Adventures of Tom Sawyer* (1876) his deformity had become a conversational commonplace among boys on the banks of the

Mississippi, Tom Sawyer remarking casually to Huck Finn on 'that old hump-backed Richard'.

The visible and dramatic proof of villainy to be seen in the Shakespearean performances of the leading actors of the day – the Kembles, Keans, Macreadys and Irvings – was reinforced on canvas. Late in the eighteenth century and throughout the nineteenth Richard became a villain in the world of art. The popularity of historical painting focussed on a small number of romantic or tear-jerking episodes in our island story: Edward IV Meets Elizabeth Woodville, the Princes in the Tower, the Death of Mary Queen of Scots and the sacrifice of the child victim, Lady Jane Grey. Of these the most enduring in popularity were the unfortunate princes, in the roles written for them by More and Shakespeare.

Painters who found this tearful subject both congenial and profitable included Samuel Wale, John Opie, Richard Westall, E. M. Ward, James Northcote, Thomas Stothard and C. R. Leslie. Northcote's *The Burial of the Princes in the Tower* was engraved and lives on in a famous Boydell print, but the hardiest survivors from this school of goo are by Delaroche and Millais. A Parisian fellow student of Richard Parkes Bonington, Paul Delaroche was responsible for *Flora Macdonald succouring the Young Pretender* (c. 1825), *Cromwell gazing at the body of Charles I* (1831) and *The Execution of Lady Jane Grey* (1834). His *Edward V and the Duke of York in the Tower* (1830) is still on public view in Paris and London, the original in the Louvre, a smaller version in the Wallace Collection.

Sir John Everett Millais (1829–96) is said to have been short on genius, but possessed of great talent and a sound commercial sense. Starting as a Pre-Raphaelite, he became recognised as the best of the Victorian anecdotal painters and ended his career as President of the Royal Academy. Today he is remembered for *Christ in the House of his Parents* and *Bubbles*, *The Order of Release* and *The Blind Girl*, but above all for *The Princes in the Tower* (1878) which, in Dr Roy Strong's judgment, epitomises the Victorian obsession with violated childhood.

These beautiful boys, their pale faces and long fair hair contrasting with sepulchrally black velvet suits, stand apprehensively hand in hand awaiting a fate which they can only suspect but the viewer knows all too well. Is that a shadow on the wall above the creepy stone stairs winding out of sight behind them? Egham, Surrey, is well worth a visit to view the original of this haunting picture. It hangs in the gallery of Royal Holloway College and, much reproduced, will doubtless do Richard III's reputation no good for several more centuries. Yet, as Henry Thomas Buckle observed in his *History of Civilisation in England* (1857), 'there must always be a connection between the way in which men contemplate the past and the way in which they contemplate the present'. It is as relevant to relate this thought to Millais as to More and Shakespeare, and to remember that, despite the spell of Millais' magic, his princes tell us more about the 1870s than the 1480s.

Musically the spin-off from the Tudor saga has been surprisingly meagre. In 1857/58 the Czech composer, Smetana, wrote his symphonic poem, *Richard III*, which contains a (*maestoso quasi andante*) passage memorably illustrating the Shakespeareanly misshapen monarch's limp. The only operatic *Richard III* is not, alas, the work of Verdi. It was written by the barely known French composer, Salvayre (1847–1916), and performed only twice: once at St Petersburg in Italian in 1883 (the year of composition) and once at Nice in its original French in 1891. According to Winton Dean's *Shakespeare in the Opera House*, it 'begins with a funeral march followed by a drunken orgy, and ends with Richard interrupting Henry VII's coronation by whipping the crown off his head and falling dead on the steps of Leicester Cathedral. The numerous choruses include large formations of gipsies, huntsmen, clergymen, Welshmen and ghosts. . . Perhaps the most startling episode is Richard's attempted marriage to his own niece, which begins with a grand wedding march led by Cardinal Bourchier and four bishops to the tune of *Rule Britannia*.' A less sensational note was struck later in Sir William Walton's *Elegy and March – Richard III* in his music for the Olivier film of Shakespeare's *Richard III* (1956).

As a boy Charles Dickens was introduced to Richard III at the Theatre Royal, Chatham, where he learned 'as from a page of English history, how the wicked king Richard III slept in war-time on a sofa much too short for him, and how fearfully his conscience troubled his boots'. Seated in a box on the stage, the young Dickens's heart leapt with terror as Richard backed against it in the final battle scene while struggling for life against the virtuous Richmond.

Later, in *A Child's History of England*, first published in instalments in *Household Words* during the early 1850s, Dickens merely copied the traditional account of Richard's accession and reign, adding some melodramatic flourishes of his own. Tyrell (perhaps the shadow in Millais' picture) 'went creeping, creeping, like a guilty villain as he was, up the dark stone winding stairs and along the dark stone passages. . .' When Richard decided to marry his niece, Elizabeth, he 'took good care' that his wife Anne should die. Richard, however, was 'not ill-looking', and at Bosworth, as at Chatham, 'he was as brave as he was wicked'. *A Child's History* was mostly borrowed from Thomas Keightley's two-volume *History of England* (1837–39), a popular educational work which was itself largely derived from Lingard's multi-volume *History*, purged of popish proclivities.

John Jesse in his otherwise sympathetic *Memoirs of King Richard the Third*, published in 1862, is another who cannot bring himself to question More's veracity. 'It is impossible to believe that the great and upright Lord Chancellor – he who suffered martyrdom for the sake of religion – would knowingly and willingly falsify historical truth.' Jesse therefore has a split personality on his hands, and one chapter heading reads: The Greatness and the Sin of Richard of Gloucester. 'To us Richard figures, at two different points of his life, as a different and distinct person. As much as the Diana of the Greeks differed from the Astarte of the Carthaginians, and as the Satan of Milton differs from the cloven-footed bugbear of the nursery. . .'

The most popular and influential historical work of the second half of the nineteenth century was *A Short History of the English People* by John Richard Green, first published in 1874 and reprinted no fewer than twenty-two times during the succeeding twenty-five years. Today it endures among the immovable stock of every second-hand bookseller. An Oxford graduate and associate of Freeman and Stubbs, Green was nevertheless a spare-time historian belonging to no school of thought but his own. A passionate high churchman, he enjoyed the leisure to write through his appointment to the sinecure of librarian at Lambeth Palace. From that moral vantage point he was able to look down on the fifteenth century with distaste: 'There are few periods in our annals from which we turn with such weariness and disgust as from the Wars of the Roses'. Both Edward IV and Richard III were 'ruthless and subtle'. Edward IV's sons were 'murdered, as was alleged, by their uncle's order'.

Yet in his account of Richard's legislation Green broke part of the mould of tradition by deploying, for the first time to a wide public, the arguments which suggested that, although a bad man, Richard might be judged a good king. In response to a petition from the citizens of London begging for justice, relief from oppression, and liberty under the law: 'Richard met the appeal by again convoking parliament, which, as we have seen, had been all but discontinued under Edward, and by sweeping measures of reform. In the one session of his brief reign the practice of extorting money by "benevolences" was declared illegal, while grants of pardons and remission of forfeitures reversed in some measure the policy of terror by which Edward at once held the country in awe and filled his treasury. Numerous statutes broke the slumbers of parliamentary legislation. A series of mercantile enactments strove to protect the growing interests of English commerce. The king's love of literature showed itself in the provision that no statutes should act as a hindrance "to any artificer or merchant stranger, of what nation or country he be, for bringing unto this realm or selling by retail or otherwise of any manner of books, written or imprinted". His prohibition of the iniquitous seizure of goods before conviction of felony, which had prevailed during Edward's reign, his liberation of the bondmen who still remained unenfranchised on the royal domain, and his religious foundations, show Richard's keen anxiety to purchase a popularity in which the bloody opening of his reign might be forgotten.'

Reverting to traditionalism, Green then appears to accept the allegations of infanticide as true and the enlightened legislation as nothing more than a charade of duplicity. 'But as the news of the royal children's murder slowly spread, the most pitiless stood aghast at this crowning deed of blood. The pretence of constitutional rule, too, was soon thrown off, and a levy of benevolences in defiance of the statute which had just been passed awoke general indignation.'

In another influential work, *The Constitutional History of England* (1878), William Stubbs, Bishop of Oxford, follows the Green line of qualified condemnation, while confessing that the materials for a clear delineation of Richard's character, long 'a favourite topic for theory and for paradox', are 'very scanty'. Of the princes he writes: 'How long the boys lived in captivity and how they died is a matter on which legend and conjecture have been rife with no approach to certainty. Most men believed, and still believe, that they died a violent death by their uncle's order.'

Stubb's verdict is a stern moral judgment leavened with a touch of Christian understanding, as befitted a Victorian bishop. 'There can however be little doubt of his great ability, of his clear knowledge of the policy which under ordinary circumstances would have secured his throne, and of the force and energy of will which, put to a righteous use, might have made for him a great name. The popularity which he had won before his accession, in Yorkshire especially, where there was no love for the house of York before, proves that he was not without the gifts which gained for Edward IV the lifelong support of the nation. The craft and unscrupulousness with which he carried into effect his great adventure are not more remarkable than the policy and the constitutional inventiveness with which he concealed the several steps of his progress. Brave, cunning, resolute, clear-sighted, bound by no ties of love or gratitude, amenable to no instincts of mercy or kindness, Richard III yet owes the general condemnation, with which his life and his reign have been visited, to the fact that he left none behind him whose duty or whose care it was to attempt his vindication.'

In *The Unpopular King* (1855), a two-volume revisionist work, Alfred O. Legge (author also of *The Temporal Power of the Papacy* and a Life of Pius IX) evades the problem of More's veracity by accepting Buck's view that 'Dr Morton made the book and Master More set it forth' – and, having set it forth, chose not to publish it. Legge dismisses the work which even Hume took for holy writ as no more than an historical romance written by one 'whose judgment was blinded by party hatred'. History sinks into romance also 'when it dogmatises upon the unrecorded motives of its heroes'. Here the fire-power of Victorian moralising is switched from Richard himself and redirected towards those chroniclers who libelled him.

To Legge, Richard rather than Edward was the victor of Barnet and Tewkesbury, and it is impossible that he murdered his brother's sons. Ratcliffe or Catesby is the likely culprit, possibly suborned by Buckingham. 'What more likely than that one of these creatures should, during the king's progress to York, anticipate his supposed wishes and make away with the royal princes either by death or by transportation? Such a plan would receive powerful support in London and would probably be connived at by Buckingham.'

Although transportation overseas by courtesy of Richard's supporters might seem unlikely, Legge believes that 'all the laws of evidence lend greater probability' to the claims of Perkin Warbeck than to 'the tradition that Shakespeare has imperishably enshrined in the heart of Christendom'. But his arguments failed to convince, Gairdner observing tartly that 'Mr Legge is not very careful in the use of his evidences'.

Sir James Ramsay (1832–1915), tenth holder of a Scottish baronetcy, was an Oxford don until disqualified by marriage – forced to choose between Christ Church and an heir. Tradition is likely to be safe in the hands of tenth baronets, and Ramsay's two-volume *Lancaster and York* (1892), the first substantial general history of the period 1399–1485, offers the clearest evidence that marauding revisionists had been repulsed and the Richard of the saga had survived the century, wounded but indomitable (and living, mostly, in Oxford, not all of whose causes are lost).

Influenced by Gairdner and Stubbs, Sir James inherited a low opinion of Richard III and accepted More's story of the murder of the princes with no ifs or buts, as though proven fact. 'We must record a cruel mandate sent to the Tower of London by the trusty hand of Sir James Tyrell ... the two were smothered in their beds by night'. After this it is less surprising to find even Molinet cited as an authority. Richard's accession evokes grudging admiration for a guileful hypocrite, who was clever enough to follow precedents set by his brother in August 1461.

Ramsay is also a 'guilt by association' historian. After describing Richard's offer of 'the obedience by the kings of

England of old, due and accustomed' to the new Pope, Innocent VIII, in February 1484, he adds darkly: 'The reader need not be reminded that the "obedience" originated with John, the murderer of his nephew Arthur.' His verdict after Bosworth is that 'the House of York fell as much from the repugnance excited by the lives and conduct of its sons as for any definite offences against the nation'. Lest this should be interpreted as implying any merit in Richard as a ruler, the work concludes with a comprehensive condemnation: 'Yorkist and Lancastrian alike could join in execrating the memory of the treacherous Richard Crouchback.' Moral certitude in the writing of history was a grand feature of the high Victorian age.

The nineteenth, it must be concluded, was a disappointing century for Richard's reputation. The argument was no longer wholly one-sided, but Walpole and his followers had been the harbingers of what proved a false dawn of rehabilitation. The hammer of the revisionists, the man more responsible than any other for their defeat in an era of new knowledge and improving scholarship, was another Scotsman – one who devoted a long lifetime to the study of fifteenth-century England and whose erudition and moral certitude prevailed. His name was James Gairdner.

21

Gairdner Versus Markham

On 26 January 1857 the Master of the Rolls submitted to the Treasury a proposal for the publication of material relating to the history of England from the invasion of the Romans to the reign of Henry VII, and a new cache of documentary treasure began to be opened for the advancement of scholarship. Among the resulting publications were two volumes of *Letters and Papers Illustrative of the Reigns of Richard III and Henry VII*, edited by James Gairdner, who proceeded to demonstrate that the availability and study of new sources would not necessarily bring to Richard III's reputation the benefits of reassessment proclaimed by Caroline Halsted.

Gairdner (1823–1912) was not a university man. After a private education in Edinburgh he worked in the Public Record Office in London for forty-seven years, winning acclaim as an editor of records and becoming the leading specialist on the fifteenth century. Today he is best known for his edition of *The Paston Letters* (1872–75) and his *Life and Reign of Richard III* (1878). But although a patient scholar and good narrative historian, according to a colleague: 'in treating of characters and motives he is less convincing, and to some readers seems to let a natural bias in favour of constituted authority influence his judgment of documentary evidence'.

This bias has been remarked upon also by A. R. Myers, who noted that Gairdner suffered a conversion to Anglo-Catholicism in 1862, so that a new-found respect for tradition made his Preface to Volume II of *Letters and Papers* (1863) less favourable to Richard III than his Preface to Volume I (1861). In Volume II he wrote dismissively of revisionists, among whom he had once numbered himself: 'It is true that much curious argument and research have been employed by able writers to bespeak a more charitable judgment of Richard III; but it is easier to cast doubts on a number of separate facts than to weave anew the web of history. The testimony to Richard's crimes is scanty; but so is the testimony to every occurrence of the period.'

Gairdner returns to this scanty point in his *Life and Reign of Richard III* fifteen years later. 'The scantiness of contemporary evidences and the prejudices of original authorities may be admitted as reasons for doubting isolated facts, but can hardly be expected to weaken the conviction – derived from Shakespeare and tradition as much as from anything else – that Richard was indeed cruel and unnatural beyond the ordinary measure, even of those violent and ferocious times.' Indeed 'he left such a reputation behind him that even his birth was said to have proclaimed him a monster'. The alleged monstrosities are then itemised – two years in the womb, born feet foremost, teeth already in the jaw, and shoulder-length hair – with no suggestion of disbelief. Shakespeare, it seems, was still to be respected as an authoritative historical source.

In his role as Richard's latest character assassin Gairdner is at his most self-revealing in his verdict on responsibility for the death of the Lancastrian Prince of Wales at Tewkesbury. He first admits that contemporary sources attach no responsibility to Richard, then notes the 'tradition of later times that Gloucester tarnished the glory he had won that day by butchering' the prince 'in cold blood after the battle', and comments: 'The story may be doubted as resting on very slender testimony, and that not strictly contemporary; nevertheless it cannot be safely pronounced apocryphal'. Yet even this is considered to let Richard off too lightly, and Gairdner concludes: 'But if the murder of Prince Edward was in any degree attributable to Richard, it was doubtless the first of a long catalogue of crimes, each of which rests by itself on slender testimony enough, though any one of them, being admitted, lends greater credit to the others. From this point of view I must frankly own that it strikes me as not at all improbable that Richard was a murderer at nineteen. Whoever would investigate the morbid anatomy of guilt. . .'

Richard is generally credited with rescuing his mother-in-law, the widowed Countess of Warwick, from sanctuary and giving her a home, but Gairdner will have none of this: for him even John Rous is an authority to be respected. 'Rous, the Warwick antiquary, who lived at the time, distinctly says she fled to Richard for refuge, and that he imprisoned her for life.'

Was Richard instrumental in the death of Clarence? 'Everyone knows that this is the view taken by Shakespeare, whose judgment on any point it is certainly impossible to ignore,' even though 'the colouring could not but be heightened to satisfy the exigences of dramatic art'. Similarly, with More: 'The portrait drawn of Richard by Sir Thomas, though true in the main, is highly coloured, and is perhaps not without a little exaggeration in itself.' So, on grounds of colouring, there is an accquittal on this charge: 'Gloucester had not yet lifted up his hand against his own flesh and blood'. Moreover, at that time he obtained licences to found two religious houses in the north (at Barnard Castle and Middleham), which suggests that he 'was not even yet a hardened criminal'.

Another point in Richard's favour is conceded in Gairdner's description of the struggle for power after Edward IV's death: 'It must not, however, be too readily presumed that there was no foundation at all for Richard's charge of conspiracy against the queen and her relations. Polydore Vergil, a writer who cannot be suspected of any design to palliate the Protector's misdeeds, expressly states that an act of sudden violence was at this time contemplated, in order to liberate the young king from his uncle's control.'

According to Gairdner the dramatic events of 13 June – the council meeting and Hastings' execution – took place exactly as described by More and Shakespeare: 'Strange as the story is, we have every reason to believe that the facts are strictly true.' The account is that of Cardinal Morton, in whose veracity Gairdner shows a touching faith: 'The colouring is therefore that of a partisan, though the facts, no doubt, are those of a truthful reporter.' No doubt fifteenth-century cardinals could not tell a lie. Morton, so Gairdner judged, was 'undoubtedly a statesman of high integrity'.

The executions of Hastings in London and of Rivers and two others in Yorkshire, taken together with Richard's summons of troops from the north to secure his position in the capital, are said to constitute 'a reign of terror'. 'For with us,' wrote Simon Stallworth in London to Sir William Stonor in Oxfordshire on 21 June, 'there is much trouble, and every man doubts the other'. This is evidence of uncertainty and apprehension, but the high colouring of some of Gairdner's authorities seems to have been infectious. Mancini estimated that Richard and Buckingham entered London with no more than 500 retainers between them, and the armed northerners, estimated by Fabyan at 4,000, did not reach the capital until the beginning of July and went home immediately after the coronation on the sixth, noted for nothing except the contempt of Londoners at their antiquated equipment and rusty armour. This would seem to constitute the least bloody and terrifying reign of terror in history.

About Richard as a usurper Gairdner is surprisingly unsure. 'A usurpation it certainly was in fact. . . Yet, in point of form, one might almost look upon it as a constitutional election. . . Indeed, it was rather a declaration of inherent right to the crown, first by the council of the realm, then by the city, and afterwards by parliament – proceedings much more regular and punctilious than had been observed in the case of Edward IV . . . the nation tacitly concurred.'

But then 'the news that the deposed king and his brother had been assassinated was spread with horror and amazement through the land. . . To many the tale seemed too cruel to be untrue.' 'There have been writers in modern days who have shown plausible grounds for doubting that the murder really took place,' but after rehearsing their objections and his objections to their objections Gairdner reaches the conclusion that 'the dreadful deed was done'. With the discovery of the princes' bones 'at last the truth came out'.

This *Richard III* was accepted as the definitive biography for three-quarters of a century. The prestige of the author's reputation as a scholar bolstered the cause of full-blooded traditionalism just when it was sagging. The general public takes its history from the general historian; the general historian gathers his from the specialist. Thus Gairdner's influence was pervasive: all the widely read late-Victorian authors of general histories of England – Green, Stubbs, Ramsay, Oman – took their cue from him. In the 1930s he was still, to Lawrence ('bones') Tanner, 'the chief modern authority on the reign'.

Yet leaning so heavily, as it does, on belief in the truthfulness of the fictions of More and Shakespeare, Gairdner's work is of more interest today for study of the workings of the author's mind. As a young man he had fallen under the influence of Walpole's *Historic Doubts*, begun to doubt whether Richard was really a tyrant at all and 'more than doubted' his involvement in the death of his nephews. Once convinced of Richard's innocence of the principal crime alleged against him, he could see how slender and unsatisfactory was the evidence supporting the other charges. This, though, was all youthful folly. 'I feel quite ashamed,' he wrote in the Preface to his *Richard III*, 'to think how I mused over this subject long ago, wasting a great deal of time, ink and paper, in fruitless efforts to satisfy even my own mind that traditional black was real historical white, or at worst a kind of grey.'

What then was the precise nature of Gairdner's conversion? Not, it transpires, a documentary revelation. It was simply that experience had convinced him of the untruth of Buckle's proposition that a certain sceptical tendency is essential to the discovery of truth. In one telling phrase he confesses all: 'I cannot but think the sceptical spirit a most fatal one in history.' Gairdner had come to believe that if doubts about historical facts were 'to be of any value as the avenue to new truths, they must lead to a complete reconsideration of very many things. . . The history of one particular epoch should be rewritten. . . The new version of the story should exhibit a certain moral harmony with the facts both of subsequent times and of the times preceding'. Otherwise, he concluded, traditional views of history cannot be successfully set aside. Richard's reputation, it is apparent, had fallen victim to a rigidly held philosophy which few would now embrace.

The manifest merits of Gairdner's work made the damage to Richard's reputation all the greater. It was evident that no one before him had enjoyed so deep a knowledge of the subject, and his learning was lucidly presented. The bias against Richard was modified by occasional judgments in his favour and passages setting out some good deeds and qualities, so that an appearance of impartiality was preserved: 'The prevailing notion of Richard III, indeed, is of a cold, deeply politic, scheming and calculating villain. But I confess I am not satisfied of the justice of such a view.' (Rather, Richard was 'headstrong' and 'reckless'.) The phrase 'a close and secret, a tyrannical and often a most cruel government' is applied, not to Richard's regime, but to that of the Tudors who allegedly rescued England from him.

Fortunately for Richard's good name, modern historians are still imbued with scepticism and less wedded to theories of moral harmony in historiography. To Charles Ross, Gairdner was 'a careful scholar' with 'an excessive trust in the value of tradition'. To Kendall, Gairdner's *Richard III* 'reveals an historian of great eminence, integrity and industry desperately wrestling in public to reconcile the opposing forces of his scholarly conscientiousness and his emotional predispositions. Gairdner attempts to make use of all the new fifteenth-century source material opened up by the researches of the nineteenth century and still to maintain the essential validity of the Tudor myth. It is a rather painful spectacle – a great historian beginning with a closed tradition instead of an open mind.'

Gairdner provides an object lesson and cautionary tale for all students of history. Meticulousness in the excavation and marshalling of facts affords no assurance against eccentricity of judgment, only a guarantee that any such judgment will be received with more respect than may be warranted. This historian assumed the high moral tone of the high Victorian age, but betrayed his integrity in adopting the role of prosecuting counsel, even lending the great weight of his scholarship to the absurd end of rehabilitating Shakespeare as an historical source.

His main adversary was a very different kind of person: no specialist, no academic even; as much a travelled man of action as Gairdner was a reclusive scholar; his interests and talents as wide as Gairdner's were narrow. This bold new Walpole who arose towards the end of the nineteenth century to bring aid and comfort to the revisionists and be savaged by the traditionalists was a romantic enthusiast typical of many who embrace the Ricardian cause, but his life was wholly original. He was the greatest geographer of his time, but the bust which stands outside the Royal Geographical Society's headquarters in Kensington Gore commemorates him as the historian of Peru.

Sir Clements Markham was born of clerical stock at Stilling-fleet in the East Riding of Yorkshire in 1830. His great-grandfather had been Archbishop of York, and his father was the vicar of Stillingfleet and a canon of Windsor. Markham wrote a History of England at the age of ten, and his proud father had twenty copies printed (in small octavo) and leather bound. An early friend, at school in Cheam, was a boy who was to become one of the most famous of Victorian historians, E. A. Freeman. Markham then went on to Westminster, but left early to join the Royal Navy, sailing for South America and the Pacific as a naval cadet at the age of fourteen and returning as a midshipman after nearly four years and more than 80,000 miles.

Relations with his superior officers were not always smooth. Markham was touchy and grew to resent the injustices of harsh and arbitrary naval discipline. His rebellious nature found a just cause in Tahiti where, despite the official British policy of non-intervention, he developed a passionate partisanship for the Tahitians rebelling against French rule.

He returned home enthused with a passion for geography and exploration. His next voyage took him to the Mediterra-nean and he later sailed in the expedition which was sent to Baffin Bay to search (in vain) for Sir John Franklyn, the Arctic explorer lost in discovering the North West Passage. He then resigned from the Navy and, resisting his father's wishes to send him to Oxford, returned to Peru, whose history and archeo-logical remains fascinated him. There he made a hazardous expedition from the coast to the remote Inca mountain site of Cuzco.

Back in England he joined the India Office, but soon re-turned to Peru, this time to collect cinchona plants for trans-plantation to India. Before this enterprise by Markham the border areas between Peru and Bolivia enjoyed a monopoly of the world supply of quinine, and he brought the plants back to England in the face of almost insuperable natural obstacles and fierce hostility from the local population. Since the plants required expert care if they were to survive the journey and

Markham had achieved this despite the climatic changes between Peru and England, he was sent on with them and supervised their planting in the Nilgiri hills in southern India. There they took root, and the ready availability of quinine in the East thereafter was due to Markham's determination and skill.

In 1863 he began what was to be a 25-year stretch of service as Honorary Secretary of the Royal Geographical Society, subsequently serving for twelve years as President until he resigned in 1905 at the age of 75. During this period he accompanied the Indian Army on its expedition to Magdala to fight the Abyssinian war – officially as geographer to the expedition, but acting also as naturalist and historian. At home he took the initiative in founding schools of geography at Oxford and Cambridge and in promoting the Arctic Expedition of 1875/76. In 1861 he became a Fellow of the Royal Society of Antiquaries and in 1873 he became a Fellow of the Royal Society.

With a characteristic Victorian gluttony for work, Markham did not allow all this activity to interfere with his writing, and the wide range of his historical works included: *History of the Markham Family* (1854), *Cuzco and Lima* (a history of the Incas) (1856), *The Abyssinian Expedition* (1869), *Life of the Great Lord Halifax* (1870), *A General Sketch of the History of Persia* (1874), *Fifty Years Work of the Royal Geographical Society* (1881), *The Fighting Veres* (1888), *Life of John Davis the Navigator 1550–1605* (1889), *History of Peru* (1892), *Life of Christopher Columbus* (1892), *Life of Richard III* (1906), *Life of Edward VI* (1907), *The Incas of Peru* (1910) and *The Conquest of New Granada* (1912).

Markham was a persistent campaigner too. According to his biographer (A. H. Markham), he was not the man to take no for an answer, especially when his heart was set on righting a wrong. A young seaman sentenced to five years' penal servitude for striking a gunner's mate (his superior officer) attracted his sympathy. He wrote to the Admiralty and was rebuffed, approached the Home Secretary without success, and then wrote to every member of parliament and to the press demanding justice. The climax of his campaign was the organisation of a public petition to the prime minister, after which the authorities at last surrendered and the seaman was released.

His efforts on behalf of Richard III's reputation were just as determined and sustained. The compilation of his Life is said by his biographer to have 'caused him, probably, greater labour and research than any other work he had written. He left no stone unturned in his efforts to arrive at the true state of affairs during that monarch's reign; for he would never believe that the king's character was such as Shakespeare had assigned to him. He probed and sifted every incident connected with the king. . . He would write and rewrite chapters already completed in order to make them as faithful as possible. . . He studied very carefully all the chronicles relating to the subject. . . He consulted the most eminent historians in England, most of whom were inclined to agree with him, many urging him very strongly to proceed with the investigations and to give them publicity.'

After nine years' work on the book he decided not to publish it, preferring to test its conclusions through the publication of a long article in the *English Historical Review*. His object was to provoke criticism, and in this he was not disappointed. The article raised a most satisfactory furore in historical circles and he replied with relish to every critic.

Towards the end of his life Markham became widely recognised and honoured as the most eminent living authority on geographical science. He became a Knight Commander of the Bath, Cambridge awarded him an Hon. LLD, and Leeds made this 'true son of Yorkshire' a Doctor of Science, acknowledging his enthusiasm, tenacity and versatility.

If Peru was his first love, and Richard III his second, his last was Polar exploration. In 1901 he promoted a successful expedition to the Antarctic, raising funds (£93,000), building the *Discovery*, and selecting Scott as leader. He became godfather to Scott's son (the naturalist and painter), who was christened Peter Markham, and Scott's death on the second expedition was a personal blow. He himself died in his bed, but not without drama, setting fire to the bedclothes while reading a book in Old Portuguese.

Driven throughout his life by what the Chancellor of Leeds University described as 'an ambition directed to the noblest ends', Markham proved a redoubtable champion of Richard III. A vigorous and painstaking case for the defence, his Life remains in print and read today. Its full title is *Richard III: His Life & Character Reviewed in the Light of Recent Research*, and the opening sentences of the Preface run: 'There are periods of history when the greatest caution is called for in accepting statements put forward by a dominant faction. Very early in my life I came to the conclusion that the period which witnessed the change of dynasties from Plantagenet to Tudor was one of these. The caricature of the last Plantagenet king was too grotesque, and too grossly opposed to his character derived from official records. The stories were an outrage on commonsense. I studied the subject at intervals for many years, and in the course of my researches I found that I more or less shared my doubts with every author of repute who had studied the subject for the last three centuries, except Hume and Lingard. My own conclusions are that Richard III must be acquitted on all the counts of the indictment.'

The first part of the book deals with Richard III's life and times, the second with the accusations made against him. One chapter acquits him of the murder of the princes, another convicts Henry. The last is a full-scale attack on the views of James Gairdner. Markham agues that much of the traditional story of the death of the princes is true, except that the murder was committed at the instigation, not of Richard III in the autumn of 1483, but of Henry VII between mid-June and mid-July in 1486, and he insists that the *History of King Richard III* 'erroneously attributed to Sir Thomas More' was, in fact, written by Richard's inveterate enemy, Archbishop Morton. Such views invited and precipitated a titanic clash with Gairdner, who was forced to make 'some corrections and additions' in a revised edition of his Life (1898), but neither of Markham's major propositions has won general acceptance.

Markham succeeded, nevertheless, in removing some of 'the accumulated garbage and filth of centuries of calumny' for which the Tudor chroniclers were responsible. 'The reckless profusion of abuse was due to the complete licence of the traducers. No one could appear for the accused. The brave young king was dead, his body subjected to cowardly insults, his friends proscribed, his people silenced. Calumny was triumphant and unchecked. Yet there was method and system in the scheme of the Tudor writers. Their accusations were all intended to lead up to a belief in the dead king's guilt with regard to one central crime. If he was to be deformed, if he was to be an assassin at the age of eighteen, the murderer of his brother and his wife, a ruthless usurper and tyrant, it was because such a monster would be more likely to commit a crime of which he must be thought to be guilty in the interests of his wily successor' – the murder of the princes.

Gairdner and Markham joined battle in 1891 in the columns of the *English Historical Review*, where much learned and detailed argument could not conceal the fact that both distinguished gentlemen were overstating their case. According to Markham, the murders attributed to Richard were out of character with the good qualities and deeds which Gairdner had conceded. Item by item, he cleared Richard of all charges and pinned the murder of the princes firmly on Henry. According to Gairdner, Richard's character was 'a very black one', whereas Markham's chief villain, Morton, 'has left a very good name behind him'; Richard was guilty of the murder of Henry VI and his son, and 'the common fame' of his murder of the princes meant that 'it was not, and could not be, contradicted' – some of the details of the More/Morton account might be inaccurate, but 'the fact itself was certain . . . everyone knew that the crime had been committed.'

To Gairdner's final magisterial pronouncement that 'to whitewash Richard III is an utterly hopeless task', Markham replied that the process should rather be described as the removal of Tudor mud from his portrait, and that Gairdner had effected some such mud removal himself, but not enough. 'It was his *Life of Richard III*, and the researches it suggested, that convinced me of the king's innocence of the charges brought against him. Whenever a first attempt is made to explode an erroneous belief, the cry is raised that if it is not retained there is an end of all history. Hume, if I remember right, raised this outcry when Horace Walpole suggested that Elizabeth Lucy was not the lady mentioned in Richard's claim to the crown. Mr Gairdner and everyone else who has given attention to the subject know that Walpole was right. Yet history has survived. History will not only survive but will be the better for the expunging of other stories from the same source.'

In attacking Gairdner Markham did not stand alone. A

broadside was fired from the unexpected direction of Boston, Massachusetts, where Senator Henry Cabot Lodge (historian and politician friend of President Theodore Roosevelt) brooded on the matter and then, in 1897, loosed off in the pages of *Scribner's Magazine*. With Shakespeare's play always on the stage, he pointed out, Richard III was the best-known ruler England ever had, 'familiar to the shoeblack and the newsboy'. But what was the truth about him?

Lodge noted that Richard reached the crown in a few weeks with no army at his back and 'but trifling opposition'. He became hated by the classes, not the masses, because 'he fought the battle of crown and people against the feudal system of petty tyrants'. 'The real rulers of England were the great nobles' and Lodge saw the Stanleys at Bosworth as heirs to the king-making Warwick. 'If Richard had survived, he would have been the king who stamped out feudalism, brought crown and people together, and opened the door to learning and civilisation.'

On the princes 'the fairest inference is that they were put to death by Richard's order, and in the darkness that covers the whole business an inference is all we have'. That apart, Richard received a clean bill of health from Boston and the guru of the Public Record Office was seen off with a back-handed congratulation. Gairdner, 'a trained historian with the new material before him and completely master of it, has done more for Richard than anyone else. He has . . . undertaken to sustain the traditional and Shakespearean account by the new evidence at his command. . . His failure to make the new and unimpeachable testimony bear out the old case is better for Richard's cause than any defence.'

22

Shakespeare: Part II

Whether Gairdner's defence of tradition was the failure Senator Lodge declared it to be or, as is more generally believed, a resounding success, his influence could not hope to rival that of the original Shakespearean Richard. The briefest of glances at the play in performance (fully surveyed by Julie Hankey in an Introduction to her 1981 edition of the text) will furnish sufficient evidence of the potency of its melodrama.

Awed respect for the perfection of Shakespeare's genius was a late development. During the seventeenth century his plays were adapted by Sir William Davenant, and towards the end of that century his *Richard III* was extensively re-written by Colley Cibber (1671–1757), a successful comedy actor and playwright and a minor poet. Cibber's version, first printed in 1700 and running to at least fifteen editions before his death, was staged at Drury Lane with such success that between 1700 and the 1870s virtually every performance of what was billed as Shakespeare's *Richard III* was, in fact, Cibber's, and this version was still being performed as recently as 1930 in the United States without acknowledgment of the adaptation.

Cibber's purpose, it was alleged, was to write himself a dominant role in which he could rant, strut and mince, whine, bellow and grunt, and indulge in all 'the distorted heavings of an unjointed caterpillar' without competition from the rest of the cast. The parts of Edward IV, Clarence, Hastings and Queen Margaret were all written out, and with them more than two-thirds of Shakespeare's lines disappeared. Little more than a thousand remaining, two hundred of them imported from other Shakespeare plays, Cibber compensated for the loss by adding more than a thousand of his own.

These new passages included seven soliloquies, containing blood-chilling couplets such as:

> I'll climb betimes without Remorse or Dread,
> And my first step shall be on Henry's Head.

and

> Hark! the Murder's doing; Princes farewell,
> To me there's Musick in your Passing-Bell.

Cibber introduced, too, what became the second most famous line in the play – 'Off with his head! So much for Buckingham!' – echoed by Lewis Carroll's Queen of Hearts and retained in Olivier's film. When he had done with it, the title role was left with forty per cent of the lines. It had become a part for an egomaniac; which was the reason for its popularity among actors, Bernard Shaw was later to observe.

Cibber out-Burbaged Burbage, playing the role triumphantly over a period of thirty-nine years. Making such an absolute villain as his Richard credible was no problem for him. He simply abandoned credibility and proved conclusively that the paying customers did not want it. The critics, however, were less appreciative, and his appointment to the poet laureateship was greeted with a lampoon (said to have been written by Alexander Pope):

> In merry old England it once was a rule
> The king had his poet and also his fool:
> But now we're so frugal, I'd have you to know it,
> That Cibber can serve both for fool and for poet.

David Garrick put a stop to the ranting. That genius of naturalism set out to revolutionise the art of tragic acting, and it was accomplished in his Richard III. He first played the part in 1741, when an elderly Pope came up from Twickenham to see the performance and pronounced afterwards that the young man would have no competitor. As had happened with Burbage and with Cibber, Garrick and Richard III became inseparable in the public imagination. After thirty-five years he chose the role of Richard to close his brilliant career at Drury Lane with a final farewell performance. Fanny Burney saw him in the part in 1772, a few years earlier, and recorded in her diary that, after his display of heroism in the second half of the play, 'the applause he met with exceeds all belief of the absent. I thought at the end they would have torn the house down: our seats shook under us.'

This success, it should be noted, was achieved with Cibber's version of the play, for despite his different style of acting Garrick rejected the suggestion that he should revert to the authentic Shakespearean text. Possibly he was influenced in this by Dr Johnson, who in his edition of Shakespeare (1765) dismissed the play as beneath literary criticism, some parts being 'trifling', others 'shocking' and 'improbable'.

Around the turn of the century the famous Richards were John Philip Kemble and George Frederick Cooke, the latter a specialist in villains, who provoked Charles Lamb into conversion to revisionism: 'I am possessed with an admiration of the genuine Richard, his genius, his mounting spirit, which no consideration of his cruelties can depress.' Kemble and Cooke were both excelled by Edmund Kean, who stunned Byron into credulity: 'By Jove, he is a soul! Life – Nature – truth without exaggeration or diminution.' Truth without exaggeration?

But Kean's awe-inspiring performance did not numb all critical faculties; rather, it stimulated them. In the judgment of Thomas Barnes, later editor of *The Times*: 'The great characteristics of *Richard* are a daring and comprehensive intelligence, which seizes its object with the grasp of a giant – a profound acquaintance with the human soul, which makes him appreciate motives at a glance – a spirit immovably fearless, because how can a mighty being tremble among animals who are but as atoms to his towering superiority?' Hazlitt was similarly impressed by what had by now become Kean's interpretation of Cibber's adaptation of Shakespeare's version of Richard's character: 'towering and lofty; equally impetuous and commanding; haughty, violent and subtle; bold and treacherous; confident in his strength as well as his cunning; raised high by birth, and higher by his talents and crimes; a royal usurper, a princely hypocrite; a tyrant, and a murderer of the house of Plantagenet.'

In this romantic Richard, which had succeeded the Gothic, some saw in Kean's portrayal a likeness to Byron, others a resemblance to the great contemporary hero/villain, Napoleon. Coleridge found his performance like 'reading Shakespeare by flashes of lightning'. However unfortunate its impact on the reputation of the real Richard, Kean's Richard made a valuable contribution to theatrical history. In his first season at Drury Lane the box-office takings averaged more than £500 a night for twenty-five performances and saved the theatre from bankruptcy.

Cooke had broken new ground for a leading actor by playing in America. The transatlantic premiere of *Richard III* had been staged in 1750, and in the United States it was to become the most frequently performed of Shakespeare's plays. It was the first choice of a company formed by the British army in New York during the Revolution, and the first black performance took place in New York at a tea garden called the African Grove in 1821, when Richard was played by a woolly-haired waiter from a neighbouring hotel. Cooke played Richard in Boston, Philadelphia and Providence, as well as New York, before dying of drink. After him an equally stormy rival of Kean, Junius Brutus Booth, took *Richard III* to America, where he played the last act with a furious brutality which alarmed and exhilarated audiences. His legacy of on-stage savagery (accentuated by insobriety and occasional touches of real insanity) passed to his son, John Wilkes Booth, who crossed the line between fantasy and reality to assassinate President Lincoln in a Washington theatre.

In England, meanwhile, the mantle of Garrick and Kean was round the shoulders of William Charles Macready, who made an abortive attempt to restore Shakespeare's unadulterated text. *Richard III* was becoming more and more of a spectator sport. At the St James's theatre in 1851 Richard and Richmond were played by Kate and Ellen Bateman, aged six and eight. The elder Booth had performed Richard on horseback in Philadelphia in 1840, and in London in 1856 Astley's presented in its famous amphitheatre an equestrian extravaganza with White Surrey in the lead. According to the playbills, 'riderless steeds gallop to and fro over the Plain; the gallant charger White Surrey, while bearing his Royal master, Falls dead in the field – the stage is covered with DYING AND DEAD HORSES'.

Rescue from vulgarity arrived in the 1860s and 1870s with the emergence of middle-class audiences. Young ladies and gentlemen queuing on camp stools replaced the fashionable and unrefined. They were waiting to see Henry Irving, whose wholly Shakespearean Richard at long last resurrected was thought 'sublime', although some critics were not so sure. A. B. Walkely thought Irving's production 'an enormously amusing tragedy', the first soliloquy being spoken 'as who should say: Please make no mistake, I am the villain of this play; sit tight, keep your eye on me, and I will see you get your money's worth.' Henry James found it not to be borne: 'The attempt to make real, or even plausible, a loose, violent, straddling romance like *Richard III* . . . only emphasises what is coarse in such a hurly-burly and does nothing for what is fine.'

While realism reigned in London, the romantic approach was still enthroned in New York. In 1920 John Barrymore chose Richard for his Shakespearean debut and was praised by the *New York Times* for conveying 'the titanic quality of a Heaven-challenging giant'.

During the second World War Donald Wolfit played a Richard with some pointed likenesses to Hitler, including a cowlick of hair over the forehead. He was followed on stage, and later on film, by Laurence Olivier, perhaps the greatest and certainly the best remembered of Richards, whose 'unholy magnetism' has cast a shadow over all subsequent aspirants to mastery of the role. Prominent among recent distinguished British actors who have struggled with varying success in an assortment of psychological and analytical Ricardian character studies are Emlyn Williams, John Laurie, Marius Goring, Alec Guinness, Robert Helpmann, Christopher Plummer, Ian Holm, Alan Bates, John Wood, Alan Howard and Edward Woodward. The lesson to be learned from modern Richards, it would appear, is that any endeavour to explain Shakespeare's creation is fated to failure. As a real human being he is beyond explanation.

For this reason the Richard who has made the deepest

impression on audiences since Olivier has been Ramaz Chkhik-
vadze, an actor conveniently bearing a strong facial resemblance to a toad. His memorable performance was seen in
Edinburgh and London (in 1979 and 1980) in a Brecht-style
recreation of Shakespeare in a new idiom, presented by the
Rustaveli company from Soviet Georgia – with added force – in
incomprehensible Georgian.

In America modern theatrical Richards have included Jose
Ferrer, Donald Madden, Michael Moriarty, Al Pacino and
George C. Scott. On film Basil Rathbone will be remembered
as Shakespeareanly villainous in *The Tower of London* (1939),
Vincent Price in its re-make (1962) and Richard Dreyfuss in
The Goodbye Girl (1978) as an actor playing the Shakespearean
role as 'a flaming homosexual' ('society crippled Richard'). A
witty modern parody was David Edgar's *Dick Deterred* (1974),
in which Richard Nixon was portrayed as Richard III, his
Watergate accomplices as other Shakespearean villains and the
Republican and Democrat parties as the two princes in the
Tower, mercilessly strangled with tapes.

Shakespeare has inspired or provoked a number of Ricardian
plays by modern revisionist authors, but none has achieved any
commercial or much critical success. Despite a theatrical
triumph for her treatment of Richard II in *Richard of Bordeaux*,
Gordon Daviot (another pseudonym of Josephine Tey, author
of *The Daughter of Time*) failed to get her *Dickon* professionally
staged. Olivia Wigram's *Sun Of York* enjoyed one acclaimed
professional production (at the Royal Court Theatre in 1955),
and Jack Pulman's *Dickon* an amateur production in 1979.
In America a Broadway production of Stuart Vaughan's *The
Royal Game* and a Delbert Mann film, *The Sun in Splendor*, with
Peter O'Toole as Richard were announced, but came to
nothing.

Of all the innumerable, incalculably damaging representa-
tions of the Shakespearean Richard there can be no doubt that
Laurence Olivier's film has been the most influential. Since its
release in 1956 it has been seen by many thousands of cinema-
goers and many millions of television viewers, and will be seen
by many millions more. When a playwright of genius and an
actor of genius come together to prove him villain before mass
audiences, one might well conclude that there is indeed no hope

for Richard's reputation. Yet Olivier's own attitude is made
explicit in the prologue:

> The Story of England
> like that of many another land
> is an interwoven pattern of
> history and legend.
>
> The history of the world, like
> letters without poetry,
> flowers without perfume
> or thought without imagination,
> would be a dry matter indeed
> without its legends;
> and many of these, though
> scorned by proof a hundred times,
> seem worth preserving for
> their own familiar sakes.

In a radio interview in America at the time of the film's
release Olivier drew particular attention to this prologue, while
praising the play as a work of art however historically untrue.
'What a pity,' he remarked, 'that all legends should die merely
because they're disproved.' But devotees of Shakespeare's
Richard III need entertain no fears on that score.

23

The Inurned Bones

> Let me not burst in ignorance; but tell
> Why thy canonised bones, hearsed in death,
> Have burst their cerements; why the sepulchre,
> Wherein we saw thee quietly inurn'd,
> Hath oped his ponderous and marble jaws,
> To cast thee up again.

In sentiment, if not in detail, the words which Shakespeare wrote for Hamlet to address to his father's ghost might well be applied to the bones which rest in Westminster Abbey today in a marble urn designed for them by a former Surveyor-General of His Majesty's Works, Sir Christopher Wren.

These human remains represent the Ricardian controversy at its most ghoulish and bizarre. Are they the bones of Edward V and his brother, as the Latin inscription records? If they are, do they prove Richard III the murderer of his nephews? Disraeli's father, a friend of Sharon Turner, is one who was in no doubt: 'The personal monster whom More and Shakespeare exhibited has vanished, but the deformity of the revolting parricide was surely revealed in the bones of his infant nephews.' Such confident assertions notwithstanding, those hot for certainty are still bursting in ignorance.

In 1674 workmen digging in or beside the White Tower, the central keep of the Tower of London, uncovered a chest containing the bones of two children. These were thrown on to a rubbish heap but recovered some weeks later, when they were declared to be the bones of the two Yorkist princes. On the orders of the reigning monarch, Charles II, they were later ceremonially inurned and took their place among the royal tombs in Henry VII's chapel.

Seventeenth-century records of the unburial in the Tower precincts are not specific, but stairs are mentioned by several sources and it seems that the bones were found in or near the foundations of a staircase leading out from the White Tower into an adjoining building since removed. Sir Thomas More had reported just such a secret burial of the princes' bodies, so that his account of their murder appeared to vouch for the authenticity of the bones, while the bones in turn served to corroborate his account. In James Gairdner's words: 'We have no doubt, therefore, that the dreadful deed was done'.

In its survey of the abbey church of Westminster the near-contemporary edition of Camden's *Britannia* (published in 1695) records the discovery of the bones in these words. 'Their bodies (though some have written they were put into a leaden coffin and cast into the black deeps near the Thames mouth by Sir Robert Brackenbury's priest) were found July 17, 1674, by some workmen who were employed to take up the steps leading into the chapel of the White Tower, which in all probability was the first and only place they were deposited in. Thence their bones (except some few of them sent to the museum in Oxford) were commanded, anno 1678, by King Charles II to be translated thence, and decently interred here, under a curious altar of black and white marble, with the following epitaph engraven on the pedestal.'

The translation of the epitaph in *Britannia* runs as follows: 'Here under lie interred the remains of Edward V, King of England, and of Richard Duke of York. Which two brothers their uncle Richard, who usurped the crown, shut up in the Tower of London, smothered them with pillows, and ordered them to be dishonourably and secretly buried. Whose long desired and much sought for bones, after above an hundred and ninety years, were found by most certain tokens, deep interred under the rubbish of the stairs that led up into the chapel of the White Tower, on the 17th of July in the year of our Lord 1674. Charles the Second, a most merciful prince, having compassion upon their hard fortune, performed the funeral rites of these unhappy princes, among the tombs of their ancestors, anno dom. 1678, being the 30th of his reign.'

This 'curious altar' is still a favourite sight for the thousands who visit Westminster Abbey every year. The authenticity of the bones is vouched for by the Latin superlative: *indiciis certissimis*, 'most certain tokens', though what these are is not stated or known. Those of the bones which were, less reverently, laid to rest in an Oxford museum are recorded in a seventeenth-century catalogue of the Ashmolean but have long since disappeared: neglected by curators or prized by thieves. In his *Collections* Thomas Hearne records a visit to the Ashmolean on 11 January 1729 to inquire about them: 'Mr Whiteside told me they had somewhere or other such bones very small, particularly the finger bones . . . but Mr Whiteside did not produce them.'

The report of the bodies being dumped in the river is taken from John Rastell's *Pastime of People* (1529) and Hardyng's *Chronicle* (1543). There is no supporting evidence, but it is of interest that the editors of the 1695 *Britannia* should have chosen to repeat it. If the princes were indeed murdered in the Tower, it would have been much easier and more sensible to take the bodies through the Watergate, row downstream and tip them overboard in a lead coffin than risk discovery – at the time or later – by digging a burial place in the heart of the Tower itself.

Westminster Abbey has the status of a royal peculiar, outside the usual episcopal and ecclesiastical jurisdiction, so that today's Dean and Chapter require only the monarch's consent and (assuming that the urn is technically a coffin) permission from the Home Office to satisfy the demands of scholarship in allowing the urn to be opened and the bones subjected to scientific analysis. In July 1933, with the consent of George V, an examination duly took place, but this, so far from settling the matter, has proven quite as contentious as every other Ricardian topic.

The investigation was undertaken by Lawrence Tanner, an historian and archivist, and William Wright, a professor of anatomy and President of the Anatomical Society of Great Britain. Their findings were presented in a paper read to a meeting of the Society of Antiquaries on 30 November 1933, *Recent Investigations regarding the Fate of the Princes in the Tower*, and subsequently published in the journal, *Archaeologica*. They found that 'the bones which filled the urn were unquestionably those of two children of approximately the ages of the princes' in August 1483, 'the generally presumed date of the murder'. Granted the 'reasonable probability' that the bones were those of the princes, 'the murder must have taken place before the close of the reign of Richard III'. Henry VII, the candidate for murderer favoured by Markham, Lindsay and other revisionists, was exonerated.

The elder prince was born (in Westminster Abbey) on 2 November 1470, the younger (at Shrewsbury) probably on 17 August 1473. In August 1483 they would therefore have been twelve and three-quarters and ten years old respectively. Supported by Dr George Northcott, a leading dental authority, Professor Wright concluded that the bones and teeth were those of two children, one aged between twelve and thirteen and the other 'about midway between nine and eleven'. The jaw of the elder child was diseased and 'could not fail to have affected his general health'. The skull was marked with a blood stain, lending support to the traditional account of death by suffocation. All in all, although it was not easy to explain 'why the urn should have contained, in addition to the human bones, a large variety of other bones such as those of fish, duck, chicken, rabbit, sheep, pig and ox', 'the evidence that the bones in the urn are those of the princes is . . . as conclusive as could be desired'.

Tanner and Wright end their paper on an elevated note, suggesting that the discovery of the bones may have been a manifestation of divine retribution, for 'while the bones of Richard III have long since disappeared, trampled into common clay, those of the princes freed from all undignified associations rest secure, in the company of those of their mighty ancestors, at the very heart of the national shrine'.

However that may be, all that Professor Wright's investigation in fact proved was that there was no reason from the scientific point of view why the bones should not be those of the princes, so that it might be thought a remarkable coincidence if they were not. Tanner nevertheless concluded not only that it delivered a verdict of 'case dismissed' against Henry VII but also that it provided evidence of a reasonable probability that More's story of the princes' murder by their uncle (a story by then generally discredited) was 'in its main outlines true'.

Himself the epitome of traditionalism, Lawrence Tanner was no doubt predisposed towards the traditionalist view. When he died in 1979 most of his long life since 1890 had been spent in the precincts of Westminster Abbey. His father was a housemaster at Westminster school, where he himself spent nine years as a pupil and later returned to teach history. He became Clerk to the Weavers Company, Vice-President of the Society of Antiquaries and President of the British Archaeological Association. For forty-three years he held the appointment of Secretary to the Royal Almonry and was rewarded with a CVO (an honour in the monarch's personal gift). At Westminster Abbey he was Librarian for sixteen years and Keeper of the Muniments for forty. His world was the world of the abbey, the public school, the city company and the learned society. That such an authority had provided seemingly convincing proof of the substantial truth of More's account of the death of the princes represented little less than game, set and match to his fellow traditionalists, while only serving to confirm the suspicions of revisionists about traditionalist figures claiming to have proved what they want to believe.

Some historians accept the identification made by Tanner and Wright. Alison Hanham is one. 'The scientific evidence strongly suggests that the remains now entombed in Westminster Abbey as those of Edward V and his brother are indeed the bones of two children of an age similar to that reached by the princes in 1483. It is highly improbable that two other children of these ages were ever buried together in unconsecrated ground in the vicinity of the royal apartments in the Tower.'

Charles Ross carries the argument further: 'If the bones now in the Abbey are not those of the princes, then whose were they? Even in the violent history of the Tower of London, the secret burial of the remains of two young persons, of approximately contiguous age, was scarcely a regular occurrence, and certainly not a recorded occurrence, for we know the fate of almost all those for whom imprisonment in the Tower eventually brought death.'

Yet Ross himself refers to another set of boys' bones, found in a walled-up room in the Tower in 1647. Whose, then, were those? At the time they too were said to belong to the princes. It is surely reasonable to suppose that not a few clandestine interments took place during the centuries when the Tower was in use as royal apartments and a state prison, as the royal treasury and armoury, as a mint and a zoo. (Another supposedly princely skeleton was later identified as that of an ape.) With a permanent garrison and royal menage of officials and servants, the Tower would have been a densely populated community throughout much of the middle ages and Tudor and Stuart times.

The objection of the sceptics to what they slightingly refer to as Those Bones is not only that the identification is mere speculation but that the findings even failed to establish either sex or century. The bones are pre-pubertal and (as Professor Wright omitted to point out) could be female. The period from which they date can only be properly described as pre-1674. There is also strong disbelief that the bones corroborate More's story. If they were where More said that they were first buried – at the foot of a staircase – why didn't Henry VII find them? More meets the point by having them secretly reinterred in a more fitting place by a priest who died without divulging their whereabouts. But if that were true, the real bones would not have been where the inurned bones were found.

'Indeed,' writes Paul Murray Kendall, 'the circumstances of the burial recorded by More do not show much correspondence with the conditions of the actual disinterment. More believed a single priest capable of digging up the bodies in secret haste; no single priest could have so disinterred the bodies in their true hiding place. "At the stair foot, meetly deep in the ground under a heap of stones" is a more accessible location than ten feet deep in the ground beneath the foundations or within the foundations of a staircase, as the skeletons were actually discovered.'

In an article in *The Ricardian* in 1976 Peter Hammond, the Richard III Society's research officer, questioned the validity of some of Professor Wright's conclusions in detail. 'It is now known that there is a much greater variation in the height which children reach by certain ages (and very little knowledge about average height in the middle ages anyway) and in the ages at which their permanent teeth erupt; even normal children can vary very much from the average. A similar situation exists with regard to the age at which the epiphysis joins on to the main shaft of the bone. The range of possible ages would allow the children to have been the correct ages for the princes, but they could equally well have been older or younger. . . Another important factor not taken into account by Professor Wright was the possible effect of bad diet and illness on the rate of growth.' Hammond's conclusion is that 'it is really impossible to tell the age of either child to within less than five years or so'.

Efforts made by the Richard III Society in 1973 and again in 1980 to persuade the Dean and Chapter to authorise another examination proved unavailing. The case for further investigation of the bones is that their authenticity or otherwise has continued to be a matter of controversy and remains of considerable historical interest and importance. Scientific advances made since 1933 offer the opportunity to obtain a much higher degree of certainty. In the field of forensic medicine there has been progress in the study of the development of children's bones as they age, and this has caused others besides Peter Hammond to question the accuracy of Professor Wright's confidently precise calculation of the ages of the children at the time of death.

Forensic examination and newly developed chemical tests could both now offer a solution to the large, unanswered question: are the bones male or female? It is now possible, too, to date archaeological material by physical means. Given a sample of fifty grams of bone (and less in the case of young bones), dating by radio-carbon testing can be accurate to within approximately twenty-five years; with as little as fifteen milligrams, to within approximately fifty years. Although not necessarily decisive, such testing would at least settle the argument whether or not the bones belong to the relevant period. Those who claim that they could date from Roman times are derided, but until there is a further investigation the possibility remains that they could be right.

In the opinion of the Abbey authorities a new examination would be neither desirable nor worthwhile. It would not settle the Ricardian controversy, reliance on the new chemical methods of sexing bones would be premature, and the present Dean and Chapter have expressed a strong aversion to disturbing royal graves in the Abbey at frequent intervals (although whether the bones are in fact royal is the point at issue, and it might be argued that half a century is not a frequent interval). Meanwhile the official Abbey guide-book continues to point the finger of accusation at Richard (the princes 'were reported to have been killed on the orders of Richard III') and unqualified assertions of his guilt continue to be made by those who guide parties of tourists round the royal tombs and, for the benefit of those with a classical education, by the tasteful Latin inscription on the urn itself.

The refusal of the Dean and Chapter to permit further examination leaves historians with the unenviable duty of obtaining second opinions, not on the bones themselves, but on the Tanner/Wright findings. Myers consulted a professor of anatomy at the University of Liverpool. Kendall called in professors of anthropology from the universities of Pennsylvania and Arizona, an orthodontist from Dayton, Ohio, and Dr Lyne-Perkis from Godalming. Ross was indebted to three experts in the university of Bristol: an anatomist, a professor of dental surgery and a student of old bones.

Not unexpectedly, this battery of experts has produced a healthy crop of doubts, qualifications and differences of interpretation. According to Kendall, 'the anatomical evidence for the age of the elder child is not sustained, and the conclusion that the stain on the facial bones upholds the story that the children were smothered is likewise not borne out. Most disturbing of all is the possibility that the elder child was too young to have been Edward V.' According to Ross, 'the medical evidence, therefore, is not conclusive, but, on balance, it suggests that the bones of 1674 might well have been those of the princes, and it certainly does not rule out the possibility or even the probability that they were.'

Whether genuine or spurious, the inurned bones have not yet proved conclusive in identifying a murderer. Those who believe in the guilt of Richard, Buckingham or Henry may all continue to believe.

24

Twentieth-Century Contestants

'Richard, Richard . . . you are the kind of man whom we should turn to, now that we move trembling towards the abyss of the future. You strove to build this England into form, you came to rule a country broken with fighting, broken almost in spirit, with all its conquests lost; from you God took all that you loved on earth, your father, your brother, your wife and your child . . . but destiny could not break your spirit, the spirit that is England. Nothing could destroy that spark that Richard carried in his breast, the spark that kept him fighting, struggling on, when he could see nothing but blackness ahead. Indomitable, heroic and lovable, the great Richard, last of our English kings . . . and even today he is not understood. It is to these men of the past that we must turn in this moment of despair.'

These are the words of one of those revisionists who are too fervent for the good of their cause. A prime example of the excessive devotion of Ricardian commitment, Philip Lindsay's *King Richard III* was published in 1933 and he is invoking the memory of Richard for the inspiration of all true Englishmen during the twilight years between two world wars, when England had fought once at a vast cost to human life and was reluctant to fight again. 'Down through the centuries he has come to us as the emblem of all villainy, as the fiend among kings – this gentle Richard, this man who pardoned too often and too unwisely, who was murdered by the treachery of those whose lives he had disdained to take, the loyal brother, the builder of churches and the patron of Caxton . . . he has come to us as a caricature, as a man who murdered for the love of murder, as a man crooked of body and crooked of mind, inhuman, bestial.'

This gentle Richard can do no wrong, and it is Lindsay and his kind whom modern historians have in their sights when they fire their salvoes of contempt at 'defenders of Richard III'. The pause in hostilities after the frenzy of the Gairdner/Markham confrontation was ended in the 1930s by the campaigning zeal of Lindsay and other self-proclaimed 'Richard-lovers' and by angry exchanges over Those Bones.

Lindsay proudly records the entry in the college registry at Magdalen College, Oxford, made after Richard III's visit in 1483: *Vivat Rex in aeternum*. He roundly describes Polydore Vergil as 'that paid liar' and Henry Tudor, who failed to distinguish himself at Bosworth, Stoke or any other battlefield, as 'the coward'. Of Henry's execution of Sir William Stanley he declares: 'That is one of Henry's executions with which I am entirely in sympathy', although in making the comment he mistakes Lord Stanley for his brother. A similar fate is wished on Margaret Beaufort, Henry Tudor's conspiratorial mother: 'If only Richard had killed that woman!' (But, it is relevant to note, the Plantagenets did not kill women. In fifteenth-century English history there was only one prominent female political victim: Joan of Arc. The Tudors, on the other hand, did not shrink from the judicial murder of Clarence's daughter and no fewer than four queens: Anne Boleyn, Catherine Howard, Lady Jane Grey – as much a queen as Edward V was a king – and Mary Queen of Scots. Would a Tudor, in Richard's shoes, have spared either Margaret Beaufort or Elizabeth Woodville? The record suggests not.)

In Lindsay's eyes Richard is also guiltless of shedding his nephews' blood. A disciple of Markham, he pins the responsibility firmly on Henry. Nor is his assessment of Richard's record as king in doubt: 'Now that he had supreme power we find continually that Richard's actions are those of a noble, just and Christian man. The laws he passed, the wrongs he redressed can be equalled by very few kings of England.'

Another favourable but more judicious assessment at this time is to be found in the *Cambridge Medieval History* (1936), where Professor C. H. Williams writes: 'Edward IV settled his son's fate by raising the Woodvilles to power. For the key problem of politics after his death was bound to be that of the custody of the royal minor, and the candidates were the Woodvilles and Richard. Whichever was in power, neither could be safe. There is no need to depict Richard steeped in crimes, the murderer of Henry VI and his son, and the destroyer of Clarence. There is no reason, even, for thinking of him as a man of one idea, and that his own advancement. There was room in his mind for many conflicting ideas. Indeed, the more we visualise him as a man of his own times the more satisfying that view will appear to be. He could be fearful for his own safety and yet at the same time anxious to act loyally by his nephew, ambitious and yet resigned to bide his time, starkly realist and yet sufficiently Yorkist to be absurdly credulous of gossip affecting legitimism [believing in Stillington's convenient tale of the pre-contract]. There was room for all these things in his mind, but for one thing there was no place. Sentiment was not a fifteenth-century virtue, and neither Richard nor his contemporaries cared much about the fate of those whom business or politics threw in their way. The dualism of the century was in Richard's personality.'

At Oxford similar views were held by Professor Jacob, the fifteenth-century specialist, but most non-specialists remained under the influence of Gairdner: 'the Plantagenets came from the devil and went back to him with Richard III' (Keith Feiling, 1950); 'with him the monarchy reached its lowest depth' (Sir George Clark, 1971). A. L. Rowse, poet and Tudor historian, curiously matched the antiRichard virulence of his near namesake in the fifteenth century and assumed the counter-role to Lindsay's.

In *Bosworth Field* (1966) Dr Rowse steps back from his own field of study to make a partisan foray into the preceding century. Imbued with Tudor literary tradition, he places much confidence in More's fidelity to fact. Although More's narrative of what occurred in April to June of 1483 is evidently a carefully contrived literary exercise with most of its history taken from Morton, Polydore Vergil or, as Dr Hanham has suggested, a common source now lost, Dr Rowse visualises it as an original first draft. More is hastily writing down in instalments an account of events as he remembered them, like an excited journalist thirty years behind the times: 'More was appalled by the story but got most of it down'.

This 'first draft' theory has the advantage of enabling all More's mistakes to be dismissed as understandable errors of detail which would have been corrected later. To A. L. Rowse, if to no one else, the traditional story of the murder of the princes in the Tower is 'perfectly plain and clear' and confirmed by 'everything that has come to light in our time'. Under 'everything', however, Dr Rowse cites only four pieces of evidence, none of which confirms anything of the kind. That Mancini supports the traditional story is far from perfectly plain and clear, as anyone who cares to read Mancini can discover for himself; that modern critical studies of Sir Thomas More support it is a scarcely less inaccurate statement. The bones in Westminster Abbey have provided evidence which is doubtful and disputed; and all Dr Rowse can find to say for the accuracy of *The Great Chronicle of London* is that it 'gives us a pretty good idea in general of what the citizens thought at the time and shortly after'.

Dr Rowse's approach to history divides the *dramatis personae* into heroes and villains, and to a champion of the Tudors the Lancastrians are naturally the Goodies and the Yorkists the Baddies. Thus, for example, Richard III's usurpation is seen in a quite different light to that of Henry IV: 'Before the middle of June the Protector was ready to strike. Like Bolingbroke in 1399 he had a very tight schedule, for the coronation of Edward V was fixed for Sunday, 22 June. But this was not going to be a constitutional revolution like 1399, with a candidate called to the throne by the magnates and the Church – really the will of the country as expressed through them; it was going to be a *coup d'état* of an Italianate kind.' Comparisons are then made between Richard 'the tyrant' and Hitler and between Richard's practices and those of Nazi Germany and Soviet Russia. 'Everyone' regarded him as a monster and those who disagree with Dr Rowse about him are denounced as crackpots, not qualified to hold an opinion, let alone express it.

Richard's good deeds in the summer progress after his coronation are nevertheless conceded by this antiRichard author: at Reading he freed Hastings' widow from forfeiture of land and the other consequences of her husband's treason; at

Woodstock he returned to the commons land which Edward IV had annexed as a royal hunting preserve; at Gloucester he gave the citizens a charter of liberties; at Tewkesbury he made a generous gift of rents to the abbey; and everywhere he refused offers of benevolences to defray his expenses. If he had done the opposite in each case, Dr Rowse would have enjoyed a field day denouncing his tyranny and drawing further parallels with Hitler and Stalin, but leniency and generosity must not, of course, redound to his credit. Richard was disgracefully purchasing favour and support.

At one point in his narrative Dr Rowse so far forgets himself as to state baldly that Richard was a competent ruler and would have made an able king if he had not murdered his nephews. Otherwise there is no letting up. It is known that after the battle of Tewkesbury the leading Lancastrian prisoners were executed by order of Edward IV after a trial by the dukes of Gloucester and Norfolk (as Constable and Marshal of England), but Dr Rowse mentions a summary court-martial under Gloucester alone. Commynes is cited as evidence that Richard killed Henry VI with his own hand because Commynes 'was in a position to hear'. The French chancellor making political capital against the English enemy with the allegation that Richard had murdered his nephews is described as Richard being 'denounced before the bar of European opinion'. It is a historic fact, Dr Rowse informs his readers, that Richard was 'but a ham-actor, for everybody saw through his acting', and indignities would not have been heaped on his corpse 'if he had not been what he was'. He makes no criticism of those who heaped the indignities.

On publication Dr Rowse's book was severely mauled by the experts. Charles Ross noted that 'inaccuracies and misconceptions abound' and in a review in the *Sunday Times* Paul Murray Kendall described *Bosworth Field* as 'non-history', 'superficially researched and badly written': 'What it comes to is the archaic notion that Shakespeare's interpretation of fifteenth-century history "is the traditional commonsense one" because the Tudor historical tradition on which it is based – Vergil, More, Hall, Holinshed – "with some few corrections in detail . . . is in keeping with the best scholarship and the conclusions of commonsense". In reality scholarship of the past half century has so enlarged our understanding of the Wars of the Roses that the Tudor tradition – "myth", E. M. W. Tillyard calls it – has been quietly relegated to the position of a useful, but prejudiced and woefully inadequate portrayal of the period. Indeed, what "the best scholarship", as represented by E. F. Jacob (*The Fifteenth Century*) for example, says is that "Richard III was very far from being the distorted villain of tradition" and that Sir Thomas More's story of the murder of the princes, which Rowse finds "perfectly plain and clear", is now discredited.'

Bosworth Field is an outstanding example of the re-statement of myth as though it were fact. As the work of a popular writer and an 'easy read' available in school and public libraries it will have been widely read, and the reputation of its author as a Fellow of All Souls and a scholar in another field will have secured a false confidence in its authenticity among the general public. Few will be aware of Kendall's finding of 'faulty dates, confusion of identities, a variety of inaccuracies, gross misinterpretations'. But to other participants A. L. Rowse's special contribution to the Great Debate has been to attach the labels of crank and crackpot, not to the Ricardians round whose necks they have usually been hung, but, by his embarrassing support for their cause, round the necks of the hard-line traditionalists, whose own traditional reputation has been for right-mindedness.

In taking the offensive against 'defenders of Richard III' G. R. Elton, Professor of English Constitutional History, has cast himself in the role of the A. L. Rowse of Cambridge. Another unregenerate antiRichard historian of the Tudor period, he is also the Polydore Vergil *de nos jours*, a foreign-born resident historian of England. As a naturalised citizen, he is characteristically over-zealous for the honour of the national bard, imagining native-born Ricardians who question the poet's *bona fides* as an historian to be antiShakespearean ('those who cannot resist pulling Shakespeare down'). As an historian himself, as he has confessed, his temper became badly frayed and his opinion of Richard III darkened as his students persisted in quoting Josephine Tey's fiction at him.

To Professor Elton, as to Dr Rowse, Richard III remains substantially the Richard of the Tudor saga, hallowed by the immortal Shakespeare. In reviews in the *Times Literary Supple-*

ment (1975 and 1982) he has expressed satisfaction at finding comfirmation of his opinions in Alison Hanham's *Richard III and His Early Historians 1483–1536* and Charles Ross's *Richard III*, although the reading of those works by others has not led them to the same conclusion. In his first review he made so much of Dr. Hanham's documentation of critics of Richard before the Tudors that Professor William Empson was driven to protest, claiming to 'express the coarse voice of the general public': 'What we learn from the review is first that no evidence is any longer offered for the belief that Richard killed the princes in the Tower. What every history book, however brief, always told about the children is now admitted to be wrong. It is insinuated instead that this does not matter because the man did a lot of other bad things, not mentioned. We learn, secondly, that the life of Richard III by Sir Thomas More, or partly in his hand-writing, contains a lot of lies; but this does not matter because the effect of them is artistic.'

As traditionalist die-hards in the twentieth century, Rowse and Elton are rowing manfully against the tide, like revisionists in previous centuries: for in universities and schools generally, Richard III is no longer nearly as black as the Tudors painted him. Nevertheless, the counter-revolutionaries still enjoy support in one important respect: it is still considered unsound to believe that Richard was not responsible for the death of his nephews. Alternative explanations for their disappearance are rightly dismissed as speculative, but often with no apparent recognition that the traditional account of their disappearance is fictional or speculative too.

To the general public a more balanced picture is now being presented. One example of a change of view, occurring over little more than a decade, is to be found in successive editions of *Kings and Queens of England: Book I* in the popular Ladybird series, which has a mass circulation among children. According to the 1968 edition, 'Richard had himself crowned as Richard III, and it is probable that the boy king was murdered by his orders. This has never been proved. Fortunately Richard's reign was short. . .' In a revised edition, published in 1981, the text about the princes becomes: 'Did Richard murder them? Or were they killed by Henry Tudor, Earl of Rich-mond? No one really knows.' The 'fortunately short' reign becomes 'Richard worked hard to be a responsible ruler; he ensured the courts operated justly, he showed respect for the Church. . .'

Stimulated by Shakespeare, foreign interest in Richard III has always been strong. From Jean Molinet (c. 1500) to *La Grande Encyclopédie* in the eighteenth century, François Guizot in the nineteenth century and *Le Grand Larousse* in the twentieth he has had an almost uniformly bad press from the French. Typically, it was the traditional account of Richard as usurper and murderer of his nephews that Napoleon recorded in his *Notebooks* in 1788. J. M. Rey, who found Richard not guilty on all charges in 1818, is a notable exception.

In Italy interest in the differences between the Shakespearean and real Riccardo Terzo resulted in a seminar on the subject conducted by the University of L'Aquila in 1979 on the occasion of the opening of a new production of Shakespeare's play by the Italian state theatre company. In Germany in 1980 Andreas Kalckhoff's *Richard III. Sein Leben und seine Zeit. Shakespeares Schurke, wie er wirklich war*, a generally sympathetic biography, provided German readers with an antidote to the classic translations of Shakespeare's play by Schlegel and Tieck.

The historiography of Richard III began with his enemies' version of him. In the sixteenth and seventeenth centuries there was much uncritical copying, with morals drawn but no assessment of the value of evidence; the eighteenth century witnessed the rise of scepticism about tradition; the nineteenth was notable for a close and long overdue scrutiny of the evidence. In the twentieth the unreliability of some of these primary sources has been recognised, moralising has become unfashionable, and scientific objectivity is the goal. These are all movements towards an improved Ricardian image, towards acceptance of a reformed character. Also favourable is a modern climate of opinion sympathetic to the criminal and conscience-stricken at the unjustly condemned, whichever Richard may be.

That the old Richard should survive submersion in these currents is a noteworthy achievement by traditionally-minded historians of the Gairdner school, but they have not been unaided. The bystander sees most of the game, and Dr Kalckhoff detects a psychological need for the Wicked King. Over the years the Richard of the Tudor saga has become transformed into the scapegoat of the English nation, and scapegoats, like legends, cannot be allowed to die.

25

Modern Biographers: Kendall and Ross

'The forceful moral pattern of Vergil, the vividness of More, the fervour of Hall and the dramatic exuberance of Shakespeare have endowed the Tudor myth with a vitality that is one of the wonders of the world. What a tribute this is to art; what a misfortune this is for history.'

These are the concluding words of a biography of Richard III published in 1955. The author, Paul Murray Kendall (1911–1973), was the long awaited answer to the revisionists' prayers. Here at last was the champion of their dreams, an historian well disposed towards Richard who could not be summarily dismissed as insane like Buck, perversely eccentric like Walpole, femininely romantic like Halsted or an interloping adventurer like Markham. Here too was the perfect complement to Josephine Tey. What she achieved at a popular level he was to match in the world of scholarship.

The worst that could be said of him by fellow historians was that his academic credentials belonged in another field, and that he was (as Dr Rowse complained) an American. Kendall was born in Philadelphia and educated at the University of Virginia. He was for many years Professor of English at Ohio University and, after retirement, held a similar appointment at the University of Kansas. He is best known, however, as an historical biographer of the Yorkist period. His *Richard the Third* was followed by *Warwick the Kingmaker* (1957), *The Yorkist Age* (1962) and *Louis XI* (1970). In working on these projects he held Ford Foundation and Guggenheim fellowships, and his *Art of the Biography* (1965) received a nomination for the Pulitzer

Prize. According to his obituarist in *The Times*, 'he had a singular gift for writing vividly and excitingly, while remaining wholly reliable as an historian'.

Others have dissented from the latter half of that judgment. Alison Hanham, in particular, has attempted a grand gesture of dismissal, denouncing Kendall's *Richard the Third* as belonging 'in the realm of fiction'. But it can scarcely be denied that this sympathetic and persuasive biography is not only immensely popular but also remarkably erudite. Setting out to eschew moral verdicts, ignore Tudor tradition and use only contemporary source material, Kendall has lent the weight of some authoritative scholarship to the revisionist cause. In doing so he painted the picture of a new Richard which caught the mood and imagination of an anti-traditionalist generation.

With Markham disregarded in academic circles, this was the first full-scale Life since Gairdner's and essential reading for all students of the period. Some of them came to it already subverted by *The Daughter of Time* and had to be cautioned by traditionalist supervisors not to be seduced into uncritical belief by the blandishments of the author's sparkling prose backed, as it was, by meticulous research.

The Kendall version of Richard would have astonished most readers of earlier histories, as the blackest blot on the fair face of England became credibly transformed into a paragon of justice and mercy. Here is the lord of the north unmasked as a royal Robin Hood, devoted friend of the poor and the oppressed: 'Richard's council appears to have acted as a court of appeal, in which these oppressed classes were able to obtain some relief of their grievances. Poor tenants, whose only claim to the land they worked was the immemorial custom of the manor, were upheld against landlords seeking to dispossess them in order to convert their holdings from arable into pasture. But the work of the council was not confined to rectifying economic hardship. Richard "offered good and indifferent justice to all who sought it, were they rich or poor, gentle or simple" . . . his verdict was sought because he offered a sympathetic hearing and fair dealing. He was a bestower of aid as well as judgment, aid to all manner of men and causes.'

Kendall holds the Woodvilles responsible for the death of Clarence and stresses the crucial effect on events of their

opposition to Richard's protectorship. He cites the relentless-
ness with which Henry Tudor later hounded Bishop Stillington
and attempted to obliterate all record of the pre-contract as
indications that Richard had good reason to believe the story to
be true. In his narrative of the Buckingham rebellion he points
out that, although rumours of the princes' death played an
important part, their actual fate was immaterial. They could
still have been in the Tower, or taken north to Sheriff Hutton, or
killed on Richard's orders at Buckingham's instigation, or
killed by Buckingham without authorisation from Richard.

Like others, Kendall finds the disappearance of the princes
and the differing speculations on their fate an overbearing
aspect of Richard's life and time. His solution is to remove the
subject from the body of the text to a lengthy appendix, which
concludes that the available evidence admits of no decisive
answer to that perennially inflammatory question: Who murdered the little princes? Either Richard or Buckingham may
have been responsible. Richard's assumption of power contained the death of his nephews within it, but although he
thereby doomed them there is reason to doubt that he actually
murdered them.

To the delight of Ricardians and the irritation of anti-
Richards, Professor Kendall's *Richard the Third* ruled supreme
for twenty-six years until, in 1981, the swing of the pendulum
brought a less favourable verdict in Professor Ross's *Richard III*,
competitively heralded on its jacket as 'the only comprehensive
and authoritative biography of Richard in existence'.

Charles Ross, Professor of Medieval History in the University of Bristol, is a leading academic specialist in the Yorkist
period. A Yorkshireman, educated at Wakefield Grammar
School and Oxford, he has spent his working life in southern
England. Fittingly, therefore, he does not take an extreme view
of Richard III, appreciating both light and shadow, the northern as well as the southern view. The swing from Kendall is not
a full back swing. Ross is far from a thorough-going traditionalist, and with the acceptance of his biography by his colleagues
as soundly representative of current thinking, it has become
apparent that among specialists in the period (although not yet
among Tudor historians and authors of general histories) that
breed has joined the dodo in extinction.

Kendall is acknowledged by Ross to be the most respectable and most scholarly of Richard's otherwise not well regarded defenders: 'Kendall's widely-read biography (1955) is the only substantial life of Richard to have been published since Gairdner wrote. Although the author admits that at times he goes beyond the facts and "reconstructs" (as in his blow-by-blow account of Bosworth), and in spite of an empurpled prose style which tends to enhance his partisanship, the book is soundly based on a wide range of primary sources, for which it shows a proper respect.'

Ross himself stands revealed as a moderate antiRichard, rapping revisionist knuckles but recognising that 'the most persistently vilified of all England's kings' was a genuinely pious man and a concerned and well-intentioned ruler as well as the product of an age of violence. So far from representing the lowest depth of the monarchy, 'Richard proved himself an energetic and efficient king' with a proper concern for justice and the impartial administration of the law, and 'no one familiar with the careers of King Louis XI of France, in Richard's own time, or Henry VIII of England, in his own country, would wish to cast any special slur on Richard, still less to select him as the exemplar of a tyrant.'

In his *Edward IV* (1974) Ross laid responsibility for the events of April to June 1483 more heavily on Edward than on Richard. It was Edward's deliberate policy which had made Richard an unchallengeably over-mighty subject. It was Edward's indulgence of their insatiable avarice which had caused unquenchable resentment of the Woodvilles among the nobility, so that 'the likelihood of a regency dominated by the queen's unpopular family was a prospect which commended itself to no one'. 'Edward IV's failure to make early and deliberate provision for the succession in the event of his own premature death is certainly consistent with his attitude to politics in general. His pragmatism persisted to the last, and he assumed too readily the influence of his own personal charm and his ability to cover all contingencies. He remains the only king in English history since 1066 in active possession of the throne who failed to secure the safe succession of his son. His lack of political foresight is largely to blame for the unhappy aftermath of his early death.'

Nevertheless, after viewing him through the eyes of contem-

porary rather than Tudor chroniclers Professor Ross, like Dr
Hanham, does not find Richard's personal image dramatically
transformed. 'Neither More nor Vergil can be accused of
inventing the "Tudor Saga", for propaganda or any other
reason. They were "improving" upon a view of Richard
already accepted in their own time, and for some years before.'
'It is a gross distortion of the available evidence to contend that
the Tudor writers *invented* the wickedness of Richard III . . . the
Tudor writers were building upon a foundation of antagonism
to Richard III which antedated his death at Bosworth.' 'We
have strong *contemporary* evidence that Richard was disliked and
mistrusted in his own time.'

This is undeniable, but it is also true that the Tudor writers
were selective in their foundation and chose to build exaggeration upon exaggeration, untruth upon untruth. Rumour, gossip
and the reports of adversaries are frail evidence, even if contemporary. Antagonism to Richard was inherent in the circumstances and conditions of the time: there were contemporaries
who disliked and mistrusted every king of England in the
fifteenth century (and most of those before and since). It would
have been astonishing if, for instance, there had been no
rumours that Richard had had his nephews put to death, but
they tell us nothing about what actually occurred, particularly
if the Croyland chronicler is correct in reporting that they were
spread deliberately to embarrass the king. In moving behind
the Tudor myths to ascertain the truth, Professor Ross seems to
place too much reliance on records which are sparse, partial,
fragmentary, untrustworthy and by no means necessarily representative. A contemporary eulogy and denial of Richard's
guilt of any crime could confidently have been expected if a
monkish chronicle written, not in Croyland but in York, had
survived. How sharply then would antiRichards have discounted the value of contemporary evidence!

Ross is right to point out that 'far too much of the proRicar-
dian stance rests on hypothesis and speculation'. But Richard's
defenders owe their existence as a body to antiRichard historians whose stance is similarly based. To pin responsibility for
the death of Clarence or the Lancastrian Prince of Wales on
Richard is no less speculative than to pin responsibility for the
death of the princes on Buckingham or Henry Tudor. Can it

conceivably be true, as Ross argues, that Richard's reputation has suffered scarcely less from the attentions of his own defenders than from the Tudors? This is a fanciful judgment which seems somewhat bizarre. To do as much damage as More or Shakespeare would be a prodigious achievement. What revisionists would claim is that by disbelief and importunity they have helped to tug historians out of the frozen attitudes of traditionalism and reliance on Moreish absurdities into a more balanced and academically seemly posture, even if in so doing some fanatics have exaggerated the case to be made in Richard's favour.

Another serious charge levelled by Ross against Ricardians is one which concerns all participants in the Great Debate. 'It has been a persistent weakness of the more extreme "revisionists" to regard anything written about Richard III after 1485 as *ipso facto* discredited and prejudiced, except when it happens to suit their case. For example, Polydore Vergil, as a Tudor author corrupted by Morton, cannot be relied upon, and yet becomes an acceptable authority when he reports a general belief that the princes were still alive and had been spirited away abroad.'

Selectivity is a naughty game which two can play, and traditionalists have been guilty of it too – whether to a greater or lesser degree it is hardly possible to judge. To aficionados it is an unfailing source of amusement to note how the author of each successive work on this tyrant or misjudged hero accepts or rejects, brandishes in triumph or derision, pieces of evidence in strict accordance with the argument to which he or she is committed. If sufficient of the evidence were hard, this would be a trick quickly exposed, but much of it is so soggy that the gates of selectivity leading to a wonderland of speculation are, if not wide open, at least temptingly ajar.

To acknowledge that Ross himself is (almost) pure in this respect is not to exonerate his deductions and judgments from being questionable. An unsubstantiated report of a general belief that the princes had been spirited away abroad would be of little value if it emanated from a source friendly to Richard III. But it surely falls into a different classification of evidence when appearing, as it does, in the most hostile of sources. This too is soggy ground, but a point in Richard's favour made by

Henry Tudor's historian must deserve closer attention than predictable passages of denigration.

Another questionable judgment is the application to Richard of a phrase from Gray's *Elegy*, made twice in this biography: once correctly as 'to wade through slaughter to a throne' and once incorrectly 'had carved his way through slaughter to a throne'. How many deaths amount to slaughter? The total tally of dead in the events leading to Richard's accession amounted to four. Can an historian of Ross's stature really be subscribing to Gairdner's 'reign of terror' theory, or is this simply an illustration of the adage, so pertinent to the Ricardian controversy, that while history may or may not repeat itself what is certain is that historians repeat each other? It would seem a much more plausible argument that Richard's assumption of the crown saved the country from civil war and that he thus averted bloodshed on a scale which could then properly have been described as slaughter.

Disarmingly, Ross shows minimal interest in the fate of the princes in the Tower, dismissing them cursorily in a nine-page chapter: what was important was what contemporaries thought had happened to them, and they blamed Richard. Ross, it is clear, also blames Richard. He does not share Kendall's scepticism about Buckingham being with Richard on his post-coronation progress until they parted at Gloucester, as stated by More and Vergil: 'Kendall was anxious to have Buckingham back in London so that he might murder the princes in the Tower.' But Ross fails to meet Kendall's point that Buckingham's name does not appear among the members of the royal party recorded at Oxford. As Robert Hairsine has commented in *The Ricardian*: 'In compiling a list of distinguished guests, the registrar of Magdalen College would hardly have overlooked the presence of the Duke of Buckingham, the second most powerful man in the land.'

Ross is also less than fair to Richard in his treatment of Mistress Shore. If, as seems probable, she was involved in the plot by Hastings (one of her bedfellows) against Richard's life, public penance was not a harsh punishment. Ross quotes part of Richard's letter to his chancellor expressing strong disapproval of the intention of Thomas Lynom, the king's solicitor, to marry Mistress Shore, but omits a significant passage of qualification which shows Richard as lenient and forgiving: 'if ye find him utter set for to marry her . . . we be content', and Richard then orders her release from imprisonment until the marriage can take place.

Arrested for centuries by the influence of literary myth-makers, Ricardian studies have made real advances in recent years. These developments are recorded and encapsulated in Ross's *Richard III*, which reflects the work of, among others, A. R. Myers in his reassessment of Richard's character, Alison Hanham in her study of the contemporary chroniclers of Richard's reign, Charles T. Wood on the constitutional issues, and A. J. Pollard on north versus south. This biography takes the form of a series of essays on Ricardian themes such as Richard's northern affinity, his exercise of patronage, the government of the realm, foreign policy and defence. Lacking the popular appeal and wide readership of Kendall, it is likely nevertheless to achieve currency for its views through accept-ance as a work of reference for much new fact-gathering and interpretation which will in time find their way into general histories and school text-books. By this process the general public will gradually become aware, for example, that Richard's peculiarity was not a hunchback, but the fact that he was and remains the only king of England from the north of the country: that the major problem of his kingship was discontent in the southern counties at the 'plantation' in the south of his northern supporters, and that his reputation is likely to have been very different had it not fallen wholly into the hands of southern chroniclers.

The current state of the argument about Richard is nicely represented in the works of Kendall and Ross. Kendall is revisionism at last triumphant, Ross a guarded retreat from the excesses of traditionalism to a more defensible entrenchment from which to launch a limited counter-offensive.

26

The Richard III Society

The most important fact about the Richard III Society is the fact of its existence. Until the twentieth century sympathy for 'the last English king', while persistent, had been sporadic and individual. The running forays of the revisionists against the established bastions of the traditionalists had kept the so-called Great Debate alive but made little headway on popular opinion, where Shakespeare's Richard reigned unchallenged. Dissenting views were generally dismissed as wayward, and converts were few.

The growth of a movement and the formation of an organisation to bring aid and comfort to the cause of a long-dead monarch of no current political or constitutional significance is itself of some significance. One historian (A. R. Myers in the journal *History*, 1968) has described the Richard III Society as 'that remarkable phenomenon of our times'. A Stuart Society, a Cromwell Association and the Sealed Knot are legacies of the civil war of the seventeenth century, but none compares with the Richard III Society in numbers, longevity and seriousness of purpose. The heat has gone out of the argument between Roundheads and Cavaliers, whereas the quarrels between white rose and red, and, specifically, the dispute about the character and deeds of the last of the Plantagenets, still arouse passions and partisanship. The Society is variously seen as a crusade for the propagation of historical truth, an academically disreputable assembly of the purblind and the parti-pris, and an amiable or ridiculous manifestation of English eccentricity.

Inspired by Walpole, Halsted and Markham, the Fellowship.

of the White Boar was founded in 1924, improbably in Liverpool, by S. Saxon Barton OBE, a surgeon with antiquarian interests: he was a Fellow of the Society of Antiquaries of Scotland. Marjorie Bowen, Philip Lindsay, Aylmer Vallance and other writers and their friends were soon attracted to the Fellowship, and they formed for the first time an articulate, pro-Richard pressure group.

In 1956 this small but vocal body was re-constituted with a wider membership under the less romantic title of the Richard III Society, and revisionists began to call themselves Ricardians. An open door policy was adopted: all who wished to join were welcomed without inquiry or reservation. No introductions or qualifications were required, no loyalty tests or oaths demanded. There have been no expulsions or heresy-hunts for Tudor moles.

The aloha principle has its drawbacks. A fanatic element is a hazard in all open-door societies. There can be little doubt that an exclusive society of scholars would have made a better impression on academic circles, or that statements and activities by some individual members, interpreted as representative of the Society as a whole, can prove an embarrassment and supply useful ammunition to those who wish to deride the Society and write off all Ricardians as cranks. On the other hand, a large membership is impressive in itself, it produces the funds necessary to make the Society effective, and there has been no take-over by a Militant Tendency minority. The policy of the elected leadership in recent years has tended towards the view that a case is best made with moderation.

In 1960 total membership was little more than 200; twenty years later it had risen to 2,500. Two-thirds live in England, where there are branches and groups in many areas, including the East and West Midlands, Gloucestershire and Kent, Lincolnshire and Lancashire as well as the prime territories of London and Yorkshire. There is a strong following in the USA, where the Richard III Society Inc. has its headquarters in New York and chapters in Washington, Chicago, Los Angeles, Seattle and other major cities. There are branches in Canada, Australia and South Africa, and individual members scattered across the globe from Germany and Italy to New Zealand, Japan and Hawaii. Since its re-foundation the Society has never needed to look for recruits. Instead, to judge from correspondence, there are thousands of would-be members throughout the world looking for it. Three extracts from letters received will serve to illustrate the desire of many to participate in the Great Debate.

'Would you kindly send me some information on your Society. I have recently learned of your existence whilst talking to someone about the controversies surrounding Richard III. I had just read Paul Murray Kendall's biography and Josephine Tey's *Daughter of Time*, and these books came as complete revelations to me, having for years accepted the stereotyped character of Richard as depicted by most historians, and this set me searching for some information about him. I am astonished at how many history books, both for children and adults, are still churning out the same old unsubstantiated stories. . .'

'About three weeks ago I turned on the radio to find myself listening to a discussion about Richard III. There I sat, muttering about Henry Tudor, and ready to spring to Richard's defence, when to my utter astonishment I realised I didn't have to – the people on the programme were actually putting forward all the arguments for Richard which I've been putting forward myself for a long time. I was delighted, to say the least, but when the presenter mentioned a society, I was positively jumping up and down with excitement. I've got so used to the facile reactions of people raised on Shakespeare's play that it never occurred to me there might be an organised group of any kind opposing the Tudor propaganda. One of the speakers on the programme remarked how strange it was that, after five hundred years, Richard should still arouse such fierce passions. I for one certainly feel very strongly indeed that a terrible injustice has been done to his name and reputation, and that the general apathy about it must be disturbed and challenged on every possible occasion. So, please, may I join your fellowship? Those members who spoke on the radio programme seemed mostly to be writers or historians, and I am neither, so I do very much hope that I don't have to be in order to join you. I simply believe in the same things you believe in and want to lend my support in any way I can. . .'

'Would a former colonial be considered for membership? I

have long been a partisan of Richard III and feel that he has been given a very poor press over the years. The reigns of Edward IV and Richard III have had a great interest for me as it was a transitional period in English history – from warrior kings to executive kings. The York family was what my grandmother would call a family of bottom – I don't know exactly what she meant by the expression, but it was great praise from her. I live in a very large not very populous state far from any centers of learning. The nearest university, Montana State University, is almost four hundred miles from here. Luckily our local library has access privileges to many college libraries, but I must wait for books until resident researchers have used them. There are so many questions I would like answered. . .'

An address for the Society appears in reference books and the London telephone directory, but the readiest access to it for newspaper readers is on 22 August each year when In Memoriam notices are inserted in *The Times* and other newspapers round the world: 'PLANTAGENET, Richard. Died gallantly, defending his country against the invader. Bosworth 22 August 1485. Loyaulte me lie. . .'

The Society does not recruit more actively for members because it is run entirely by fully-stretched voluntary labour. Throughout the 1970s an unpaid honorary secretary – a housewife in Essex – devoted eight to ten hours a day to the Society's affairs. A chartered accountant in Surrey made his professional skills and time freely available as honorary treasurer. A husband and wife team in Chiswick devoted themselves and part of their home to the work of the Society as, respectively, editor/research officer and librarian. Other members of the committee produce quarterly Society bulletins, arrange events and outings, keep press cuttings and photographic records, raise funds through craft sales, and stock and supply by mail order relevant publications and insignia – badges, ties, headscarves. In local branches in England and in the United States and elsewhere overseas there is a similar dedication by ready volunteers.

Who then are the members? They are educated men and women with a mostly amateur interest in history. They are librarians, teachers, civil servants, writers, secretaries and housewives, with a sprinkling of doctors, lawyers and accountants. Women outnumber men, but not in sufficient numbers to excuse the gibe that the inspiration of the Society is the romantic love of women for an unattainable monster. If the composition of the committee is representative, the Society includes a disproportionately large number of left-handers (those who, when articles are put into their right hands as children, firmly transfer them to the left). The membership contains its share of the distinguished: among Vice-Presidents in the 1970s were Dermot Morrah, Arundel Herald Extraordinary, and the Hon. Donald F. Lybarger, Chief Justice of the Court of Common Pleas, Cleveland, Ohio. But a more typical member would be a young, intelligent, left-handed, female librarian.

The primary aim and purpose of the Society are stated in these words: 'In the belief that many features of the traditional accounts of the character and career of Richard III are neither supported by sufficient evidence nor reasonably tenable, the Society aims to promote in every possible way research into the life and times of Richard III, and to secure a re-assessment of the material relating to this period, and of the role in English history of this monarch.' The secondary aim is 'to arrange, through the committee and through branch committees in their own areas, appropriate historical and social activities'.

Although not the journal of a learned society, *The Ricardian*, published quarterly, formerly a pot-pourri of historical articles, notices of society events, and letters, poems and gossip from and about members, has since 1975 become exclusively academic, devoted to the publication of original research. A separate Bulletin provides members with routine Society information and reports on Society activities. Otherwise the Society concentrates most of its resources on making available source material relating to the period. Its most important publication has been *British Library Harleian Manuscript 433*, the collection of state and personal papers from Richard III's signet office, in four volumes at an outlay of some £20,000.

The second stated aim covers the activities of the less scholarly members of the Society – those for whom membership brings the companionship of like-minded people at meetings and outings, those whose interests in the fifteenth century are more general (in music, costume, heraldry, palaeography) and, more particularly, those whose targets for conversion to the cause are not the academic community but the public at large. The two major events in the Society's calendar under this heading are the Annual General Meeting, held in London on the Saturday nearest 2 October, the date of Richard III's birth, and the service at Sutton Cheney church and visit to the battlefield at Bosworth on the Sunday nearest 22 August, the date of his death.

As early as 1934 the Society installed a Richard III memorial window in the church at Middleham. In 1960 it was responsible for a memorial brass and enamelled shield to mark the burial place of his queen, Anne Nevill, in Westminster Abbey, unveiled by the then head of the Nevill family, the Marquess of Abergavenny, and dedicated by the Dean. Other memorials followed: a plaque near the remaining stonework on the site of Fotheringhay castle, Richard's birthplace; an illuminated vellum for display in the Chapter House of York Minster; a commemorative tablet in Sutton Cheney church; a memorial window in the church at Fotheringhay. In 1974 the Society's regular visits to the battlefield, where it had cleared and fenced ground around King Richard's Well, led the Leicestershire County Council to obtain the necessary rights of way and open the site to the general public. In 1982 a chapel in memory of the house of York was dedicated in Fotheringhay church, and a memorial stone to King Richard – the inspiration of a member of the Society – in the chancel of Leicester cathedral.

The most ambitious of the Society's non-academic projects began in 1978, when a public appeal was launched under the patronage of the Duke of Rutland for the erection of a statue of Richard III in Leicester. Nearly £20,000 was raised and in July 1980 the statue, by James Butler RA, was unveiled by HRH Princess Alice, Duchess of Gloucester, at a civic ceremony in Castle Gardens, Leicester, attended by the Lord Lieutenant and the Lord Mayor. The duchess read a dedication address from her son, HRH the Duke of Gloucester, who had been prevented at the last moment from undertaking the unveiling himself.

'It is, of course, a source of pleasure to me,' wrote the duke, 'that the man with whom I share not only a title but also a Christian name should be honoured in this way. But there is more to this occasion than just the acknowledgment of a fine man's achievements – for the purpose and indeed the strength of the Richard III Society derives from a belief that the truth is more powerful than lies – a faith that even after all these centuries the truth is important. It is proof of our sense of civilised values that something as esoteric and as fragile as a reputation is worth campaigning for.' Later the same year the duke became the Society's Patron.

For nearly 500 years there had been no fitting memorial of this king in the place of his burial, and many people outside the Society responded to the statue appeal. A large donation from Switzerland was accompanied by a letter stating that the reason would be understood when the signature was read: the name at the foot of the letter was Brackenbury. Money came from a Metcalfe in Australia: the fifteenth-century Metcalfes were loyal supporters of Richard III. The motivation of an Italian pharmacist from Cortina d'Ampezzo who came by taxi to the Society's London address and handed in 50,000 lire was never discovered. Another valued contribution came from Lord Olivier, who wrote a long letter of support and offered the use of his name as sponsor.

The uneasy relationship between the Society and professional historians improved gradually throughout the 1970s. While some historians of the Tudor period continued hostilities, a useful dialogue developed with specialists in the fifteenth century who lectured to members and took part in symposia organised by the Society at Leicester University (1976) and Trinity College, Oxford (1981).

In America in the 1930s members of the then styled Friends of Richard III Incorporated included such luminaries as James Thurber, Salvador Dali, Cornelia Otis Skinner and the film stars Tallulah Bankhead, Helen Hayes and Robert Montgomery. But the most committed of famous American Ricardians has been Rex Stout, long recognised before his death in 1975 at the age of 89 as one of the best crime writers of the twentieth century. He was prominent as a champion of authors' rights and a determined crusader in a variety of other causes. In *Death of a Doxy* his overweight Johnsonian detective, Nero Wolfe, banishes *Utopia* from his bookshelves because of More's maligning of Richard III. The author had taken the same action after investigating the merits of the case and concluding that More was a liar.

Stout became an honorary member of the Richard III Society and, in a characteristic departure from the standard format, wrote the obituary notice which appeared in the *New York Times* on 22 August 1970: 'PLANTAGENET – Richard, great king and true friend of the rights of man, died at Bosworth Field on August 22, 1485. Murdered by traitors and, dead, maligned by knaves and ignored by Laodiceans, he merits our devoted remembrance.' As every schoolboy no longer knows, the Laodiceans were members of one of the seven early Christian churches of Asia, condemned in the Book of Revelation for being lukewarm. They were to be spewed out because they were neither hot nor cold.

In the 1930s the movement on both sides of the Atlantic may have reflected the general reaction among liberals against government propaganda of the day, both fascist and communist. Since World War II the climate of opinion has continued to be anti-authoritarian. A mood of scepticism towards what previous generations had perceived as established truths was reinforced by experience of the systematic cultivation of the official untruth by Marxist regimes. Rebelliousness in questioning what was taught at school came to be seen as healthy in a democratic society.

Within this favourable ambience there were special stimuli to the spread of the revisionist gospel. The most widely influential publication and the largest single factor contributing to the steady flow of recruits to the Society since the 1950s has been a novel, Josephine Tey's *The Daughter of Time*, inspired by Markham's denunciation of Henry Tudor as the real murderer of the princes.

First published in 1951 by a small publishing house (Peter Davies), *The Daughter of Time* gathered popularity by word of mouth and has achieved the status of a classic through 'reader recommendation'. The Penguin paperback edition appeared in 1954 and was reprinted twenty times between 1956 and 1980. In 1982 the BBC broadcast a radio adaptation, the *Radio Times* accurately describing the original as 'strangely compulsive'. The author's real name was Elizabeth MacKintosh. Born in the Scottish Highlands and educated at the Inverness Royal

Academy, like Markham she spurned a university education, in her case preferring to attend a physical education college. She claimed that she started to write very soon after beginning to walk, but her working life was spent in hospitals and schools, 'straightening spines for bread-and-butter and writing for fun'. A shy person intent on protecting her privacy, she used two pseudonyms. As Josephine Tey she wrote eleven novels, mostly crime stories, including *Miss Pym Disposes* and *The Franchise Affair*, of which a film was made. In Sir John Gielgud's phrase, her detective stories were her 'yearly knitting'. As Gordon Daviot she achieved success in the theatre with *Richard of Bordeaux*, a play about Richard II produced in London in 1932 with Gielgud in the title role. When she died in 1952, at the age of 55, he and Edith Evans were among the mourners at her funeral.

Another major stimulus to revisionism was the mounting (by Dr Roy Strong and Dr Pamela Tudor-Craig) of a special exhibition on Richard III at the National Portrait Gallery in 1973. Members of the Society assisted in the preparation of the exhibition and the catalogue, and the large attendances led to an expansion in the membership, which continued into the following year, augmented by public interest in the opening of the battlefield site at Bosworth.

From this exhibition two pieces of new evidence emerged. The Windsor Castle portrait of Richard III was lent by Her Majesty the Queen. No physical deformity is portrayed, but the set of one shoulder prompts the suspicion that a view from behind might reveal a hunchback. Permission to x-ray the painting was obtained, and it was discovered that the high line of the right shoulder was an overpainting by a later hand. This piece of faking indicates that even thirty years after his death, when the picture was first painted and the libels of More and Vergil had already been written, the king's physical normality was known. The over-painting is evidence, not of deformity, but of the Tudor legend of his monstrosity gathering pace during the sixteenth century.

Secondly, a previously unremarked privy seal warrant from Richard III to his chancellor was exhibited. Dated 29 July (1483) from Minster Lovell, it refers mysteriously to an unspecified 'enterprise', undertaken presumably in London, by 'certaine personnes' then in custody, concerning whom the chancellor is instructed 'to procede to the due execution of our laws'. Evidently this was a matter of such importance that it was not to be named even in official correspondence. There are two such known events to which the warrant may refer: a conspiracy to remove Edward IV's daughters from sanctuary in Westminster Abbey, or the disappearance of the princes from the Tower. In either case it would suggest that Richard was taken by surprise, but there is no record of any due execution of the law which would elucidate the matter.

As the Society's volumes of cuttings prove, press coverage of this long-dead monarch is prodigious. In terms of column inches in newspapers, magazines and journals, serious and popular, the patron of Caxton has been amply recompensed. Nationally, as well as locally in places like York and Leicester, he seems seldom out of the news, made relevant to all occasions. When, for instance, the Argentine forces in the Falkland Islands were cut off from reinforcements during the war in the South Atlantic in 1982, Galtieri, the leader of the junta, was, almost inevitably, portrayed in a newspaper cartoon as Richard III crying out for a horse.

The correspondence columns of *The Times* provide a regular battleground for Ricardian skirmishing. In 1980 a (not wholly serious) letter from the Chairman of the Society was published in the context of public controversy over two television programmes. It inquired whether after apologies by the Foreign Secretary for *Death of a Princess* ('mixing fact with fiction . . . can be dangerous and misleading') and by the Independent Broadcasting Authority for *A Man Called Intrepid* ('dramatic licence should not lead to a travesty of the truth') an apology might be expected from the governors of the National Theatre for staging 'Shakespeare's scurrilously inaccurate docu-drama *Richard III*, which is deeply offensive to many people today'.

Parliament itself has recently taken note of the strength of feeling about Richard III's reputation. The Broadcasting Bill which became law in November 1980 originally contained a provision enabling complaints about unfair treatment in television and radio programmes to be made on behalf of the dead. When the bill was published, it became apparent that it would open an avenue for legally based complaints on behalf of

Richard III whenever Shakespeare's play was broadcast. In the debate on the bill in the House of Lords several speakers referred to Richard III in forecasting that this provision would arouse much historical controversy. It was pointed out that the laws of libel have never permitted legal action to be taken in the name of a dead person. One noble lord, weak in history, inadvertently referred to Richard II and was immediately corrected: 'Richard III, my lord!'

Forewarned, the government tabled an amendment, and the Act as finally passed stipulates that complaints on behalf of the dead may be made only in the case of programmes first broadcast within five years of their death. Shortly after the bill received the royal assent the Chairman of the BBC, referring to this amendment in a speech, said that it was known as 'the Richard III clause'. Revisionists consoled themselves for lost opportunities with pleasure at the thought that Richard III was still exercising a sensible influence on his country's legislation.

All in all, many have been busy during the last half century repairing the omission noted by Bishop Stubbs, that this king 'left none behind him whose duty or whose care it was to attempt his vindication'.

27

Richard III Today

The English are by inclination a backward-looking people, and between 1945 and 1980 the study of history was a growth industry, stimulated by an overall expansion in higher education and the development of technical aids such as the photo-copier and the computer. Specialist historians were better equipped with resources and facilities than ever before, and the publication of large numbers of popular biographies and other historical works, the birth of a history book club and the success of a magazine such as *History Today* were evidence of a wider interest among the public at large. Concern about current events provoked a delving into background and precedents, and disenchantment with the present induced escapism into the past. Some embraced history purposefully for its relevance; others for relaxation and its apparent irrelevance.

Distance in time lends enchantment to a violent age such as the fifteenth century. The student is safe but not unmoved, for the Wars of the Roses have bequeathed a legacy of Yorkist and Lancastrian partiality, to be detected not only on the cricket ground on summer bank holidays. Yorkshire folk are very conscious that the superiority they feel over other Englishmen was once demonstrated in the ascendancy of a ruling house of York. In Lancashire the triumph of the red rose is marked on formal occasions by a loyal toast to 'The Queen, the Duke of Lancaster'.

In such circumstances it is not surprising that the second half of the twentieth century should already have seen the publication of two full-scale biographies of Henry VI and each of the

two adult Yorkist kings as well as Lives in popular Kings and
Queens series and reprints of Mancini, More, Buck, Walpole,
Hutton, Halsted, Gairdner and Markham. The public appetite
has been whetted as never before. 1983, the quincentenary
of the year of the three Yorkist kings and, most especially,
of Richard III's accession to the throne, is likely to witness a
further crop of publications and commemorative events stimulated by, and arousing even more, public awareness. But what
conclusions are being reached?

'The Tudor fables are now discredited and dying, but they
are dying hard.' These words, apt today, were written by
Markham nearly a hundred years ago. In fact, as we learn from
the example of Aesop and the Greeks, fables and myths are
indestructible. The story of the innocent royal babes and their
monstrous Wicked Uncle can never be killed, even by the truth.

By way of contrast Richard III also stands today in danger of
becoming a cult figure. The scholarship of Kendall has bestowed on revisionism an accolade of respectability, hailed by
Ricardians as a vindication of their cause and proof positive of
the sad state of historical studies over so many generations. In
an age of scepticism about traditional knowledge and accepted
wisdom he is widely seen as a man martyred by biased historians. The excesses of tee-shirt slogans and car-stickers (Richard
Rules OK?) are yet to come, but Ricardian commemorations
are ardently supported, Ricardian places have become the
destination of what are sometimes little less than pilgrimages,
and for the last two or three decades it has taken what has been
estimated as an average of six new titles a year to satisfy the
market for romantic historical novels with Richard as hero.

Poems too are numerous, if seldom published. The following
sonnet by George Awdry, a dedicated Ricardian, is a characteristic expression of faith and mood:

Uphill, the Welshman's hirelings cut their way;
The traitor baron and the knight draw near;
The faithless earl stands idle in the rear,
As if afraid to succour or betray.

And now, the Household, marshalled in array,
Aims for the dragon banner, takes career.

The King will make an end to treason, here;
Put to the touch his crown and life, today.

Farewell, King Richard! Failing victory,
Today the rightful English kingship ends,
And here you die, in valiant company,
To be remembered, silently, by friends.

Though fouled with lies, to prop a stolen throne,
Sleep safe in honour, till the truth is known.

A guide to the places associated with Richard is published by
the Richard III Society in *Ricardian Britain*, currently in its third
edition. Here too the romantic appeal is strong. Those interested in the past, seeking havens from their own century and
involvement in another at a comfortable distance in time, can
discover enjoyment in many evocative sites and deserted ruins
a short drive from modern centres of overpopulation.

In the north, haunting the landscape, stand the stone car-
casses of great medieval castles at Middleham, Richard's
home, and Raby, his mother's birthplace. Barely a stone is left
above ground at Sandal, where his father met his death, or at
Pontefract, Richard's headquarters when he became Constable
of England and Steward of the duchy of Lancaster in northern
parts in 1472, but the magnificence of the sites remains. At
Sheriff Hutton, the seat of Richard's Council of the North, only
a few fragments of castle break the skyline, but in the obscurity
of the parish church is the tomb of Edward of Middleham,
Prince of Wales, his son and heir, whose premature death
signalled the downfall of a dynasty.

At Nottingham, in the king's Castle of Care where he learned
of his son's death, the foundation of his building work ('a right
sumptuous piece of stone work') may still be traced, known
today as Richard's Tower. At Warwick castle much of the
external splendour of the Bear and Clarence towers which he
erected has survived, and at Ludlow, another Yorkist stronghold and headquarters for the government of Wales, the castle
ruins crowning this hill town on the marches are among the
most picturesque in England. The ruins of Francis Lovell's
Minster Lovell and Hastings' castle at Ashby-de-la-Zouche

and his never completed Kirby Muxloe are scarcely less romantic.

With Leicester (wrote Caroline Halsted) Richard's name is 'inseparably connected'. A letter which he wrote to the Duke of Burgundy in August 1483 is dated from his castle of Leicester, and he was there again two months later, before his tragic return in 1485. Today only the sadly neglected castle mound and one stone gateway survive, and all trace of the house of the Greyfriars where he was buried has been obliterated, his place of interment now a car park. Even the stone horse-trough which was traditionally supposed to have been his coffin (although as far back as 1720 Rev. Samuel Carte, father of Thomas, could find no evidence for the identification) has long since disappeared. Instead his statue stands defiantly, sword in hand, on the site of the castle bailey and in the cathedral he is honoured with a finely inscribed memorial.

By comparison with the place of his death Richard's birthplace is little known. The castle of Fotheringhay in Northamptonshire was granted by Edward III to his fifth son, Edmund of Langley, whom Richard II created the first Duke of York. The duke rebuilt the castle, and in 1411 Edward, the second duke, founded a college there, to which his own body was brought back from Agincourt and which became the mausoleum of the house of York. Richard's father, the third duke, made Fotheringhay his principal home. Four of his children were born in the castle, and there Richard probably spent his childhood. In 1476 he followed the corpses of his father and brother Edmund at the head of a solemn procession from Wakefield to Fotheringhay for their re-interment at a ceremony attended by 20,000 people. Today, although the college buildings and original memorials were destroyed in Tudor times, the church is outwardly unchanged, its tower surmounted by an octagonal lantern topped by pinnacles displaying Yorkist emblems. In the south aisle is the new chapel of All Souls with its memorial window to the house of York dedicated in the presence of today's Duke of Gloucester. Of the castle all but a single piece of fallen masonry has vanished, but plaques record the connection with Richard III and with Mary Queen of Scots, who was executed in the great hall. Surrounded by its double ditches and flanked by the river Nene (together forming the shape of the Yorkist fetterlock), the castle mound rises today beside farm buildings. From its vantage point there is an unbroken panorama over the still empty heartland of England.

There are strong Ricardian associations with London too: at Crosby Hall (the centrepiece of his town house in Bishopsgate, now removed to Chelsea embankment) as well as the Tower, Guildhall, Westminster Hall and Westminster Abbey, where he was crowned. The other great ecclesiastical buildings of England associated with him include York Minster, King's College chapel at Cambridge, St George's at Windsor and the recently repaired abbey ruins at Crowland, where the chronicler wrote. Inside the abbey church at Tewkesbury lies the body of his fickle brother, George, Duke of Clarence, and outside lies Bloody Meadow, where the battle was fought. Battlefields are less spectacular than castles and abbey churches, but they offer more of a challenge to the imagination. At Mortimer's Cross, Towton and Barnet memorials stand beside modern roads; at East Stoke one must search the hedgerows for a marker and identify Red Gutter and Dead Man's Field unguided.

Only at Bosworth itself is the supposed disposition of the rival armies set out and an account of the progress of the battle provided. At weekends in the summer Richard's and Henry's standards fly from flagpoles to mark the positions of their respective camps, and a death stone has been erected in the field beside a brook where, according to ancient lore, the middle ages ended so abruptly one August morning with the killing of a demon king. In the nearby church of Sutton Cheney this same king is lovingly commemorated by a plaque, adorned by the faithful with laurel wreaths and white roses. Throughout the church and on the steps of the altar are hassocks embroidered with Yorkist emblems and the badges of his ministers – Lovell, Ratcliffe and Catesby – stitched as a labour of love by ladies in Washington, D.C.

The spell of ancient buildings and sites on the romantically inclined is magical, and the innocent self-indulgence of revisionists in such an unscientific and unintellectual pastime as the exploration of Ricardian Britain is seen by traditionalist historians as typifying defenders of Richard III. Yet what this activity illustrates most graphically is the influence of the past on the English consciousness and on Anglo-Saxon attitudes. Strong threads of continuity in the fabric of English history are not woven into the Great Debate about Richard III alone, but reminders of him in the twentieth century and awareness of them are unusually pronounced.

Despite his reputation, Richard's portrait is displayed on pub signs: one hangs outside the Kings Arms on King's Staith beside the Ouse in York, and another identifies the York House in London Road, Gloucester. In Ludlow the restaurant in the town's historic hotel, The Feathers, is named after him. Facing the sea at Scarborough is the fondly preserved King Richard's House, a reminder of his role as Admiral of England. Even in far-flung Tenerife there has been no escaping him. John, whom loyalty binds across time and ocean, would in the 1970s be pleased to welcome you at his Richard III bar in Puerto de la Cruz. Nearer home is The Gloucester Arms in Penrith.

A different kind of peculiarity in this bridging of the centuries is the recurrence of personal names. It is noteworthy but readily understandable that a Brackenbury in Switzerland and a Metcalfe in Australia in the twentieth century should contribute towards the cost of a statue of Richard III in memory of the long-past loyalty of their families to that king. There is no mystery about the link between the sympathy of Sir George Buck in the seventeenth century and the death of John Buck, his ancestor, at Bosworth. But what is to be made of the names of two modern antiRichard historians – A. L. Rowse and Charles Ross – echoing that of a contemporary antiRichard chronicler, John Rous (or Ross) of Warwick? Or the similar sharing of a name between a pro-Richard modern historian – Paul Murray Kendall – and Richard III's secretary, John Kendale (or Kendall)?

A lesser coincidence is the foreshadowing of William Hutton, the eighteenth-century historian of Bosworth, by Dr Thomas Hutton, the diplomat employed by Richard III in his negotiations with Brittany. But there is also the strange case of the two Legges: Dr Thomas in 1579 (*Richardus Tertius*) and Alfred O. in 1882 (*The Unpopular King*). And one might almost imagine that Caroline Halsted's involvement in the controversy in Victorian times was pre-ordained when Robert Fabyan retired three centuries earlier to compile his chronicle at Halstedys, his estate in Essex.

Most mysterious of all, of course, is the repetition of the name of Tyrell in two of the most dramatic events in English history. Despite their often violent lives, few kings of England have failed to die of natural causes. It does not seem a credible coincidence that two of those few – William II and Edward V – separated by four hundred years, should have been killed by men with this far from common name. Here there must be room for suspicion that the belated casting of Sir James in the role of principal murderer of the princes was not unconnected with his bearing of a name already tainted with regicide. It would have been a characteristic piece of opportunism by such a subtle politician and wily myth-maker as Henry Tudor.

Half a millennium has been too short a span of time to arrive at a consensus on Richard III, but long enough to establish the fallibility of tradition in general and historians in particular, and to reach the conclusion that in the absence of certainty people believe about him what they wish to believe. Mostly, the views held by historians and non-historians alike are more revealing of their own characters and attitudes than of his. The searchlight of history which has played upon him has illuminated very little. His mind and motives are still a mystery, theirs – whether actuated by bias or striving for impartiality – often all too apparent. Unreliable sources are combed and fragments of evidence eagerly seized upon or scornfully discarded according to theory or prejudice. To adapt a saying of the fourth Earl of Chesterfield: Tell me what you think of Richard III and I will tell you what you are.

Was he honourable or a villain? Puritan and pious or a hypocrite? Ruthless or over-merciful? Ambitious for the crown at any cost or driven by circumstances to accept it? The victim or perpetrator of violence? Loyal or faithless to his brother and his brother's sons? Sharp or dull witted? A man who strongly influenced others or was strongly influenced by them? A man of learning, practised in the guile of statecraft or a simple soldier and country gentleman? A man whose character his contem-

poraries could read at a glance or an example of another of Lord
Chesterfield's mots: *volto scuolto e pensieri stretti* (an open countenance and close thoughts)? Some of the accusations made
against him are plainly untrue, others unproven. But can there
really be so much smoke without any fire at all? After centuries
of controversy the truth remains elusive and the king himself a
persistent enigma.

Laodiceans will inquire with a shrug why such questions
matter. Is it not the problems of today which require solution?
Why spend time and passion on an old puzzle which has proved
insoluble? Surely the only relevant history is social and economic, and how can thousands of pounds spent on the statue of
a long-dead king be justified at a time when millions of people in
the world are living in misery and dying of starvation? In reply
it will be asked of those who stand silent on the touchline or turn
their back on the contest whether they feel no concern for the
truth. Without truth, traditionalists and revisionists may unite
in asserting, the compass of life is broken and humanity lost.
Today's lies about crimes are nourished by yesterday's. Myth-
making is infectious: whenever it masquerades as truth it must
be unmasked. Generations of school-children should not have
been mistaught.

There are those who look upon the Ricardian controversy as
no more than a game of chess, white versus black, with first one
side then the other crying check but neither conceding check-
mate. Others see it as the stuff of courtroom drama and mount
mock trials with Richard in the dock. But to those caught up in
it the Great Debate may be a feverish affliction. Some graduate
from mild interest and amusement through rising degrees of
absorption to obsession. They become enthralled, like alchem-
ists seeking the philosopher's stone or Arthurian knights in
pursuit of the Holy Grail. Hot for certainties of Ricardian
truth, they suffer the rebuff of dusty answers. Then their
predelictions become articles of faith and harden into dogma.
Richard the usurper and infanticide becomes Richard the
wickedest man in English history or Richard the maligned king
becomes Richard the martyred saint.

Should evidence conclusive enough to end the debate ever
come to light, it will be a triumph for learning and a tragedy for
the imagination. Meanwhile one can conclude only that in real

life Richard appears to have been a cultivated, conscientious and courageous man of his time, which was rough and tough. The last of the soldier kings, he was quickly out of his depth in politics, and it was political floundering as much as miscalculation on the battlefield which cost him his crown, life and reputation. He died young after a brief reign; yet few have led such a vigorous, robust and enduring life after death as this English king who was crowned in Westminster Abbey on 6 July 1483 and killed in battle little more than two years later. For him *requiescat in pace* is an unanswered prayer.

The question *Good King Richard?* is not an idle one. To a dedicated and growing minority the 'good' attaches to both king and Richard and, since the best of rulers are seldom the best of men, the verdict of 'good king' may receive assent even from those who do not acquit him of some villainies. As acknowledged by many who would not call themselves revisionists – across the centuries from Camden to Ross – the record of his legislation suggests that Richard was indeed a good king and, if he had not botched Bosworth, might even have become a great one. All in all, it seems, more people will answer this question in the affirmative today than at any time since the memory of his rule was lost in the mists of legend.

As Sir George Buck first observed more than three and a half centuries ago: 'Malice and ignorance have been the king's greatest accusers.'

Select Bibliography

General

AWDRY, George: *The Richard III Society* 1974

BACON, Francis: *History of the Reign of King Henry the Seventh* 1622

BUCK, Sir George (ed. A. N. Kincaid): *The History of King Richard the Third* 1979

Calendar of Charter Rolls (Vol. VI) 1927

Calendar of Patent Rolls (1476–85) 1901

CARTE, Thomas: *A General History of England* (Book XIII) 1747–55

CHAMBERS, R. W.: *Thomas More* 1935

CHRIMES, S. B.: *Lancastrians, Yorkists and Henry VII* 1964

CHRIMES, S. B.: *Henry VII* 1972

CHURCHILL, G. B.: *Richard III up to Shakespeare* 1900 (1976)

COMMINES, Philippe de (tr. Michael Jones): *Memoirs – The Reign of Louis XI* 1972

DAVIES R. (editor): *York Records* 1843

Dictionary of National Biography (Compact Edition) 1975

FABYAN, Robert (ed. Henry Ellis): *The New Chronicles of England & France* 1811

GAIRDNER, James: *History of the Life and Reign of Richard the Third* 1878 (revised 1898)

GRAFTON, Richard: *Continuation of John Hardyng's Chronicle* 1543

HALL, Edward: *Hall's Chronicle* 1548 (1809)

HALSTED, Caroline A.: *Richard III as Duke of Gloucester and King of England* 1844 (1977)

HAMMOND, Carolyn: *Ricardian Britain* (third edition) 1977

HANHAM, Alison: *Richard III and his Early Historians 1483–1535* 1975

HAY, Denis: *Polydore Vergil* 1952

HICKS, M. A.: *False, Fleeting, Perjur'd Clarence* 1980

HOLINSHED, Raphael: *Chronicles* (second edition) 1587

HORROX, Rosemary and HAMMOND P. W. (editors): *British Library Harleian Manuscript 433* 1979–83

HUME, David: *The History of England* (Vol. II) 1762

HUTTON, William: *The Battle of Bosworth Field* 1788 (1974)

INGULPH (tr. Henry Riley): *Chronicle of the Abbey of Croyland* 1854

JACOB, E. F.: *The Fifteenth Century 1399–1485* 1961

JENKINS, Elizabeth: *The Princes in the Tower* 1978

JESSE, J. H.: *Memoirs of King Richard the Third* 1862

KALCKHOFF, Andreas: *Richard III. Sein Leben und Seine Zeit* 1980

KENDALL, Paul Murray: *Richard III* 1955

KENDALL, Paul Murray: *The Yorkist Age* 1962

KETTON–CREMER, R. W.: *Horace Walpole* 1940

LAMB, V. B.: *The Betrayal of Richard III* 1959

LANDER, J. R.: *Conflict and Stability in Fifteenth-Century England* 1969

LANDER, J. R.: *Government and Community: England* 1450–1509 1980

LEGGE, Alfred O.: *The Unpopular King* 1885

LEVINE, Mortimer: *Tudor Dynastic Problems 1460–1571* 1973

LINDSAY, Philip: *King Richard III* 1933

MANCINI, Dominic (ed. C. A. J. Armstrong): *The Usurpation of Richard the Third* (second edition) 1969

MARKHAM, A. H.: *The Life of Sir Clements Markham* 1917

MARKHAM, Sir Clements: *Richard III: His Life and Character* 1906

McFARLANE, K. B.: *The Nobility of Late Medieval England* 1973

MOLINET, Jean: *Chroniques* 1827–8

MORE, Sir Thomas (ed. R. S. Sylvester): *The History of King Richard the Third* 1963

MURPH, Roxane C.: *Richard III: The Making of a Legend* 1978

MYERS, A. R.: *England in the Later Middle Ages* 1952

MYERS, A. R.: *English Historical Documents 1327–1485* 1969

RAINE, Angelo (editor): *York Civic Records* (Vol. I) 1939

RAMSAY, Sir James: *Lancaster and York* (Vol. II) 1892

RAPIN-THOYRAS, Paul de (tr. N. Tindal): *The History of England* (Vol. VI) 1728

ROSS, Charles: *Edward IV* 1974

ROSS, Charles: *Richard III* 1981

ROUS, John: *The Rous Roll* 1859 (1980)

ROWSE, A. L.: *Bosworth Field* 1966

RYMER, Thomas: *Foedera* (Tom. XI & XII) 1710, 1711

SHAKESPEARE, William (ed. Julie Hankey): *Richard III* 1981

STRONG, Roy: *And When Did You Last See Your Father?* 1978

THOMAS, A. H. & THORNLEY, I. D. (editors): *The Great Chronicle of London* 1938

TILLYARD, E. M. W.: *Shakespeare's History Plays* 1944

TUDOR-CRAIG, Pamela: *Richard III* (Catalogue of National Portrait Gallery Exhibition) 1973

VERGIL, Polydore (ed. Henry Ellis): *English History* 1844 (1968)

WALPOLE, Horace: *Historic Doubts on the Life and Reign of King Richard the Third* 1768

WARKWORTH, John: *A Chronicle of the First Thirteen Years of the Reign of King Edward the Fourth* 1839

WILLIAMS, D. T.: *The Battle of Bosworth* 1973

WILLIAMSON, Audrey: *The Mystery of the Princes* 1978

Fiction

BOWEN, Marjorie; *Dickon* 1929

CARLETON, Patrick: *Under the Hog* 1937

EDWARDS, Rhoda: *Some Touch of Pity* 1976

FARRINGTON, Robert: *The Killing of Richard III* 1971

JAMES, G. P. R.: *The Woodman* 1849

JARMAN, Rosemary Hawley: *We Speak No Treason* 1971

LYTTON, Edward Bulwer: *The Last of the Barons* 1843

OMAN, Carola: *Crouchback* 1929

PALMER, Marian: *The White Boar* 1968

PENMAN, Sharon K.: *The Sunne in Splendour* 1983

POTTER, Jeremy: *A Trail of Blood* 1970

SCOTT, John Reed: *Beatrix of Clare* 1907

STEVENSON, Robert Louis: *The Black Arrow* 1888

TEY, Josephine: *The Daughter of Time* 1951

WHITTLE, Tyler: *The Last Plantagenet* 1968

Journal

The Ricardian, quarterly journal of the Richard III Society (4 Oakley Street, London SW3).

Index